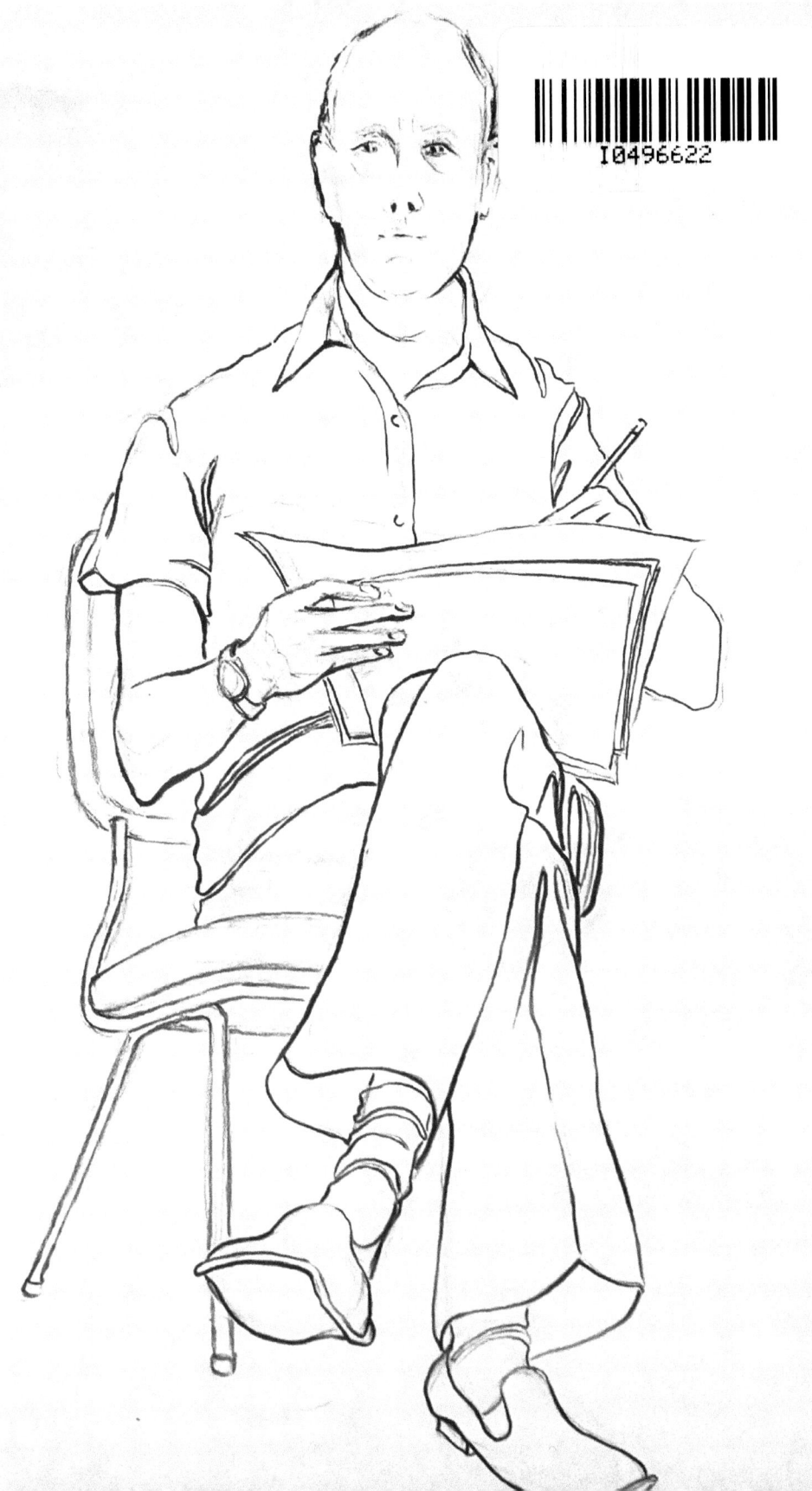

# Dale Gibson:
## The Artful Codger

A LAW PROFESSOR'S POETRY AND ART

COMPILED BY
SANDRA MOSHER ANDERSON

DALE GIBSON: THE ARTFUL CODGER
A *Law Professor's Poetry and Art*

Copyright © Sandra Mosher Anderson, 2025

All rights reserved. No part of this publication may be reproduced, stored in a retrieval system, or transmitted in any form or by any means, electronic, mechanical, photocopying, recording, or otherwise, without written permission of the copyright holder and publisher.

Published by Sandra Mosher Anderson, Edmonton, Alberta, Canada

ISBN:
    Paperback   978-1-77354-575-2
    PDF   978-1-77354-664-3

Publication assistance in Canada by

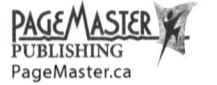

PUBLISHING
PageMaster.ca

# Chapters

Introduction ............................................................. 1

The Poet's Craft ....................................................... 7

Self-Contemplation ................................................ 13

The Law ................................................................. 35

Social Commentary ............................................... 45

Beasts in Human Form ......................................... 65

Love ....................................................................... 73

Guilt ...................................................................... 95

Friends, Others ................................................... 123

Relatives .............................................................. 131

The Prairies ......................................................... 151

Other Places ....................................................... 171

    Canada ........................................................ 173
    China & Asia .............................................. 195
    Europe ........................................................ 201
    Ireland ........................................................ 209
    United States ............................................. 217

Nature, General .................................................. 229

Art ....................................................................... 253

Dale's First Court Case ...................................... 277

Index of Poems .................................................. 285

Curriculum Vitae ............................................... 293

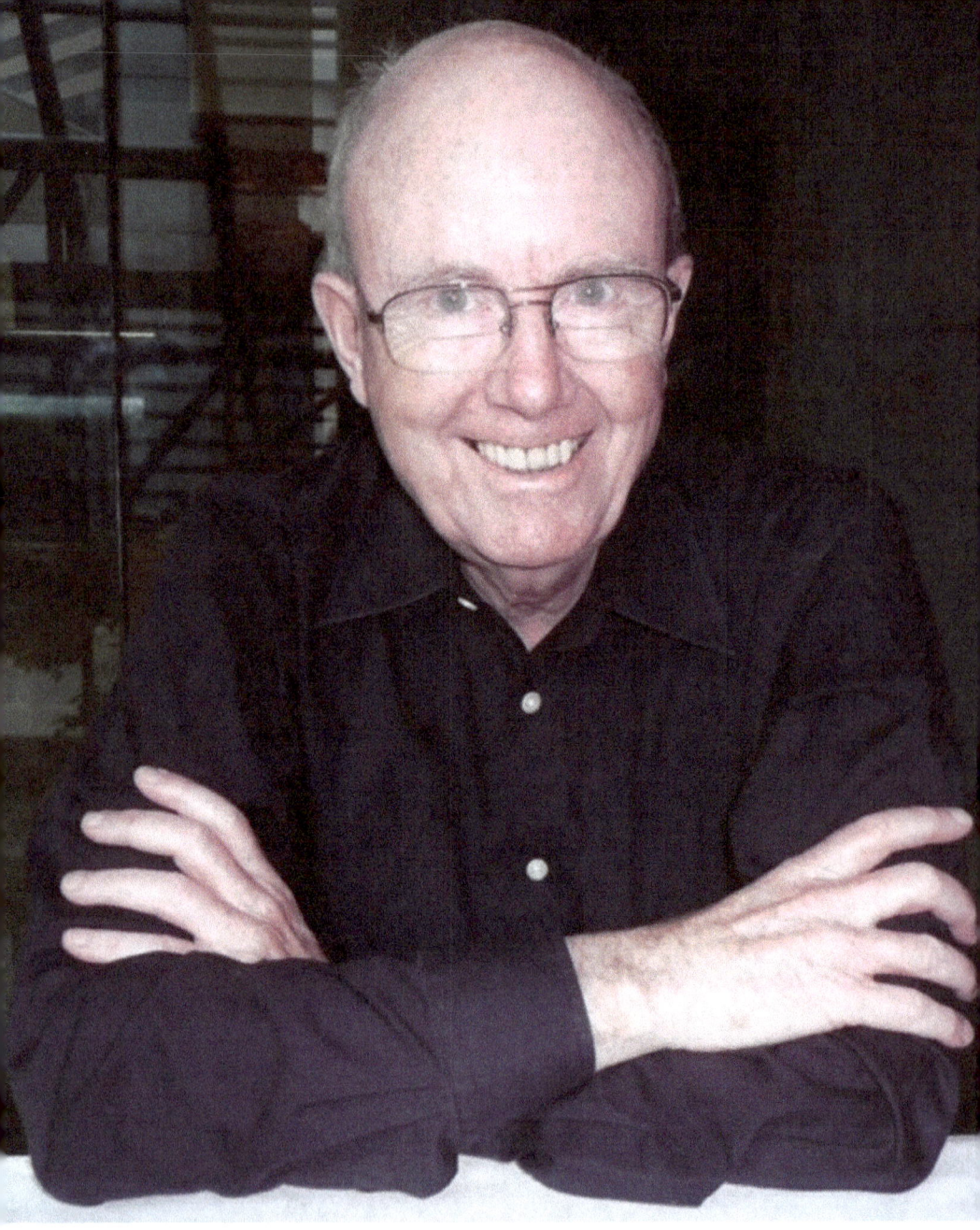

Dale Gibson, 2008

# Introduction

Professor Dale Gibson (1933-2022) led an illustrious life along many dimensions. He was well known as a leading constitutionalist, advising the Federal and Manitoba governments on the 1982 patriation of the Canadian constitution, a storied law professor admired by his students for his brilliant and clear mind and willingness to invest himself in them, a Distinguished Professor (later Emeritus) of the Faculty of Law, University of Manitoba, and the first Belzberg Professor of Constitutional Law at the University of Alberta. He published some of the earliest legal texts on the *Canadian Charter of Rights of Freedoms*, one on its general principles and another on the equality rights it enshrines, and they and others of his writings have been frequently cited by Canadian courts at all levels in their judgments.

Indeed, his published works span almost every area of Canadian law, and, especially in his later years, his fervour for prairie Canadian legal history resulted in massive contributions in that area as well. His published articles in legal journals run into the hundreds (Curriculum Vitae). He was counsel in numerous significant civil cases at all levels of Canadian courts; a favourite story is that his first appearance in a court as a young lawyer, substituting for a lawyer conflicted out at the last minute, was in the Supreme Court of Canada, where he not only won his case but was also handed a note from one of the justices congratulating him on his presentation ("First Court Case").

But Dale had another side little known to anyone other than those closest to him. His supple mind and creative energy led him to compose reams of poems, travel narratives, and stories, drawings and water-colours, and to experiment with stained glass and models of buildings, furniture-building, elaborate gift-wrapping, and photography. Moreover, for decades, he kept journals of fascinating complexity and detail, the earlier half of which he donated in 1988 to the Manitoba Archives at their request, with the remainder of his written output eventually to follow.

His wit and erudition sparkled in the titles and contents of his books and published articles, extending, for example, to inventing an imaginary conversation between René Lévêsque, Sir John A. Macdonald, Lester Pearson, and Bora Laskin, published in 1992 as an extension of a symposium report. It begins:

> "Perhaps it was a case of intellectual indigestion. A day and a half's discussions about Canada's constitutional future with a score of sophisticated constitutionalists would be enough to upset anybody's mental metabolism, whatever the cause. As I sat contemplating the highlights of the constitutional symposium in the warm amber light of a single-malt scotch, I was visited by an extraordinary vision...."[1]

Dale's creative output over a long life was prodigious; it simply flowed from him, self-expression as necessary to him as breathing. Especially in his poems, he tried to make sense of his choices, his feelings, his adventures, the world, and the people around him, by capturing them in elegant, pithy, often humorous wordplay. This body of work, only a small portion of which appears in these pages, reflects the now-rare practice that, since ancient times, the community's stories and self-understanding have been handed down and delivered to future generations in the language of poetry.

However painful to himself and to others, these poems are honest in confronting the effects he visited upon others, good and bad. In particular, the regret and guilt he felt about his decision in 1991 to tear apart his life in Winnipeg and remake it anew with me in Edmonton is palpable in his poetry, in even more distilled form than in his equally forthright journals from that period.

In these pages, I have paired the visual materials thematically with the poems without regard to time and place of either; the reader should be

---

[1]  "'As I see it, René...' said Sir John" (1991) 3, 1 Constitutional Forum 18

aware that there is very little direct correlation between the themes of Dale's poetry and his visual art and vice-versa. Nevertheless, it is to be hoped that they reinforce and enlarge each other's impact. To underscore this, I have removed dates from the poems and placed them in a separate index, arranged alphabetically by title or, in cases where he left a poem untitled, by its first line. Dale revised a number of his poems multiple times, refining their wording, sometimes over years, without substantially altering their meaning. I have endeavored to combine the variations in such a way as to be true to his original intent or to provide, in the few cases of variations too extensive simply to meld, two or more versions.

Due to space constraints, it is not possible to do justice here to Dale's essays, stories, journals, and autobiographical writings (with such wonderful titles as: "My Sporting Life," "Adventures in Lawyering," "Hey! It's Our Constitution Too!," "Dale the Sailor Man," "Picnic Ant: Memories of a Small Life," "The Much Defended Border," "Legal Jungles, Academic Groves & Other Spaces: A Varied Life," etc.), nor is it possible at present to publish the voluminous autobiographical materials Dale left behind, nor yet to write the biography he deserves.

However, a fair amount of accessible biographical material can be found in:

> "Dale Gibson: Scholar, Teacher, Lawyer, and Man of Principle," by The Honourable Justice [now Chief Justice of Alberta] Ritu Khullar, (2022) *Alberta Law Review*, 59:4, pp. 785-805; and

> "Interview with Dale Gibson: The Metamorphosis of Legal Education in Manitoba: An Eyewitness Account" by Bryan P. Schwartz & Cameron Harvey, (2016) *Manitoba Law Journal*, 29,1, pp. 25-76.

As well, Barry Strayer's last book, *Canada's Constitutional Revolution*, Edmonton, University of Alberta Press, 2013, contains, among a number of references to Dale' work advising the Federal and Manitoba governments on the patriation of the Canadian Constitution, a description of him, in connection with the response Dale wrote on behalf of the Canadian Government to the U.K. House of Commons' hostile "Kershaw Report," as "one of the fastest pens in the West."

Curating Dale's massive output of artistic expression of all kinds, especially his rich poetry and visual art, is a privilege as well as a comfort. It is an exhilarating opportunity to rummage inside his brilliant, multi-faceted mind in a systematic way that our constantly unfolding active lives and our intensely companionable marriage did not always fully afford. As I choose them for this book, I feel as though I were in:

<u>Aladdin's Cave</u>

Having brought an end
To earthly pleasures,
Grief sits small
Among *these* treasures.

Dale's was a deeply contemplative life expressed in myriad ways that seem even more profound when experienced as a whole, as I am fortunate to be doing as I curate his legacy. I offer these selections to you in joy and in loving tribute to a remarkable human being.

*Sandra Mosher Anderson*

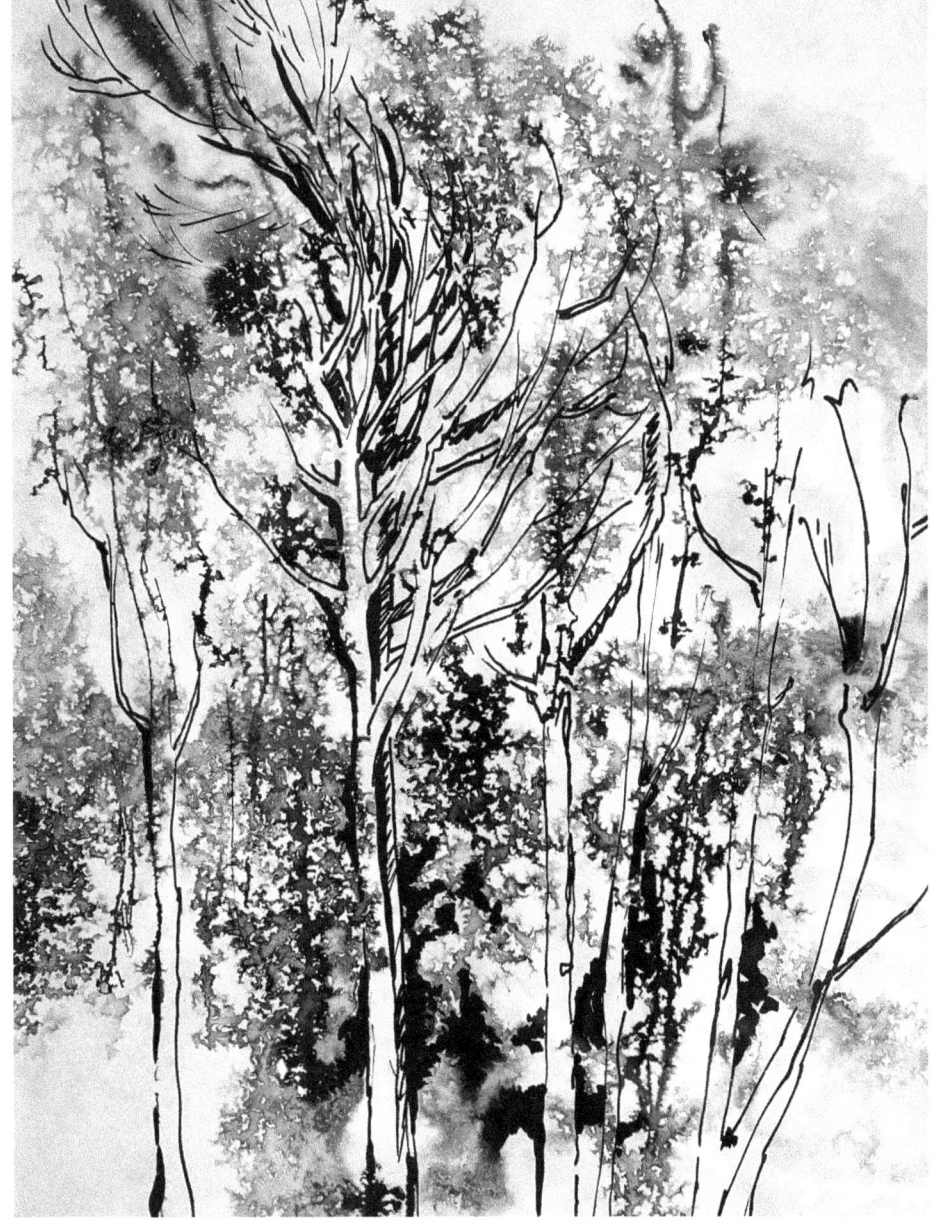

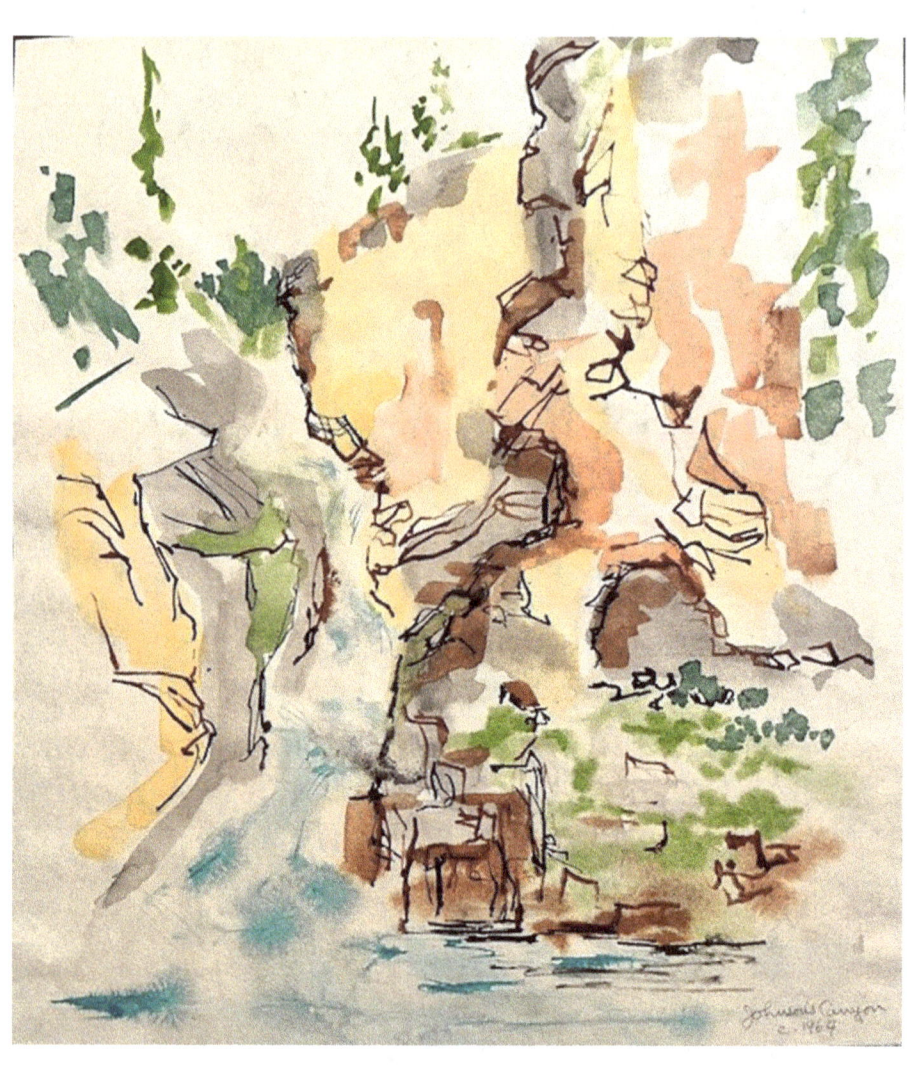

# The Poet's Craft

Poems are the least of things
unless they're apropos,
in which case they have infinite
capacity to grow.

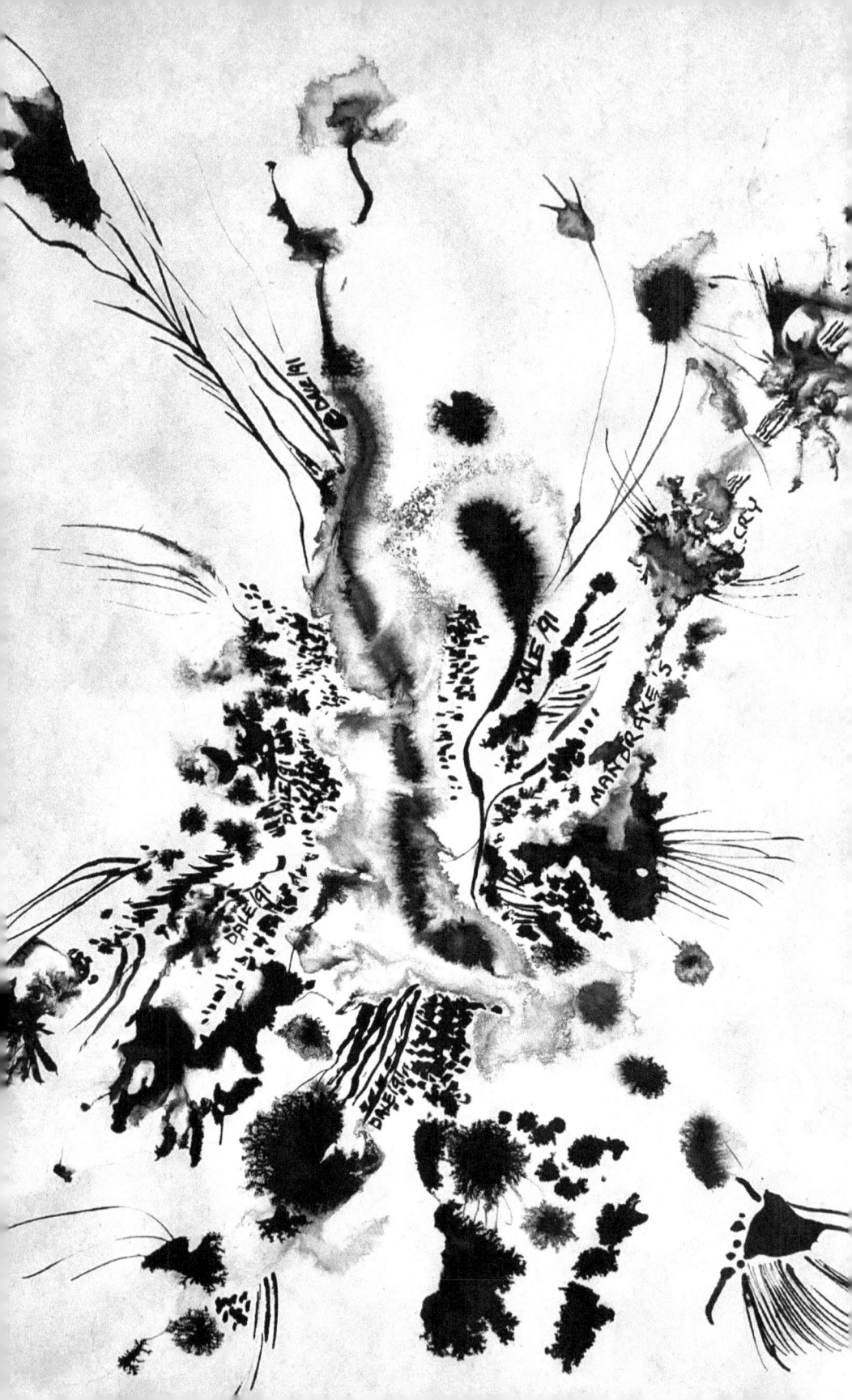

# World Without End

Starting's always easy
what I cannot do is finish.

Beginnings
tempt
accumulate
intimidate
deter
and rot.

Spring brings only disappointment
that the winter's work's not done.

I'd like
to manufacture
simple things,
like chairs, or shoes, or something
I could finish,
but there would always be
unhappy customers,
demanding alterations.

You
must be my seasons,
completions,
and conclusions.

# I've got the flu

or something worse
and a terrible urge
to put it in verse.

It feels like God
is standing on me
which is especially unpleasant
for an atheist.

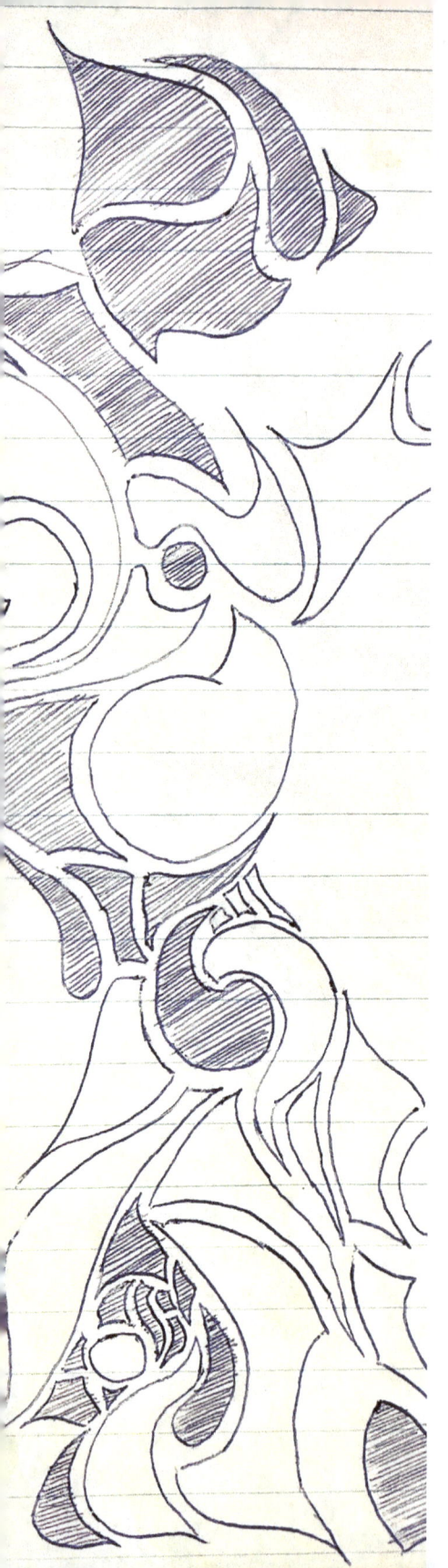

# Running

At first, I ran to learn,
and then to prove,
then to celebrate,
and finally to run.

And then?
It isn't wise to forecast.
Unformed expectations
can't be disappointed.

And besides,
the running's best
when you forget
you're running.

But whether you know it or not,
you're leaving the place where you started
at double the rate you realize.

Poetry and running
are both solitary sports
and in both the trick
is knowing when to stop.

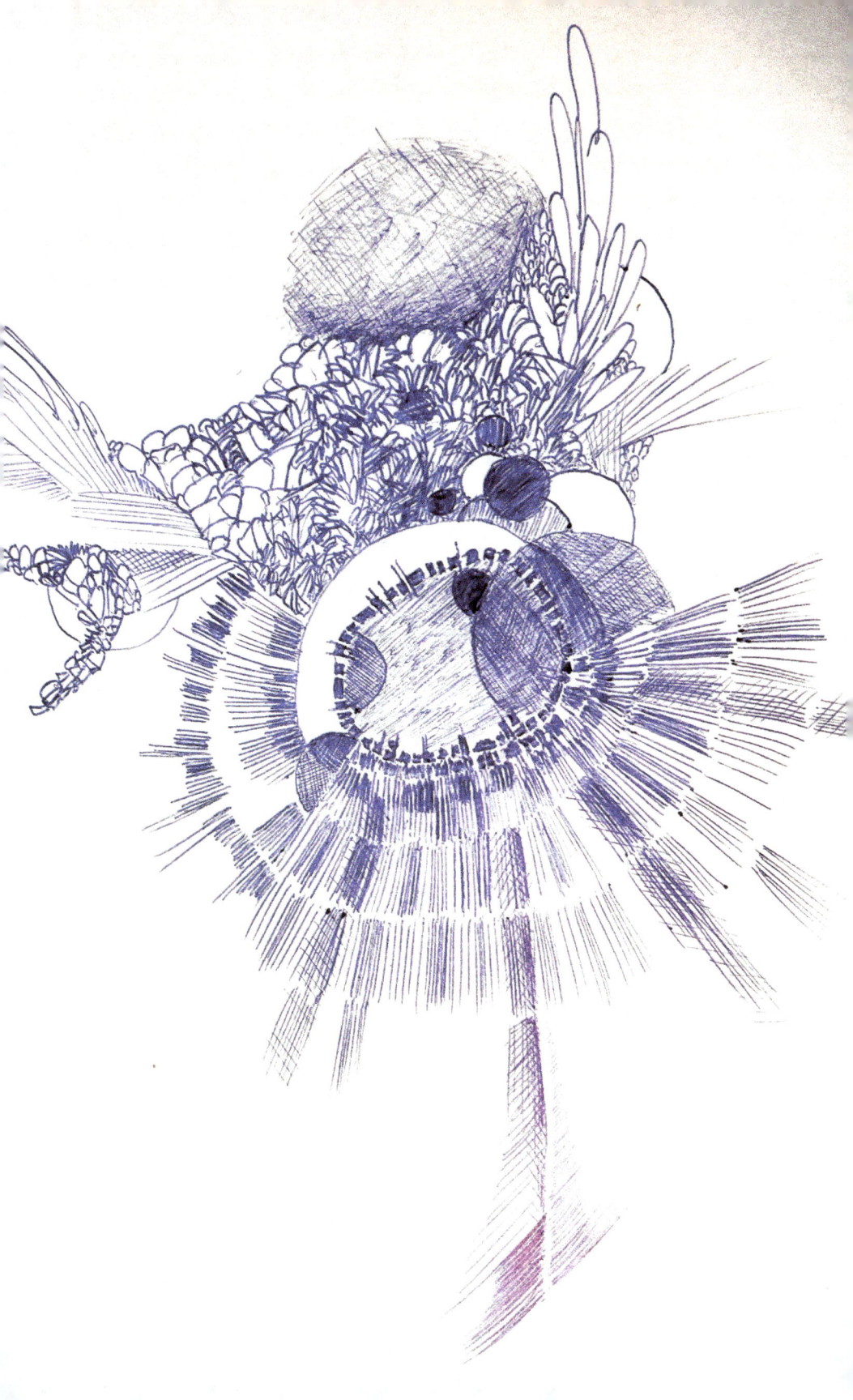

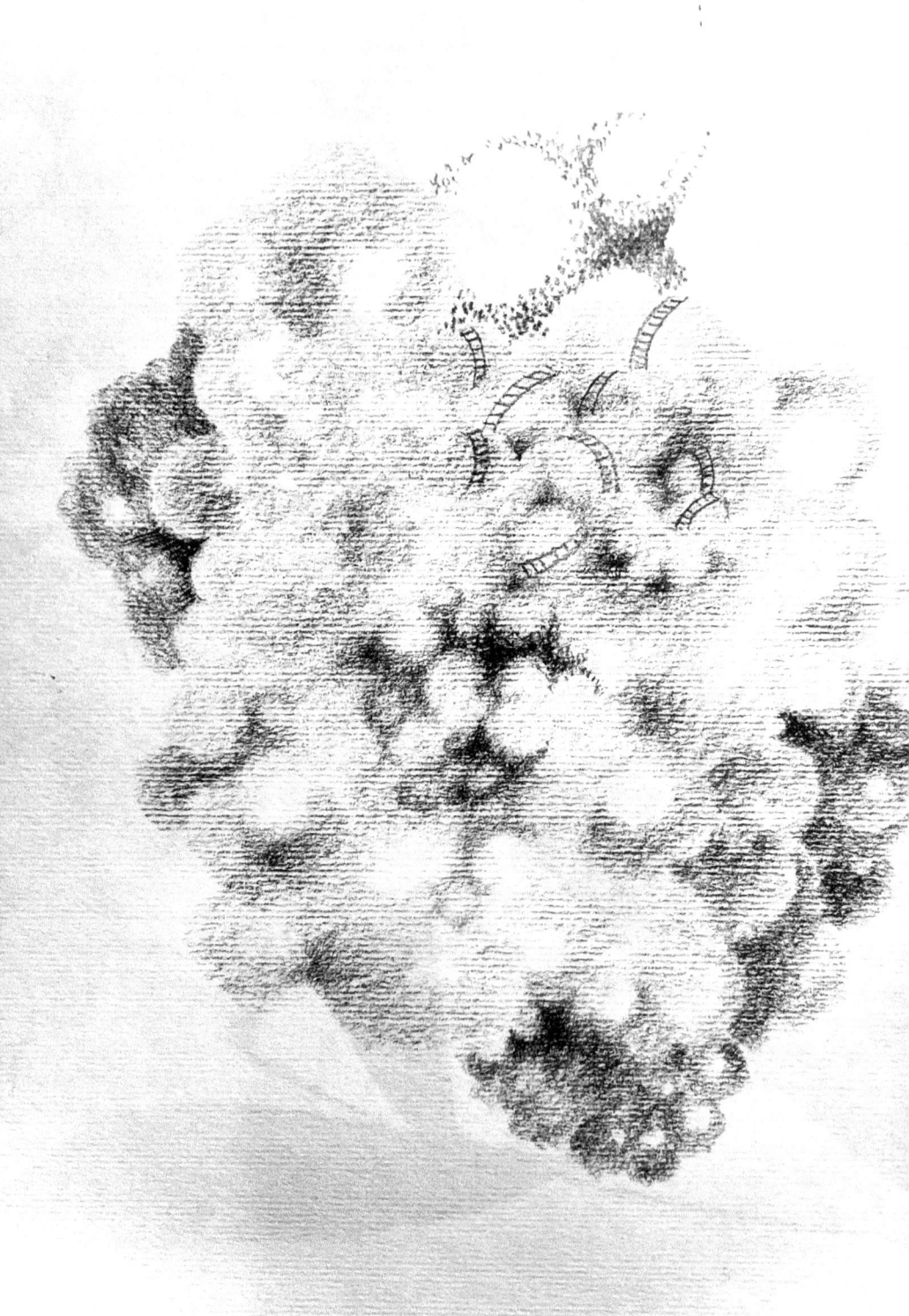

# Self-Contemplation

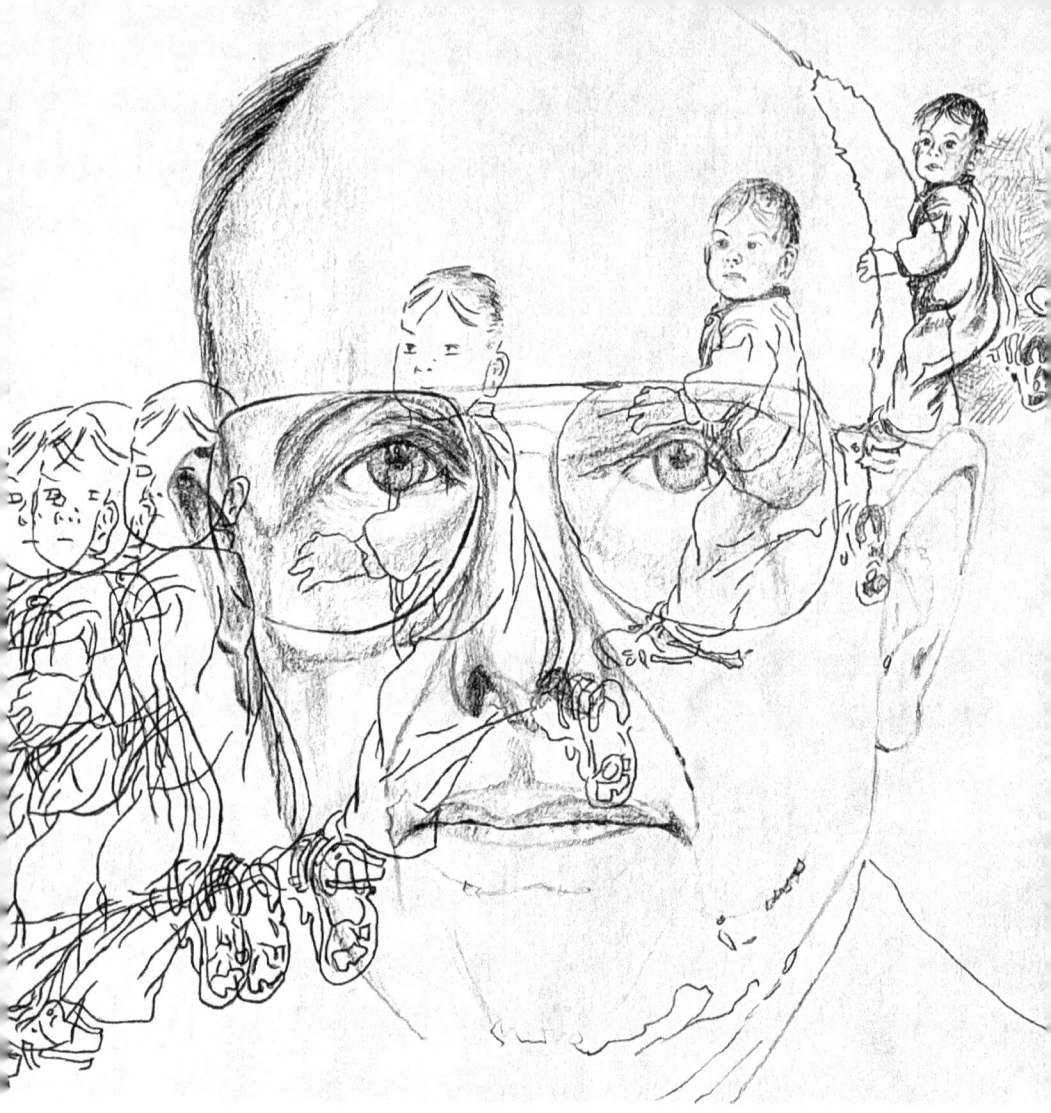

# Sorting Myself Out

I've become
the curator of me

What I do
is try to preserve
what I did

Who I am
seems to be
who I think
I used to be.

# Symbol Searching for a Poet

A cantering horse
emerges from fog
along the Yellowhead Highway
runs introspectively
as from a Colville painting
right at our Honda,
uncompromising
as a locomotive.

then veers, dissolves,
as Alex Colville situations do,
moments before
fact and symbol
crash

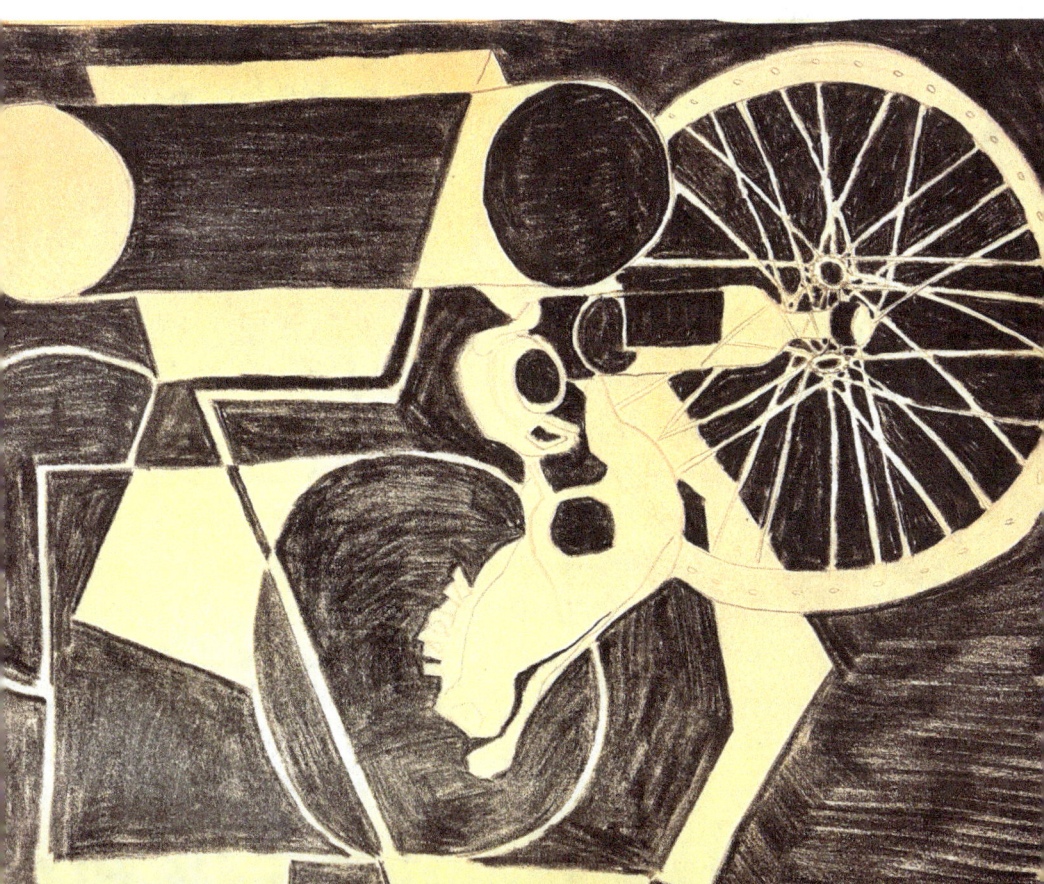

# Schizography

There were four of me
when I was small:
Waneetz, Hempreenge
Bullshick and Dale.

People smirked when
one of us walked past
in four-way conversation.

Bullshick
(corruption of a neighbour's name
much to Mother's burning shame)

was who I didn't want to be:
self-centred, clumsy,
not too bright.
Bullshick it was
who stood on Reg's
baby bird.

And once he threw a brick
at Bobby Lockie's Mom.
Another time
he stole a book with
photographs of genitals
that scared us all.

Waneetz was who I wished I were:
loyal, loving, cautious [careful]
well-behaved.

Hempreenge
was also well-behaved
but not so nice:
omnipresent,
book in hand,
observant, uninvolved.

Dale was somehow separate
from the others, though
I don't know how.

And now
sometimes Bullshick
shows up at parties
spilling drinks and
dropping verbal farts.

Waneetz is bald and seedy
not so timid or so virtuous
trying hard as ever
to be liked.

Hempreenge has weathered best
and changed the least,
judgmental even of himself.

And Dale is still not sure
that these are the friends
he really needs.

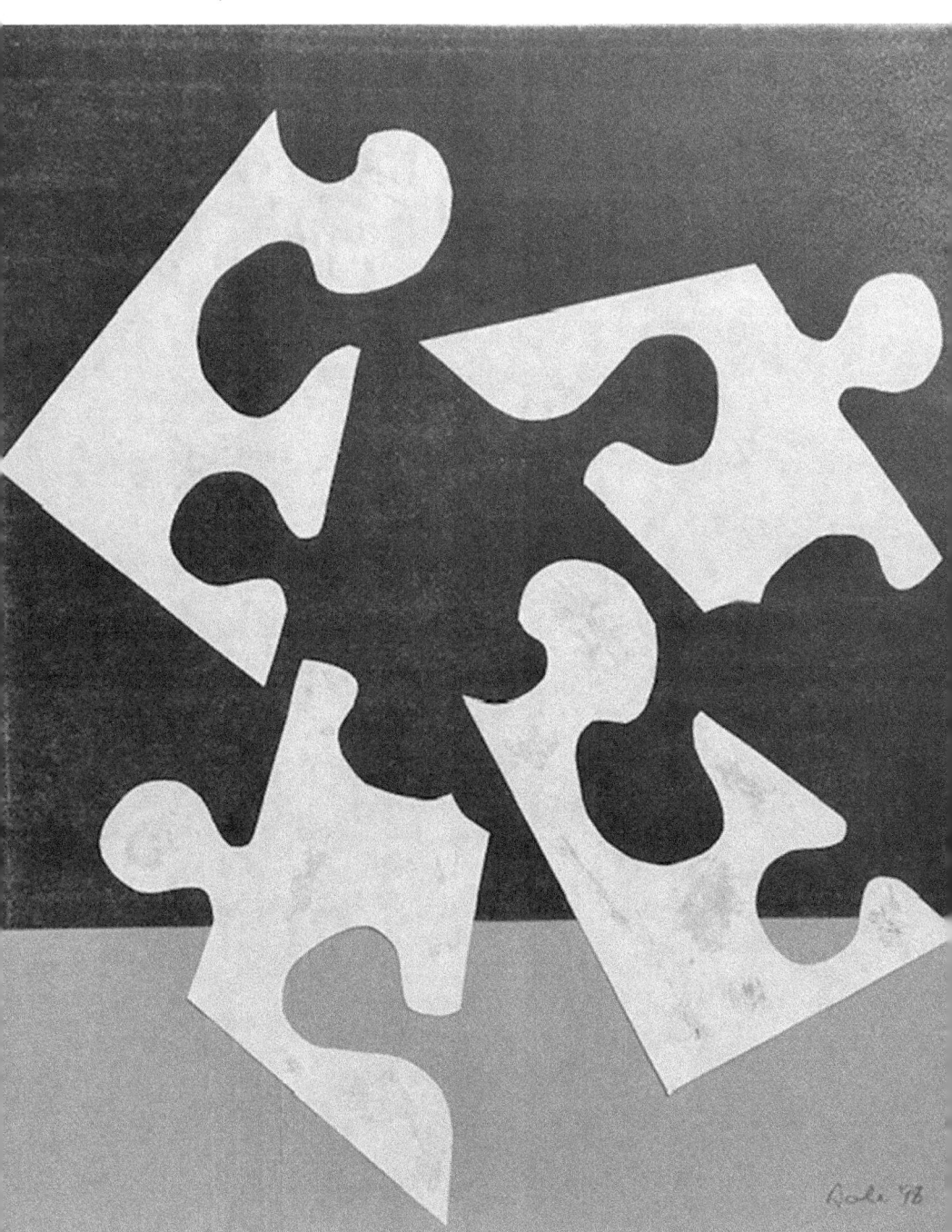

# the Stone, You See, Wasn't Thrown

The stone, you see, wasn't thrown
at the bus, but by it.
My target was,
I'd know a lot later,
what artists refer to as
negative space –
the too-often overlooked zone
squeezed in between the frame
and the object of principle interest
(in this case a 50 or 60 passenger bus):
that chunk of the world
which, if the bus were removed,
would be scarred by
a bus-shaped cavity.

The distinction was lost
on the driver, and Dad,
and the rest of the
blunt-sided world.

Now why was I throwing
a stone in front of a bus?

Well, that is really the point.

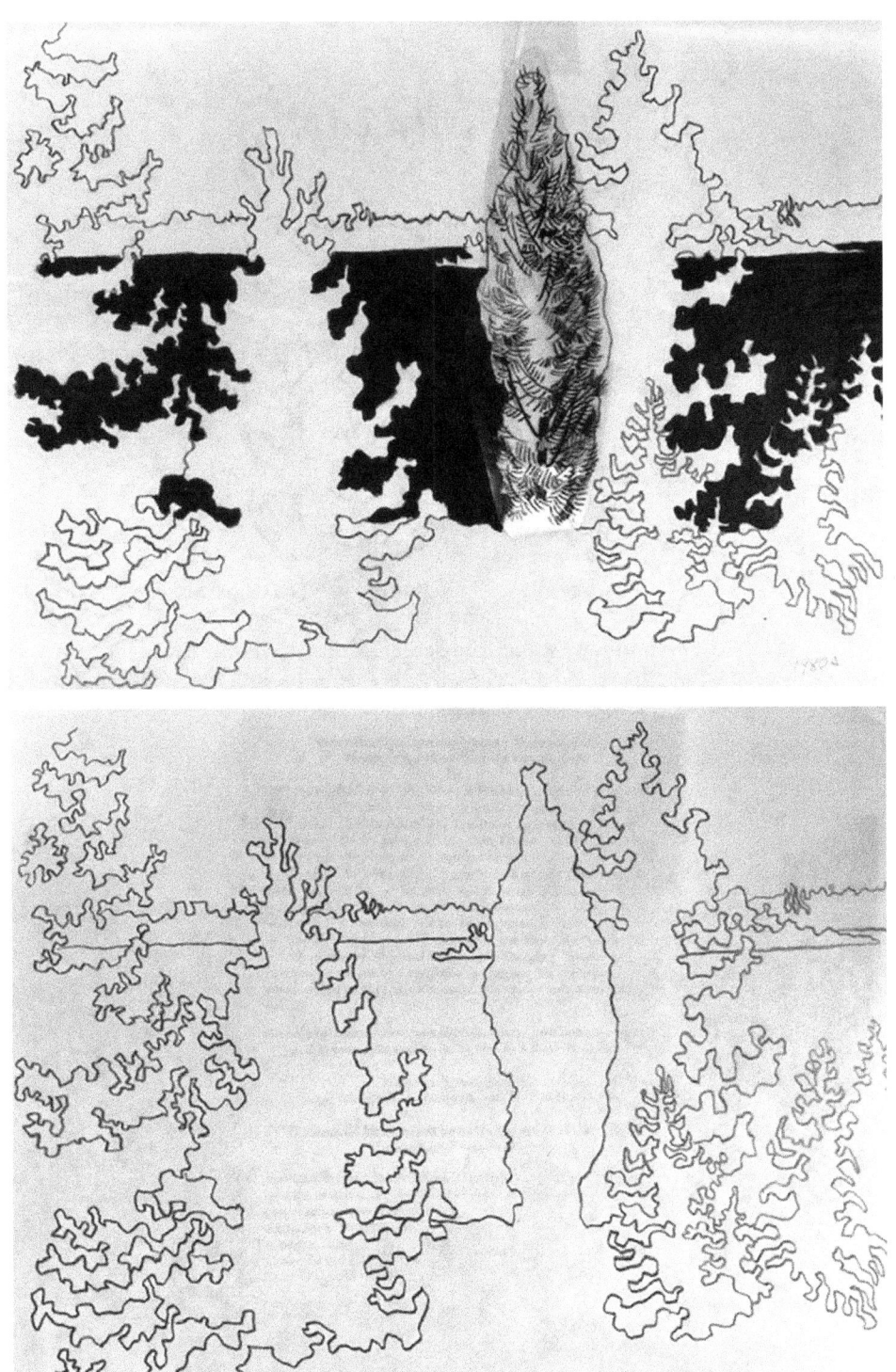

# Shazam!

We never walked
>back home
>from matinees in 1943 –

We swaggered, slashed & soared.

>Propelled to dazzling daylight
>we beat back waves of evil,
>smashed hordes of alien snowbanks,
>crushed fleets of tin-can spaceships
>as easily as Billy Barson
>>changed to Captain Marvel.

Nor did we walk from Seeger's concert Wednesday night.

>Rather small at first
>& palely foreign
>in a chamber darkly lined with life,
>he fed upon us,
>>swelled,
>>>& filled the chamber,
>which eventually exploded,
>>hurtling us
>>>into the midnight air.

My Chevrolet was a golden mount
whose saddle I shared with a naked nymph,
and we raced through Winnipeg's snowy streets
affirming life &
>showering love upon the Philistines
>>scattered by our steed.

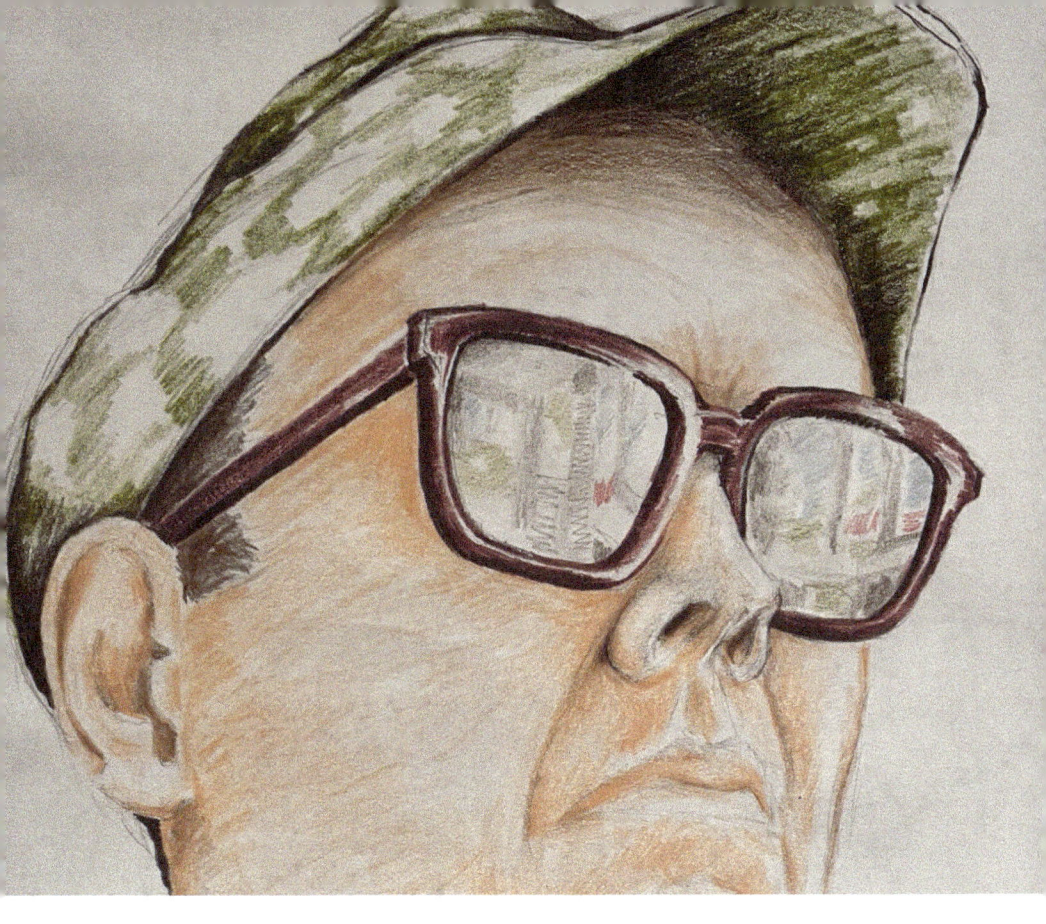

# The Magic Hat

I bought a winter cap,
a warm one
with a peak and ear flaps,
something like
the ones that postmen wear.

And when I wore it
Presto!

To my lawyer friends in felt fedoras,
to academic colleagues in their toques,
I disappeared.

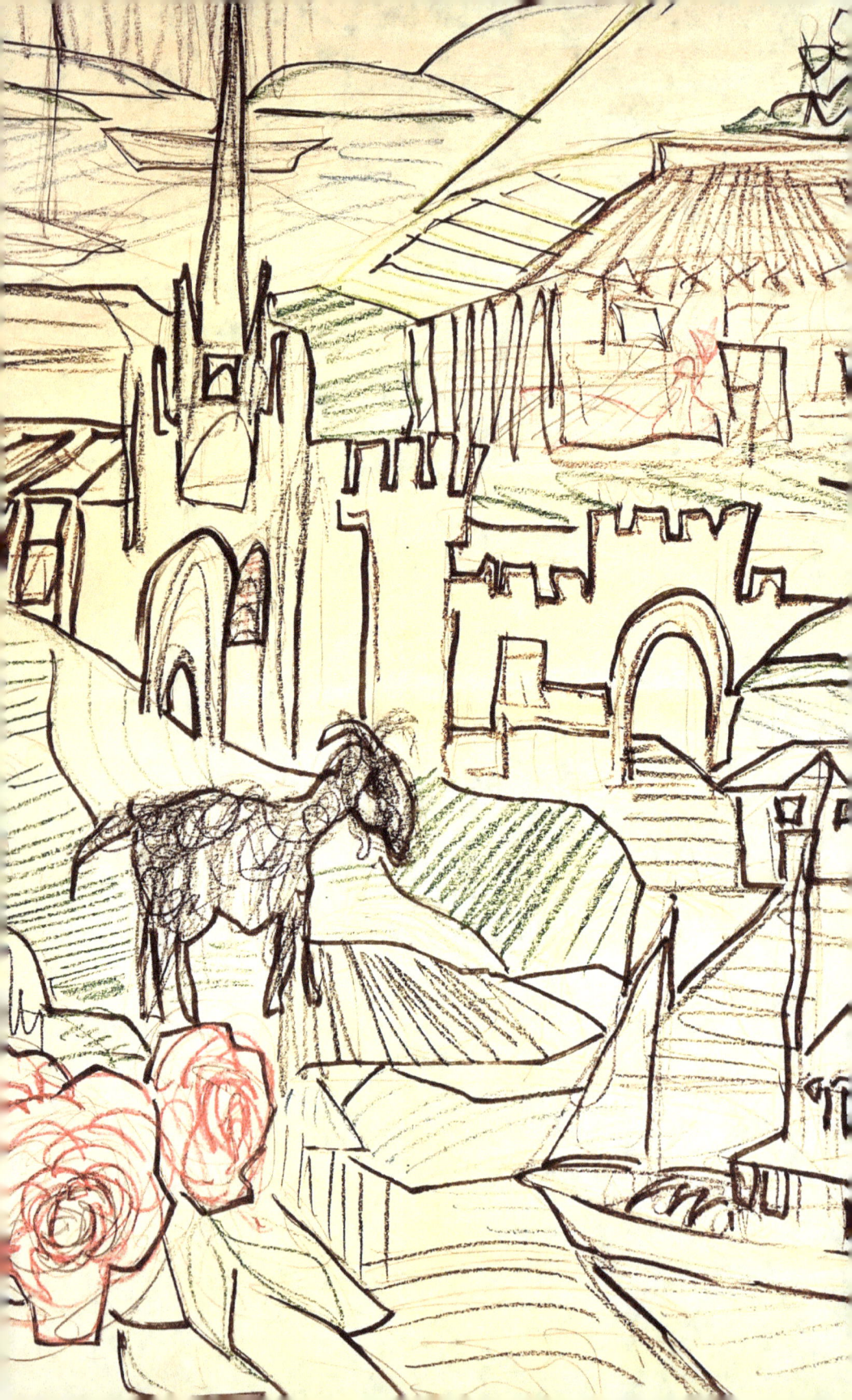

# The Day I Became an Atheist

My mother, puffing a little,
had gone on ahead
to find us an inconspicuous pew
which I knew would be hard
on the bum, wherever it was.

My dad wasn't there.
He never was there.
Not because he didn't believe –
I imagine he did, but he'd
"got enough of that stuff as a kid"

and seemed to think it
a natural division of labour
for him to hold down a job
and shovel the walk, while
my mother cooked & looked after
the wash, and religion,
ensuring that I "got enough of that stuff."

I dawdled
kicking a can, thinking,
but still I arrived while
other last-minute worshippers, panting,
ran up the steps
past black gothic sign
that announced: "This week:
'He is the Breath of Life.'
Genesis 2:7"

As for me,
instead of using the steps
as others were,
I opted to scale the granite
wall that sloped from
below the yawning entrance
to the apex of the steps.

As I got near the top,
an elder who didn't approve
that means of ascent
shouted.

I turned
in response, misjudged my footing
and fell
to still-frozen ground
eight feet below,
flat on my back.

I found myself emptied of air.
Though I gasped and wheezed, my lungs
refused to function, just as if a punitive
God stood on my chest.

Above me a circle of faces floated
Expressing concern until an elder
who'd apparently seen the whole thing,
assured them I'd only
"had the breath knocked out" and
deserved it,
for "larking."

Had I known anything of
Milton's Paradise Lost,
I might have thought,
as I fell, about
Lucifer's non-conformity.

As it was, I had only
a grim awareness that
cause would be followed by consequence.

This consequence
was not as dramatic as hell,
but it sure wasn't the
"Breath of Life."

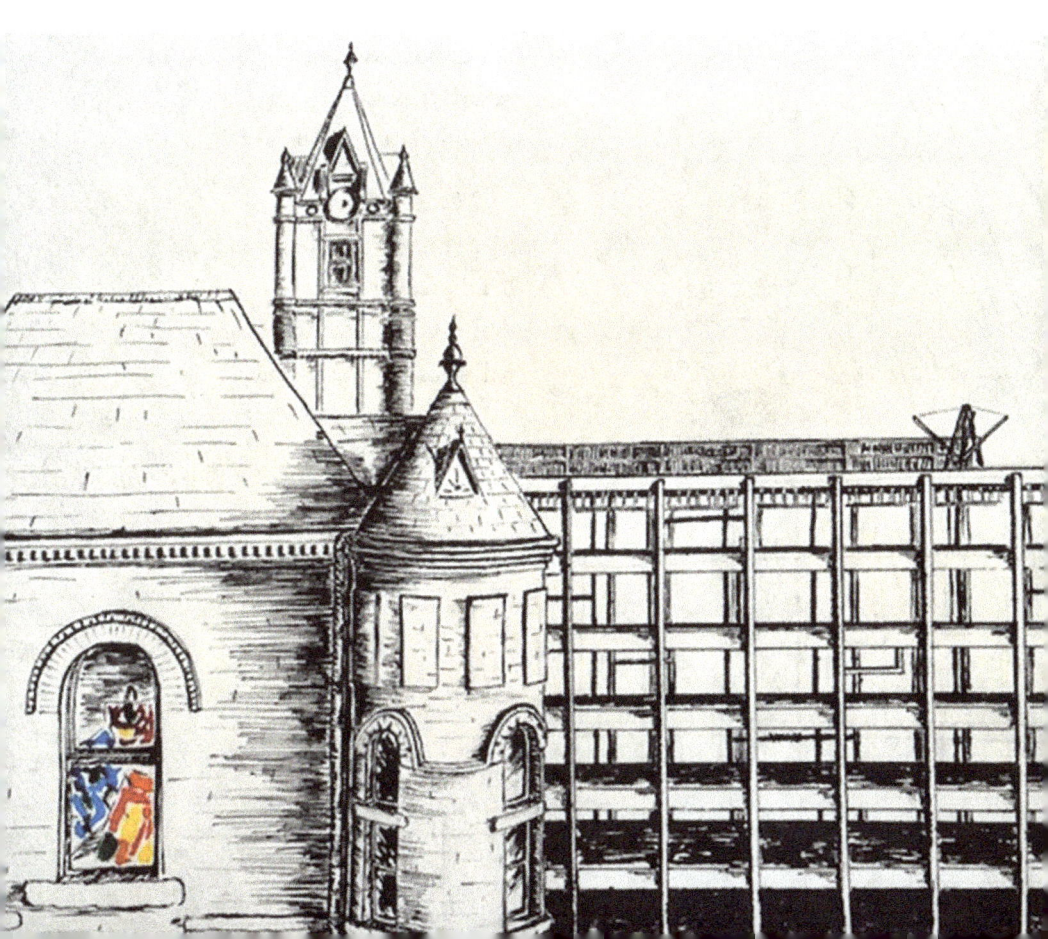

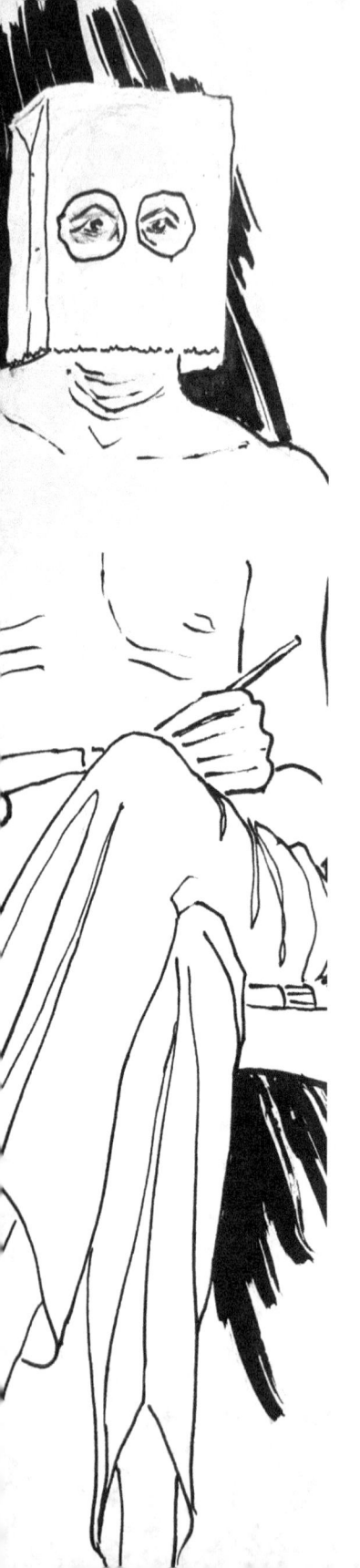

# Seven Dales

The boy
is said to be
father to the man

This boy?
Bland as pablum
soft as arrowroot
timid as tissue
tentative as trust?

This man?
Acrid as Lagavulin
stubborn as reality
assertive as advertising
opinionated as pedantry?

More than genes
caused this metamorphosis:
failure and success
guidance, ridicule, encouragement
love, disillusionment, betrayal
Happenstance?
No
just inexorable if unpredictable
causation

# Going to the Cottage to Get Some Work Done

Walking through the early woods,
branches tear the file cards
from my grasp.

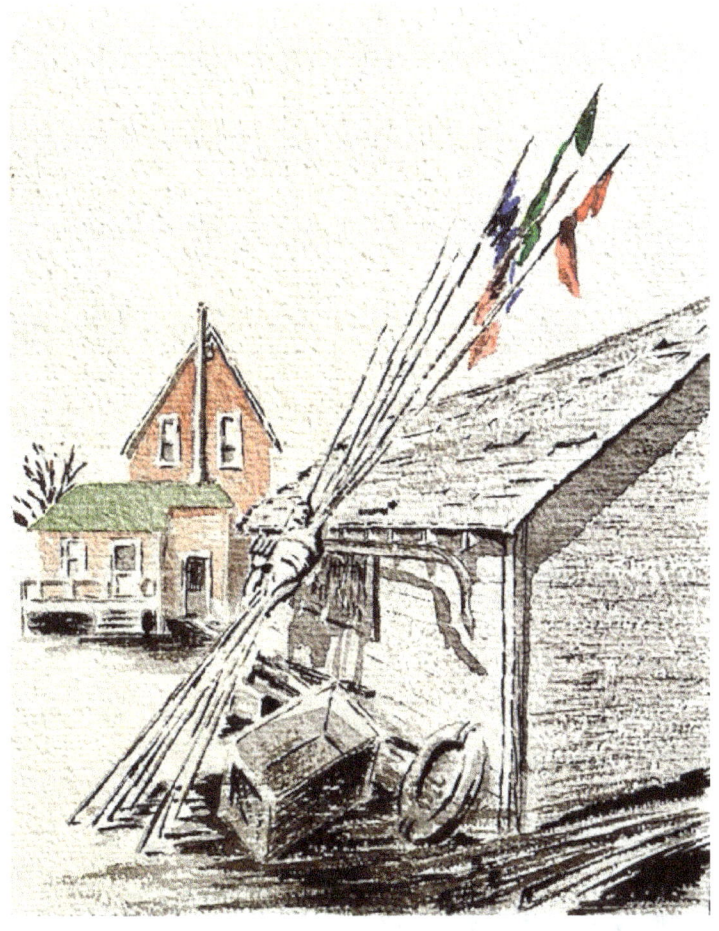

# Loons Are Laughing

The loons across the bay
are laughing
at my nakedness

as I flinch along
the splintered dock
to launch a swim
awkward as a loon on land.

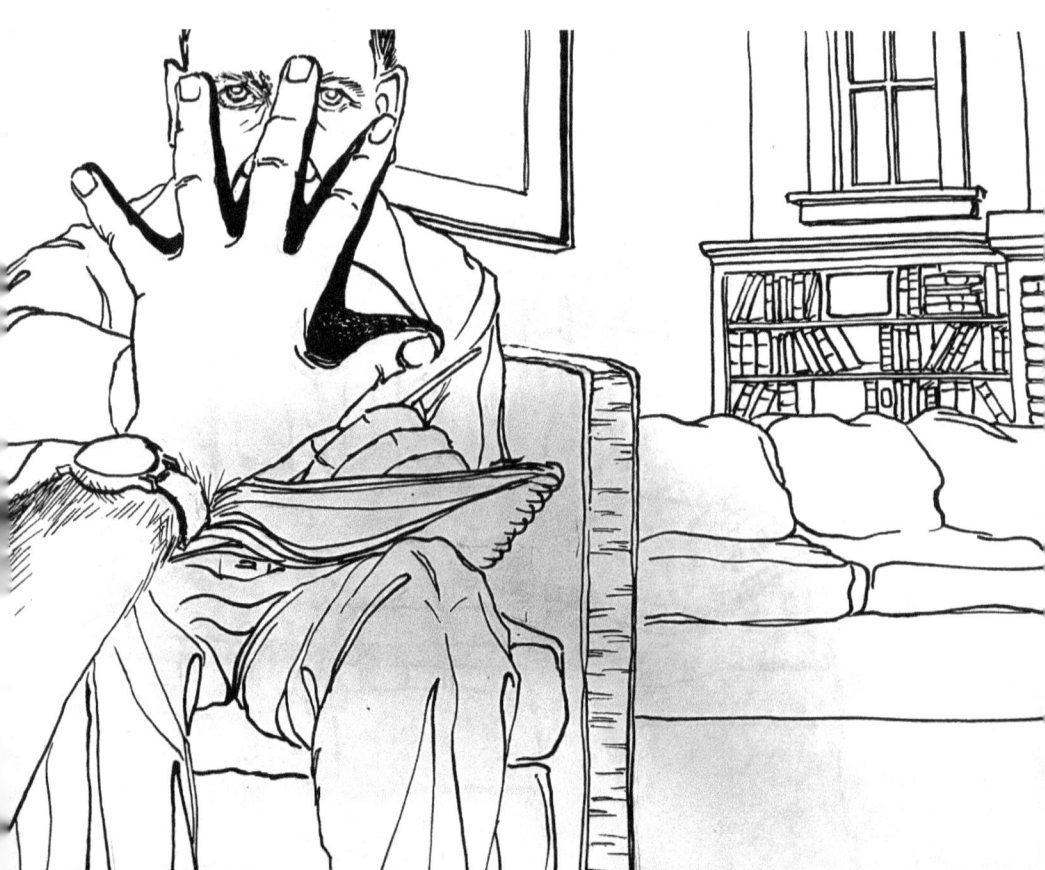

# Yesterday I killed a bird,

Yesterday I killed a bird,
a sharp-tailed grouse.
When he rose, cranky from his lair of scrub,
I pointed my borrowed gun
and fired,
as I had done – ineffectually – several times before.

He paused in flight,
then glided to the ground,
as if to show contempt
for so unskilled a foe.

I wrapped his entrails
in yesterday's headlines
and put them out of scent.

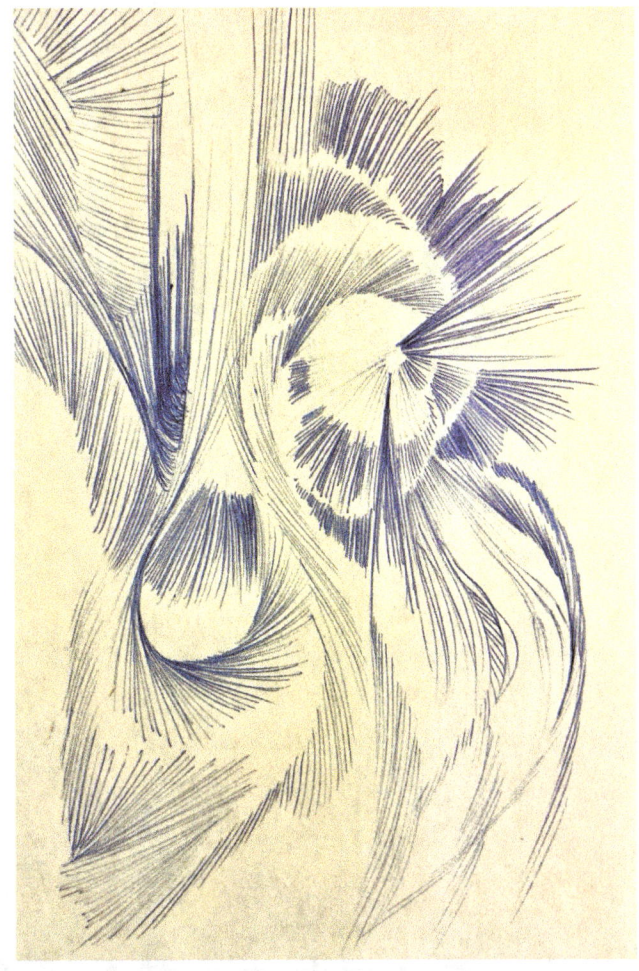

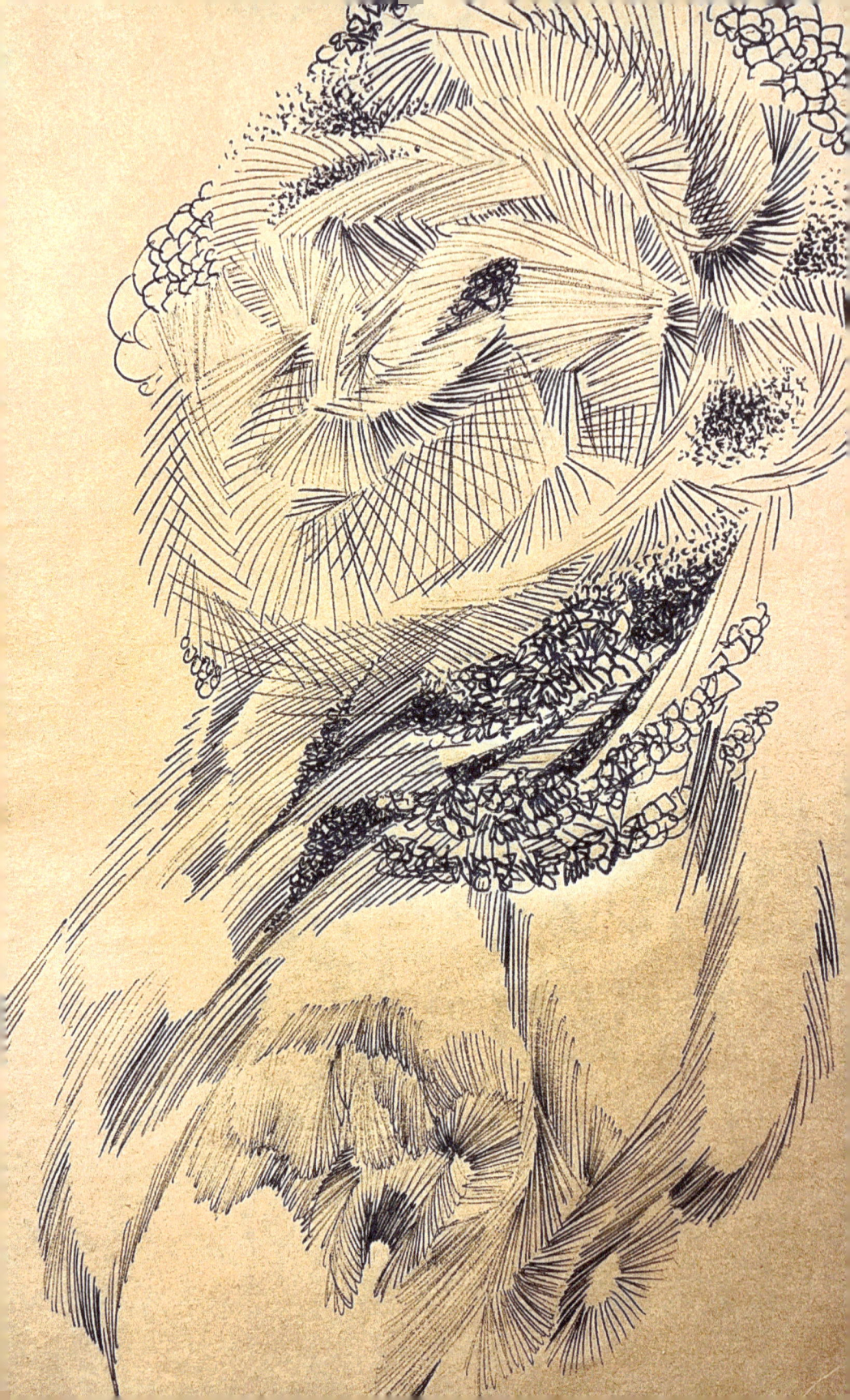

# Don Quixote's Mid-Life Crisis

Don Quixote's mid-life crisis
also
started at the age of fifty

He too thought
that he was special
that he was hurting no-one

To him as well it must have seemed
his new preoccupations
were somehow adding to
the world's worth


"So long as the rivers flow,"
they were told, and
although the water rushes past,
the river's always there,
hurrying from secret origins
to unknown destinations,

or is it?

Is this the river that flowed here yesterday?
Am I the man who stood here yesterday?

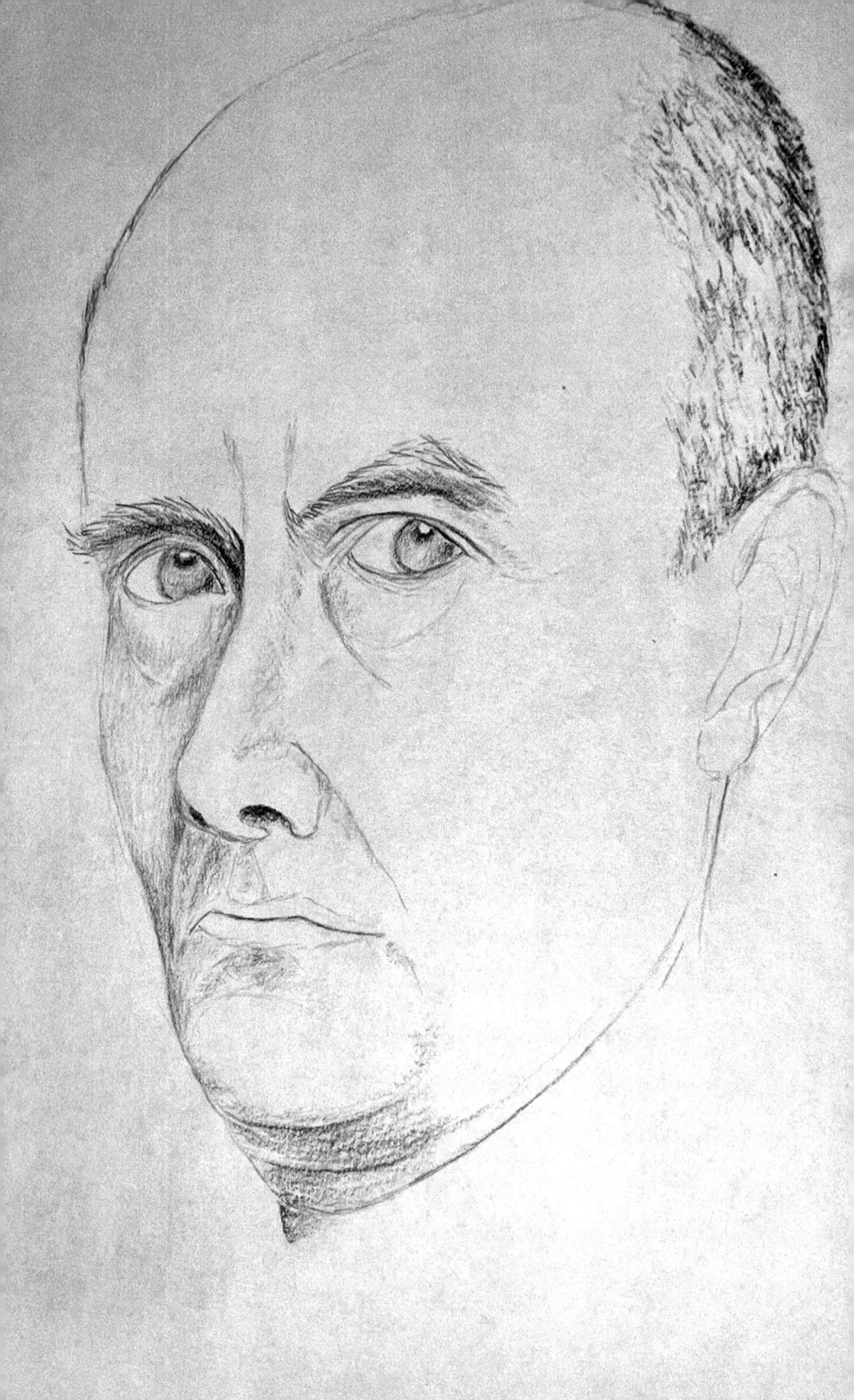

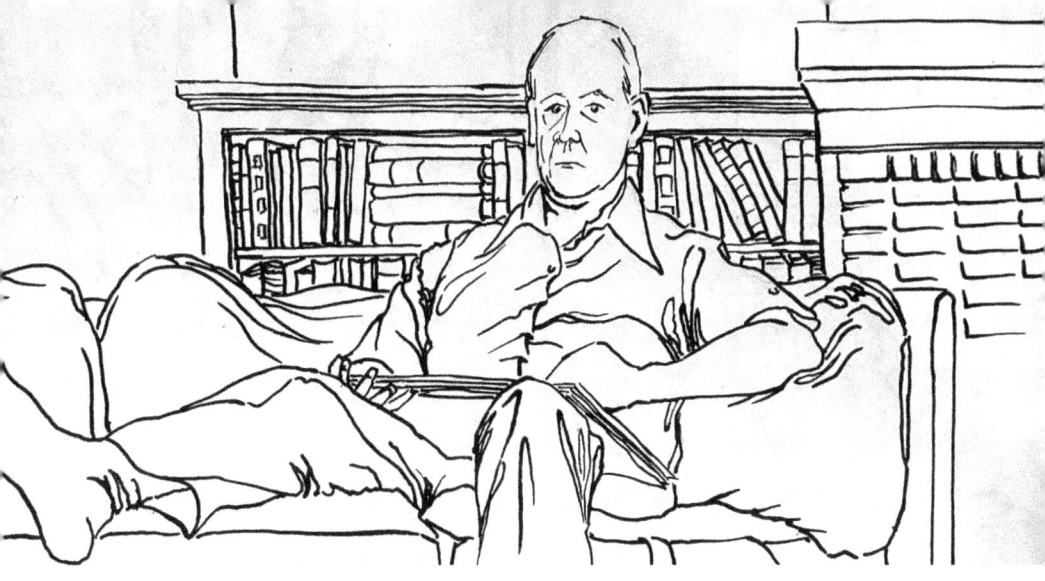

# What Have I Learned?

Towards the end of my years
they asked me to forecast
conditions a century from now.

Maybe they thought
that only someone my age
could even conceive
of a century.

They may have been right.
I have, after all, seen almost
three-quarters of this one.

And what have I learned
in that time
that's worth passing on?

That men govern laws
That justice shouldn't be blind
That decency's the obverse of evil
That learning soon spoils
if not put to use.

# The Law

# Some Say Law

Some say law
has always screwed
the citizen.

I'd rather think
that law makes
loving possible.

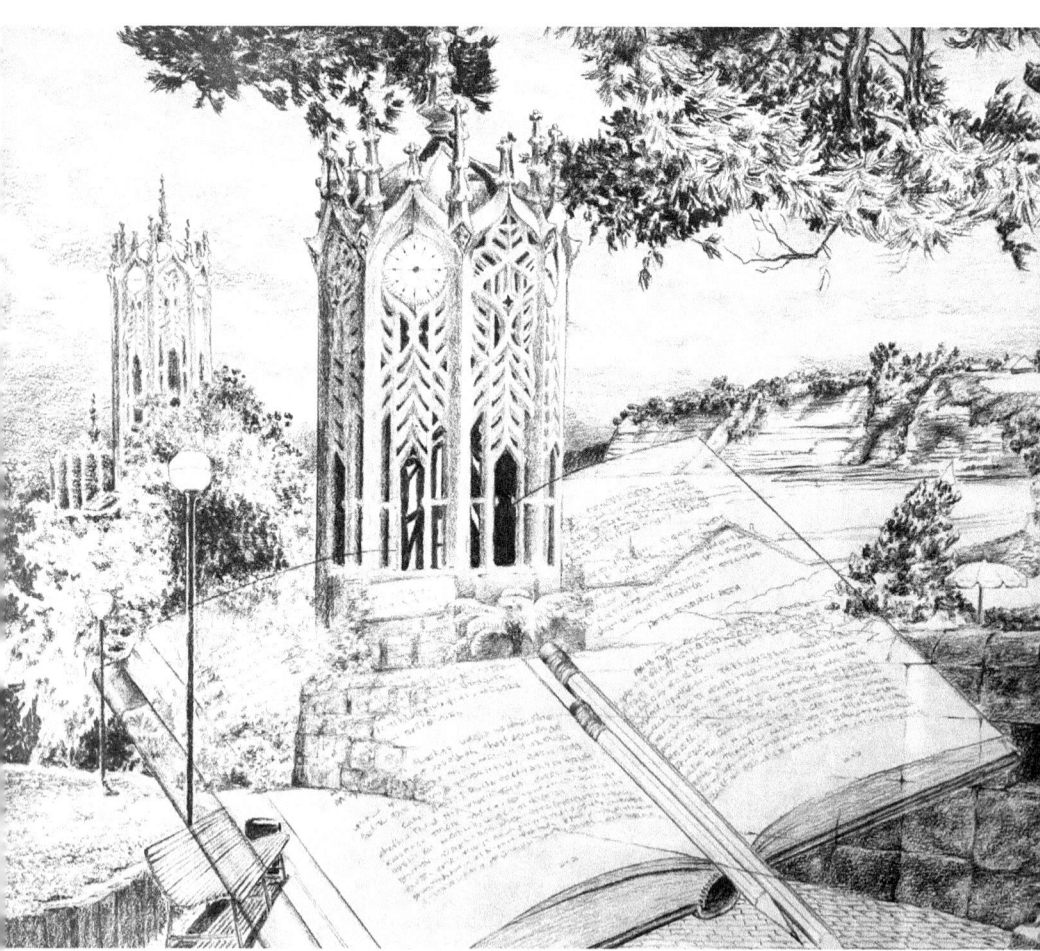

# The Canadian Charter of Rights and Freedoms

like any other poem
will mean more
or less
than was intended.

The words are sown
but the crops will be spoken
by others.

Woodrow Wilson once told us
that constitutions
obey the laws of Darwin,
not Newton.

The words will take root
or shrivel or blossom or mutate.

We overflew the sunrise,
underlit cloud beds
roiling like lava
threatening to thrust
another Iceland
forth

and landed on
a flinty British day
through
the Commonwealth Arrivals gate –
past luggage, boxes, trunks,
around dark dots of frightened immigrants
and non-committal officers,
but we Canadians
were waved right through.

Outside,
the rain
was laced with snow
and crocuses lay wisely low.

Even
the property agents
were cautious;
where signs would say "sold"
in America,
here they read:
"Offer being considered."

Their architecture
since Wren and Nash has been
organic

Their Constitution, too.

Charters
and similar promises
are not understood
any longer

Runnymede
was so long ago.

Why,
they wonder,
can't Canada
muddle along
with makeshifts
as they have?
Why ask for trouble?

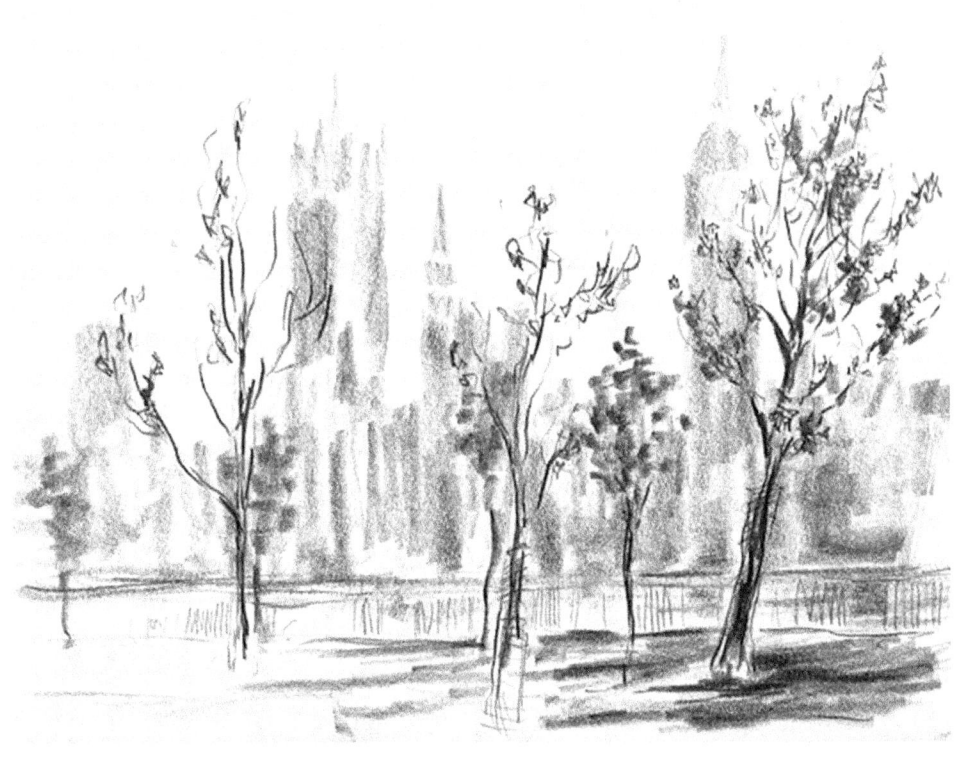

# The Client

The crime was grave;
the guilt was clear.

This, though, is no criminal.

This is a man
who committed a crime.

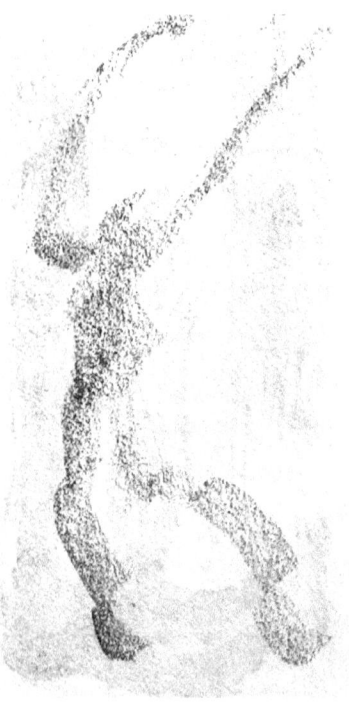

# He was only 16

He was only 16
on his first date in Court
He arrived on time
and was given 8 years.

His second date was yesterday.

To answer why he
carried on the street
the weapon that he needed
for defence in prison,
his mother appeared
as the Court convened
to explain that he wouldn't
be able to be there
due to being shot dead
at a party the night before.

# Good Friday

Good Friday.
The hawks are soaring again
beautiful, threatening

Sweeping the sky
in elegant amber arcs
like radar

Ignoring
nest-building geese
for now

Searching
for creatures
who've shed their fears

like winter coats
in the warmth of the
traitorous sun.

\*\*\*

And the lawyers
are also working
despite the holiday,
reconnoitering
opponents' briefs for
vulnerabilities,

fat, squirming non-sequiturs
to feed
to the judge.

# Endgame

I was never
much good at chess

My openings were bold
my mid-game gambits
were sometimes surprising

but checkmates
seemed to
elude me

As a lawyer I filed more
Statements of Claim
than Judgments

As a scholar
I thought about more than I wrote
and I wrote considerably more
than I published

And now
that I'm playing an opponent
I can't hope to beat,
I've thought about castling,

but I'd much rather

skip round the board
taking as many pieces of his as I can

before
succumbing
to checkmate.

# Senior Partner

Smiling
pleasantly enough,
speaking softly
though authoritatively,
and acting just as moderately
as he thought the circumstances justified,
the senior partner
sat down on
the junior's head.

Or thought he had;
in fact, the junior had declined
to lie down as expected, and
the senior ended sitting on a
barren floor.

"Never mind,"
he told the junior's disappearing
back
with a not unpleasant smile.
"There are many more
who'll lie down than who won't."

Which was true,
but only partly relevant,
since both lived happily thereafter.

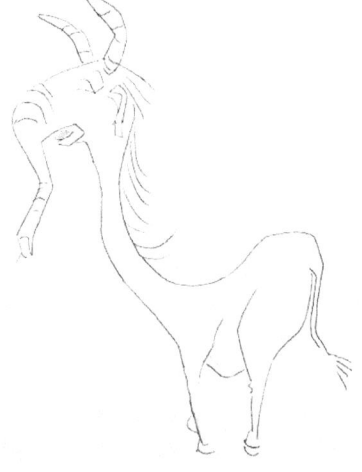

# Social Commentary

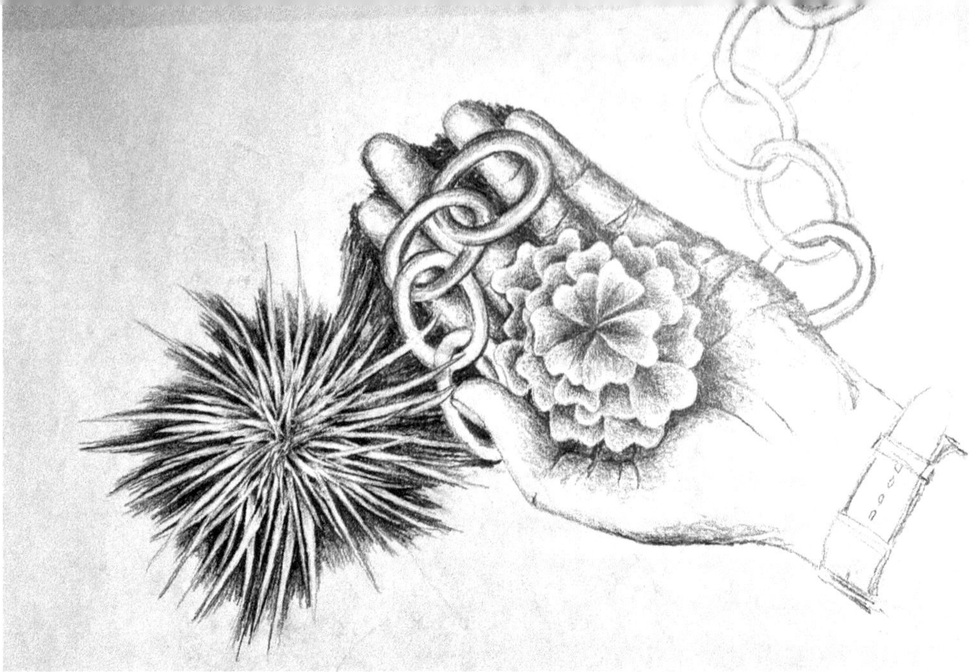

# Mobius

Once I had a cat
so compulsively self-curious
he crawled right up his bum
and disappeared.

I named him Mobius
in retrospect,

and
thought
that if he ever
finds out how to put
the process in reverse
he'll bring us back
the secret of the
universe.

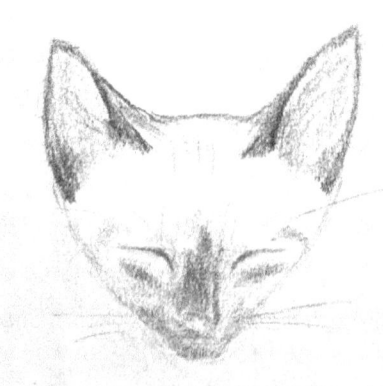

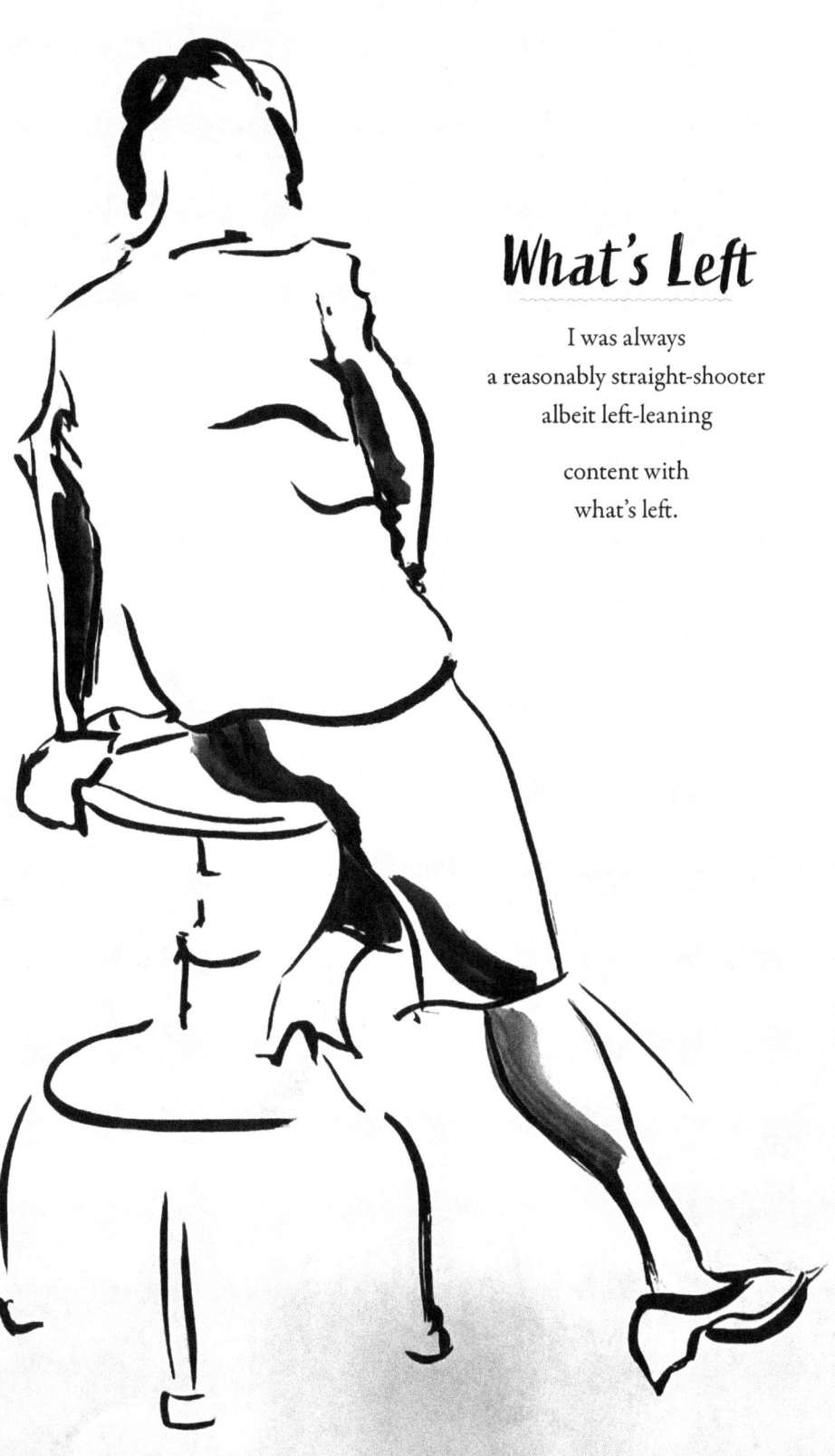

## What's Left

I was always
a reasonably straight-shooter
albeit left-leaning

content with
what's left.

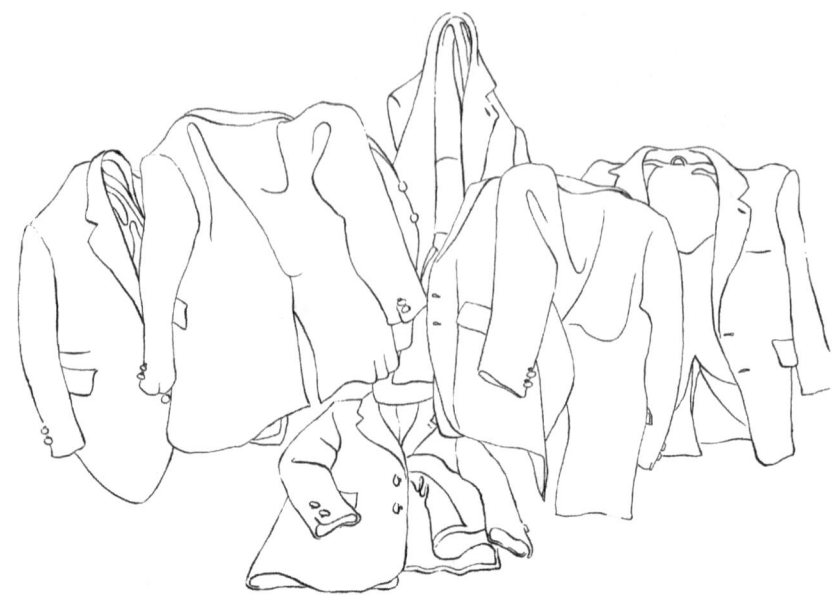

# Fe(de)ral Bureaucrat

One
must never bite
the hand that feeds
the future.

Nor
except in
special circumstances
and
with excess caution
the hand that feeds
the present.

But
it is always quite
permissible
to bite the
hired
hands.

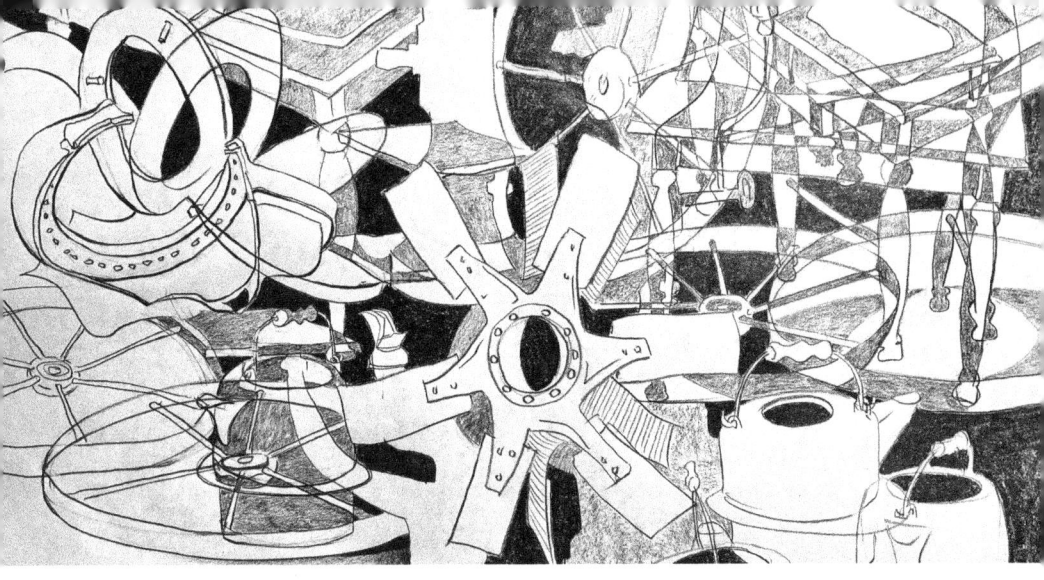

# Policy Evaluation Seminar [1]

Everywhere were inputs.
Why isn't there an outcome?

Because the
orientation
globally speaking,
while emphasizing systemic interface,
optimizes internalization,
thus constricting the throughput
and clogging the infrastructure.

# Policy Evaluation Seminar [2]

Everywhere are inputs.
Why isn't there an outcome?

Because
the orientation
of the dialectic
is teleologically inhibitory.

Maximizing interface
like this conduces
multifurcation of the issues
on an almost
exponential scale,
clogging the infrastructure,
constricting throughput,
and
ultimately inducing
systemic gridlock.

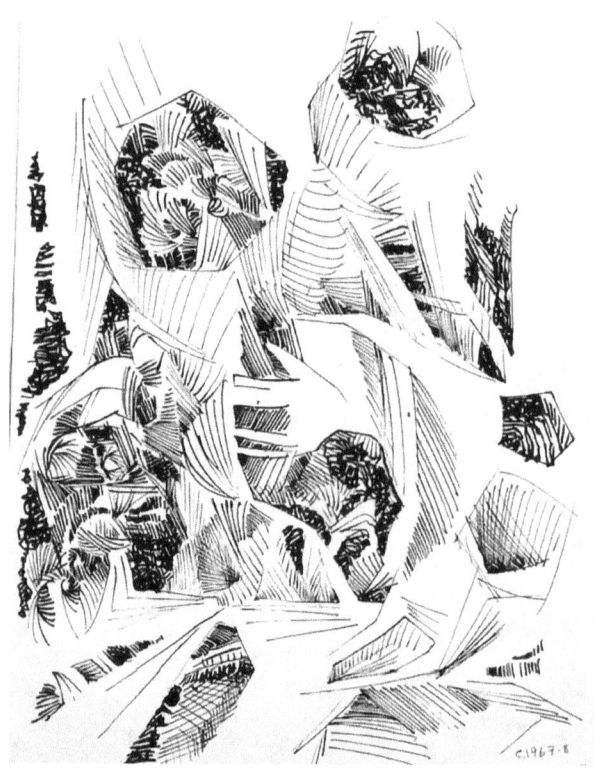

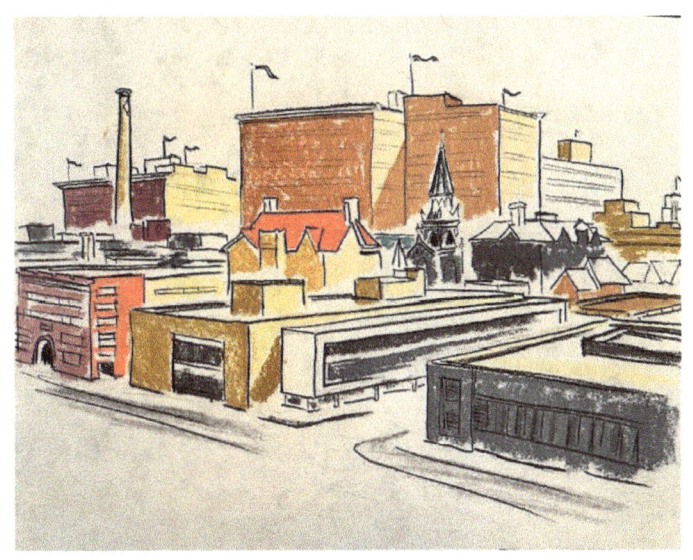

# One Prairie Province Conference

Three hundred veterans
of the conference circuit
congregate at Lethbridge
to debate a union of the prairies.

They gather in a hockey rink
which, judging by the smell,
has also witnessed many other
livestock shows.

And when the talking stops,
the scoreboard over centre ice
records a scoreless tie,

which isn't strictly accurate,
because the sparrows,
darting high among the rafters,
scored at least a dozen times.

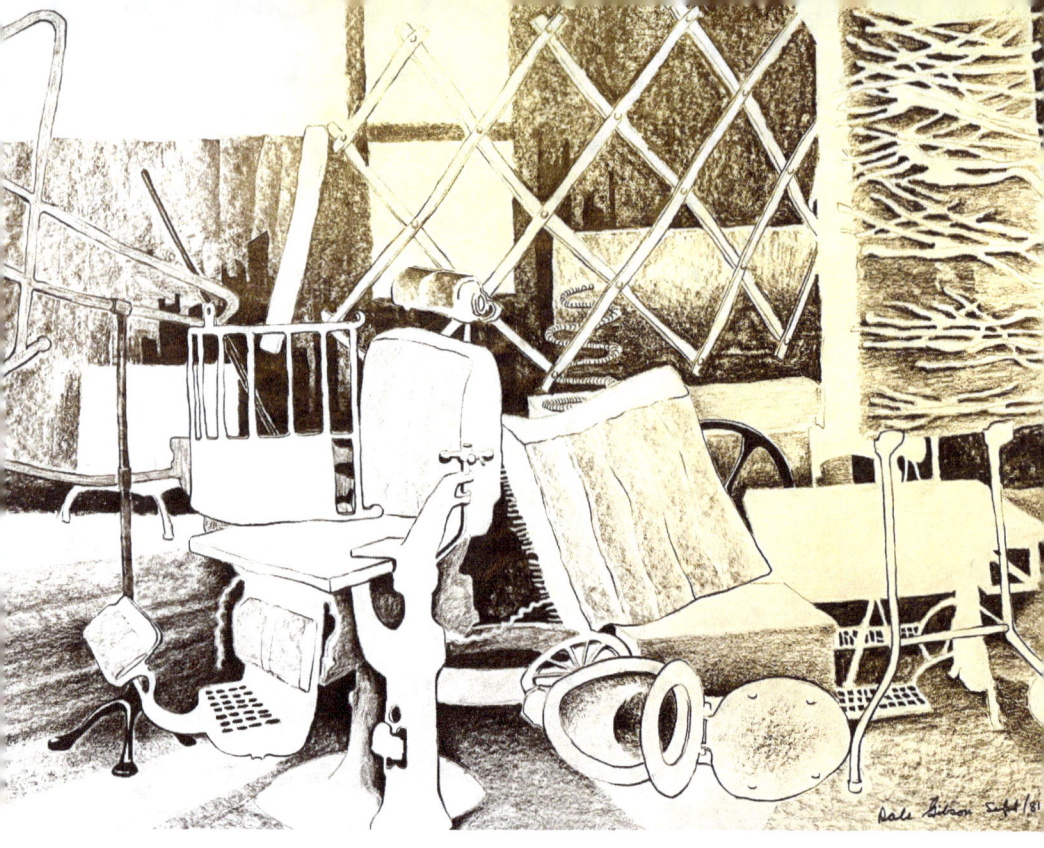

# Accommodating the French

The paper band across
the hotel toilet seat
reads: "Pour votre protection."

The fire precautions are in English.

# The Clerics Explain Cycle

And God so loved the world
that he ordered its inhabitants
to slaughter each other
to gain life eternal
in another world
where they'll all be together once again.

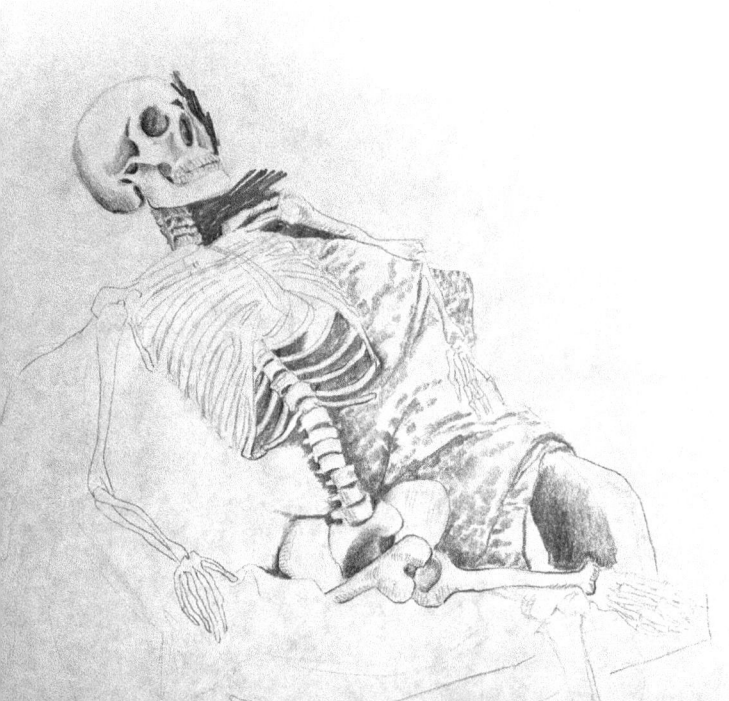

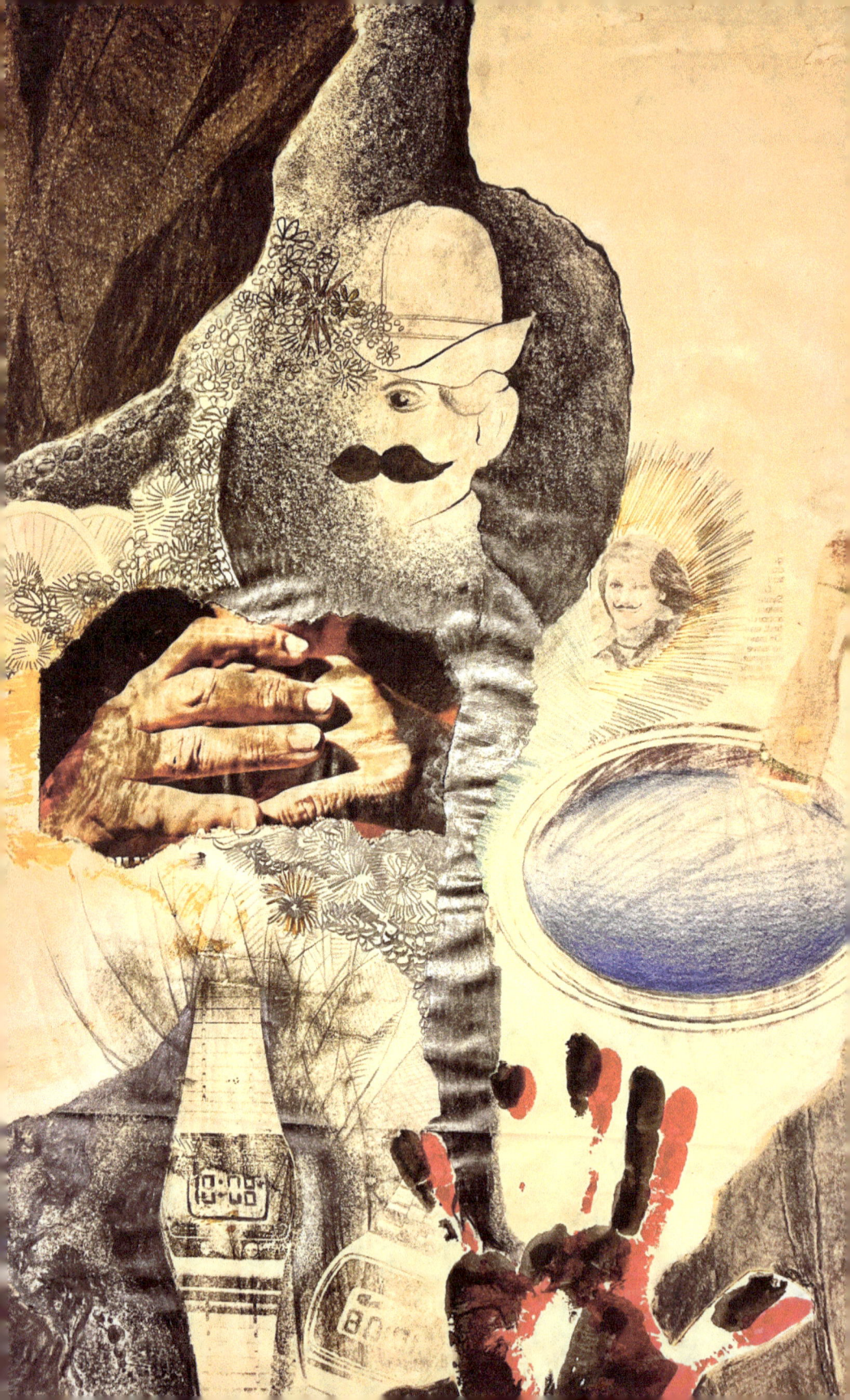

# After the Play

(Niagara-on-the-Lake)

After the play
a peach-coloured dusk
silhouettes
the Queenston-Lewiston bridge
across
the cleft escarpment

and the pompous plinth memorializing
Canada's victory
at
Queenston Heights
in 1812:
outlines
as flat as stage sets
as simple as history.

Bar music throbs
from the U.S. side
breaching
the world's longest undefended frontier
while
General Brock
moulders
beneath his
two-dimensional monument.

# Bayeux Tapestry

The embroidery began
with a needle plunged
through Harold's eye.

The thread was dyed
in peasants' blood
vivid now as
when it ran
at Hastings
and at Agincourt

and Omaha Beach
where American graves now
hold the heights:
with woven rows of
motionless sentries
listening to waves

of bombers and beach craft
shell bursts and screams

of kids on the beach
while their parents
queue up at museums for the Conquest
and D Day and similar
works of art.

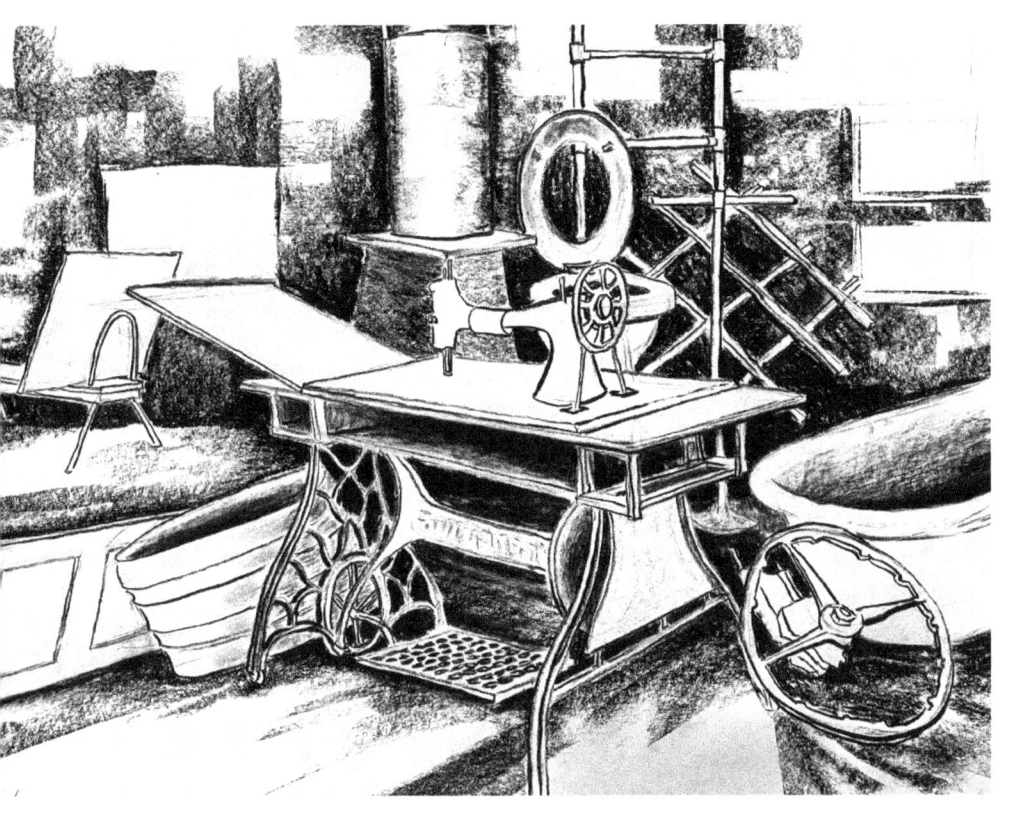

# September/ Walking to the Class

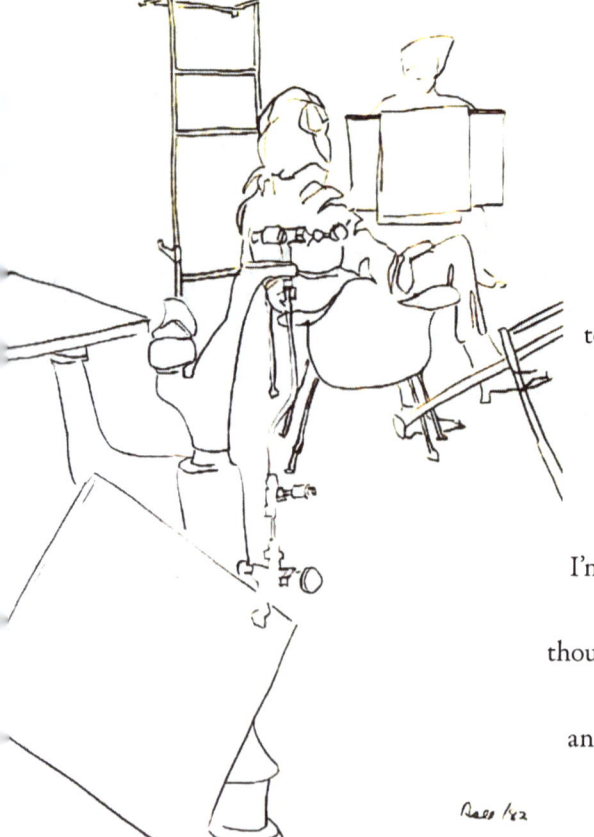

September, but
at universities
it's spring.

The students
hurry past
in avid groups
or hand-in-hand
in pairs

along an avenue
of mountain ashes,
overwhelmed by
autumn fruit.

They're rushing on
– the students are –
to where I've been before
and where I hope
to meet them now.

But as we enter
I can see
I'm in a different classroom
than they are
though I can watch them fidget
as the old man drones
and all my pungent insights
are delivered
to an empty room.

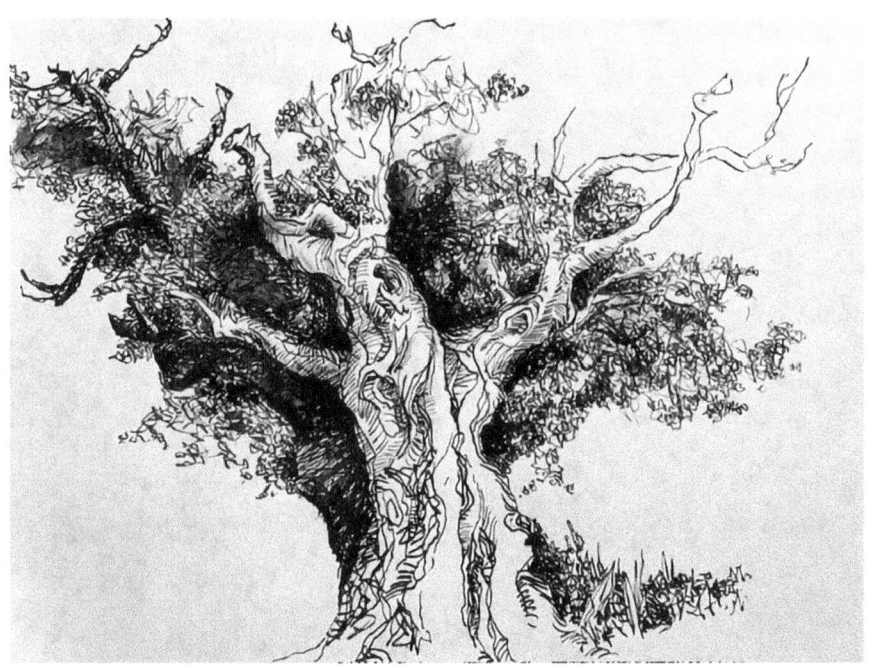

# End Game

Suppose
that on the 6th day,
He'd stopped to reconsider

"Wait a minute.
What am I getting into here?"

And what if
on the 7th day
She didn't rest
or pause to savour
what she'd made,
but spent the day
preparing for the eighth?

Well,
what, if anything,
would have been the point of
days one to six?

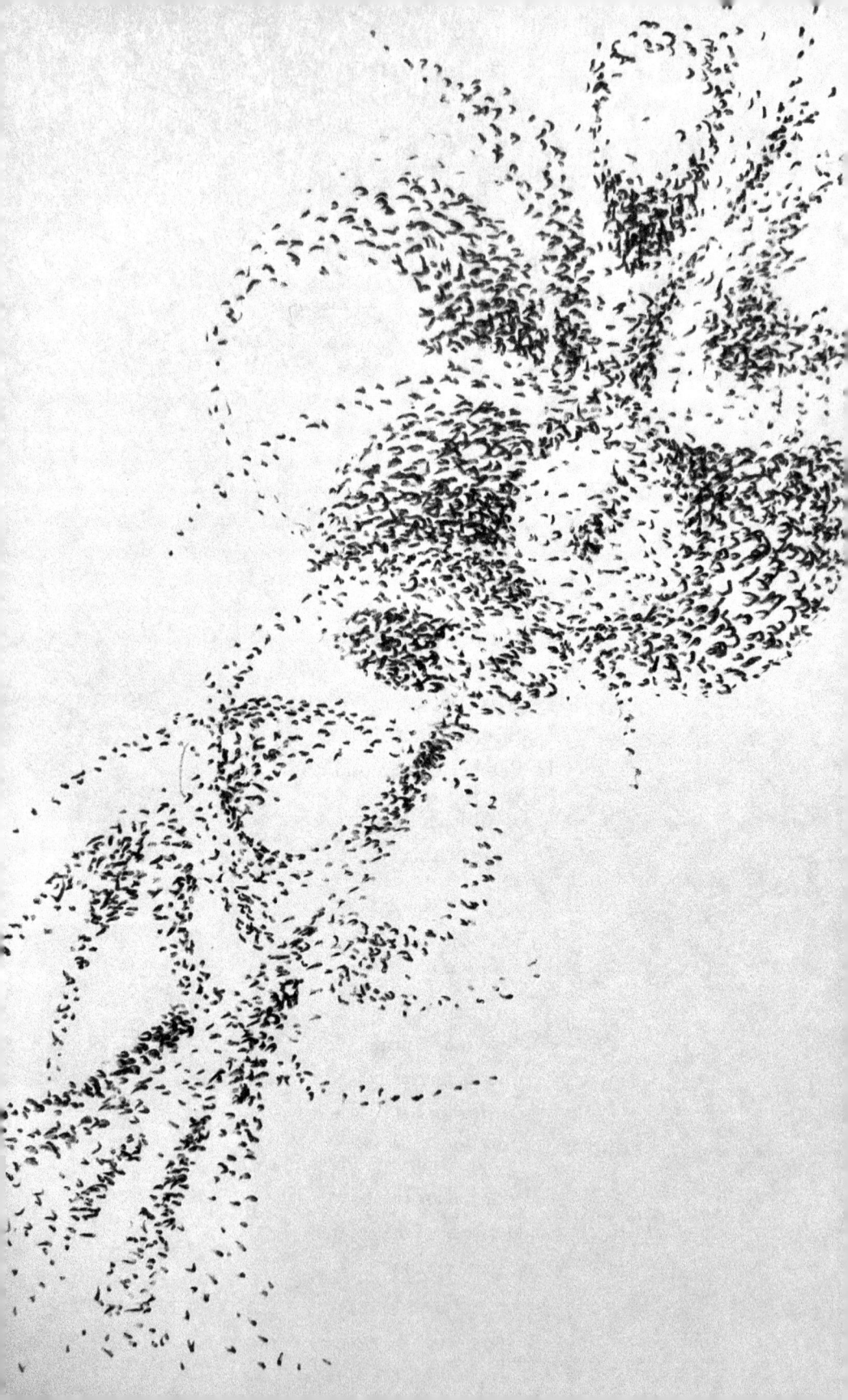

# The Dual Aspect Tango

(Poetic parry and thrust by a frustrated professor and an unsatisfied class)

## Part I: Ultra Vires (By Dale Gibson)

Trying to teach this bunch
about the constitution
is much like making love
to someone with a headache.

Perhaps a
tantalizing dance
would help.

Shamelessly
I leap upon the lectern,
stripped to pith and substance.
After taking some preliminary liberties
and exhibiting certain colorable devices
I begin – licentiously – to dance
the dual aspect tango.

With sinuous movements
and sensuous rhythms
I urge them all
to flout convention, challenge laws,
embrace the body politic –
take an active interest in our
most fundamental act.

Eventually
I note a slight response:
a spreading – almost imperceptible –
of barely lubricated minds,
and I dare to think
that I may occupy the field, after all.

But then the hour ends.
Intellects are hastily re-zipped
and I withdraw – functus.
No, not even that: ultra vires.

# Part II:
# An Aroused Response (by Class 2b)

We sat in the dark, in anxious anticipation.
For many it was the first time.
A man with a dual purpose began clutching at us.
As the subject aroused our interest, our minds spread open.
He seemed to take forever to get to the pith and substance.
We glanced at our fingernails as he got all tangled up trying to unhook
our necessarily incidentals.
With assistance this was accomplished, and we faced him prepared
to accommodate section 92.
But his knowledge would not rise within us,
"Perhaps a cigarette would help" we soothed.
"No, we will expand on this matter today!" he
cried in frustration.
In forced resignation, we stooped to contemplate his possible emergency powers.
By oral elucidation, we encouraged a growth in understanding.
Inch by inch, our grasp of the expanding jurisdiction solidified.
It extended to us.
His bald head now glistened in the fluorescent light,
the point of the matter became clear.
"Is that all there is to it?" we asked, aghast.
"Don't worry – I have amendments to make the Act complete" he countered,
and he fumbled for them under the podium.
We expertly navigated him to matters of absolute jurisdiction.
At last the give and thrust of intellectual debate began, ....and ended
prematurely.
"Too soon!" we cried.
Alas the outpouring of provincial powers was complete, leaving only a residue:
as he went dribbling off to another topic.

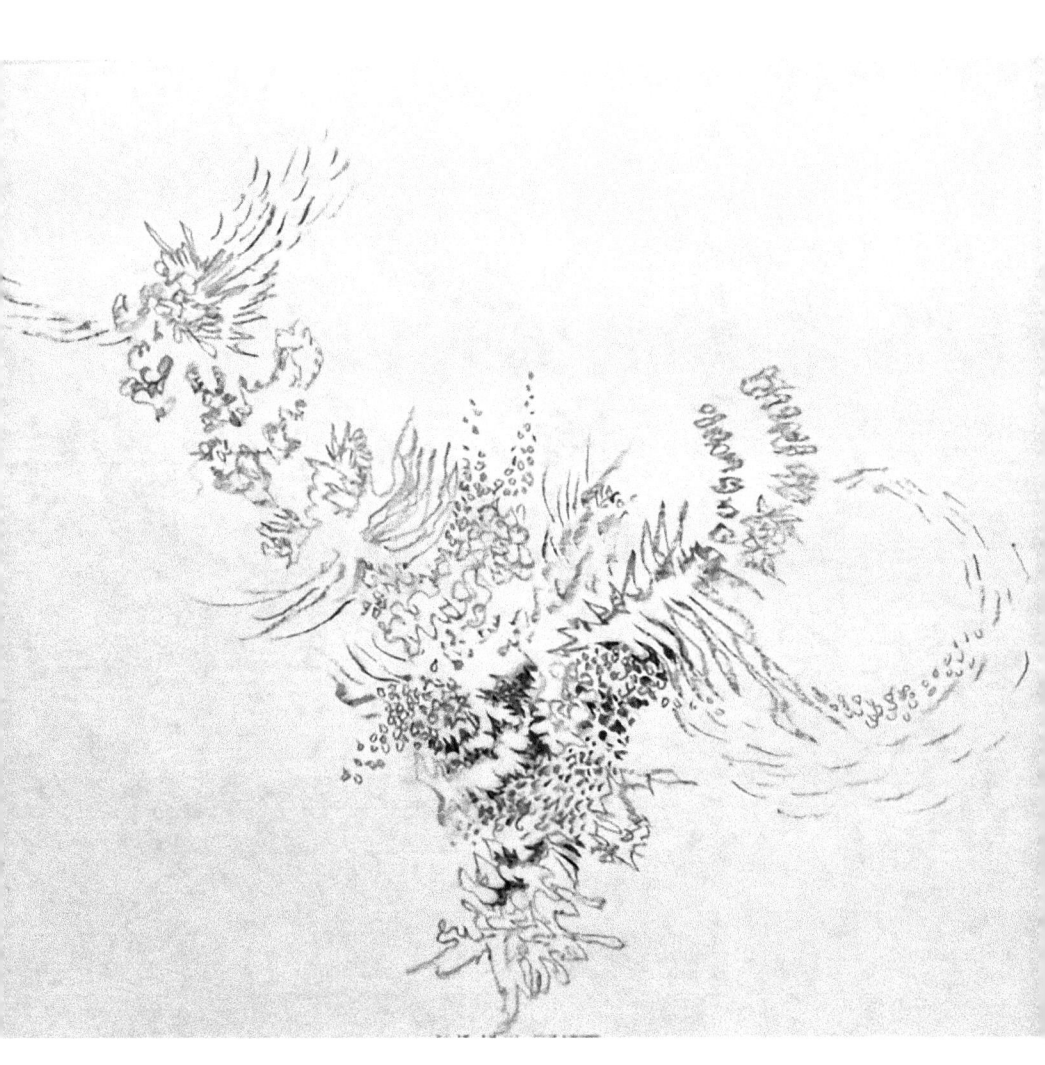

# Beasts in Human Form

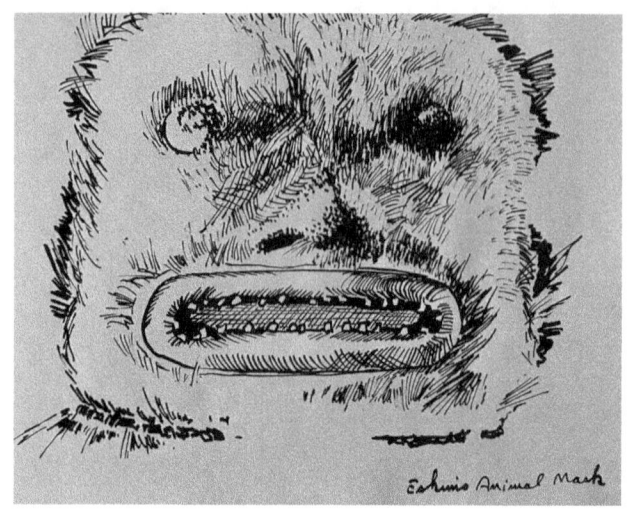

*Eskimo Animal Mask*

# A Conceptual Bestiary

For a fortunate few
life can be pastoral
strolling meadows and groves
thinking thoughts that are ast[o]ral.

But for too many people
that description's a bungle.
Their daily landscape
is chiefly a jungle.

The creatures that lurk there
the birds, beasts, and fishes
are rarely much friendly
and frequently vicious.

E.g.: the slimy-scaled jokester
who aims demeaning
noir at less advantaged folks

Or the forked-tongued politico
who promises gold....

# Beasts of Academe

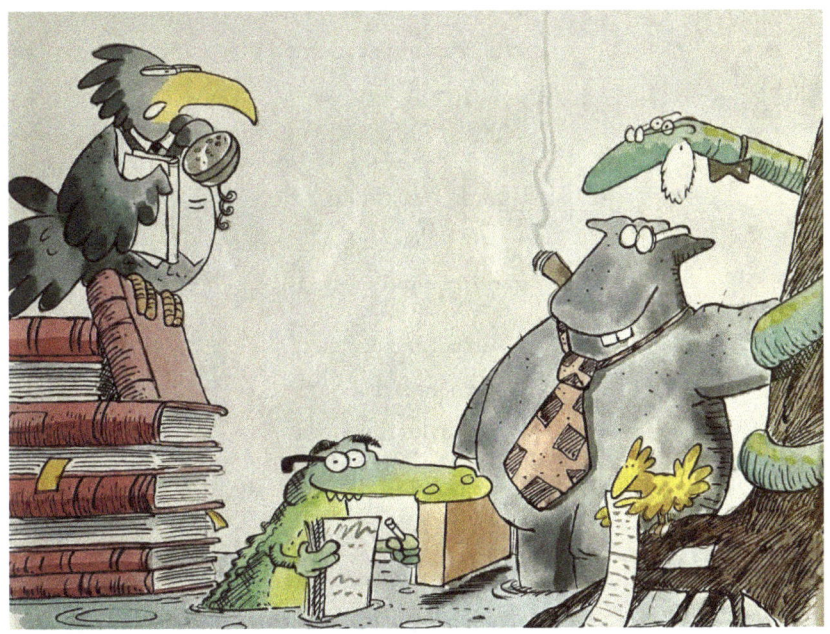

THE CARTOON THAT THE CANADIAN BAR NATIONAL COMMISSIONED IN 1986 TO ILLUSTRATE THE DOGGEREL POEM "BEASTS OF ACADEME" THAT I SUBSTITUTED FOR AN AFTER-DINNER SPEECH IN RESPONSE TO MY AWARD FROM THE CANADIAN ASSOCIATION OF LAW TEACHERS AND LAW REFORM COMMISSION OF CANADA THAT YEAR HAS BEEN HANGING AROUND, NEGLECTED BUT NOT FORGOTTEN, EVER SINCE. I FINALLY HAD IT FRAMED THE OTHER DAY, ALONG WITH A SLIGHTLY-REVISED VERSION OF THE VERSE, AND IT LOOKS GREAT. I PLAN TO HANG IT LATER TODAY. THE VERSE CURRENTLY READS AS FOLLOWS:

(JOURNAL, NOVEMBER 26, 2012)

The scholarly life
is said to be pastoral:
strolling meadows and groves
thinking thoughts that are ast(o)ral.

But I'm here to assert
that description's a bungle:
the groves of academe
are really a jungle.

The creatures that lurk there
the birds, beasts and fishes
are wildly exotic
and frequently vicious.

Take, for example,
the scholarly boar
who impales the unwary
on fine points of yore.

Or the white-thatched committee-bird
whose malevolent best
keeps more gifted than he
from the tenure-track nest.

Law schools are teeming
with socratical panthers
who spring cruel questions
but offer no an(th)ers.

Now, some of these fauna
are strictly conceptual,
and those are the ones
I find most perplexual.

For instance, a beast that
I'd vote for extinction
is the slinking and slithering
common law distinction,

which renders its victims
perceptually lame,
seeing everything different
and nothing the same.

But of all these fierce creatures
of fin, fur or feather
there's one more ferocious
than all put together.

More fearsome by far
than three hippopotami:
the venomous, full-fanged
fallacious dichotomy.

Dichotomies devastate
devour and destroy ya.
They're especially crippling,
it seems, for the lawyer,

who's reduced, post attack,
to utterances feeble,
such as: "Ours is a system
of laws, not of people."

Now, a lawless society
would sure be draconic
but discretionless law'd be
simply moronic.

Wisdom or street smarts,
whatever you style it,
law that's without it's
a plane without pilot.

An opposing dichotomy that
stalks legal tomes
long ago ambushed
the great Justice Holmes.

An attack by that beast
turned Holmes demagogic,
saying: "Law's all experience
rather than logic."

When lawyers talk nonsense
plain folks don't trust us.
They know logic's consistency
and consistency's justice.

Experience keeps law
in touch with reality,
but law without logic's
a cloak for brutality.

The great Charter debate
becomes quite monotonous
when combatants resort to
reasoning dichotomous

.

Some keep declaiming
with dull repetition:
"The only safe guardian
of right's the politician."

While other protagonists
won't ever budge
from placing sole faith
and trust in the judge.

There are sadly a few people
aware the sound growth
of freedoms and rights
needs the efforts of both.

So my message, dear friends
in case you have missed it:
if tempted to dichotomize
do your best to resist it.

For the venomous, full-fanged
fallacious dichotomy
it is more to be feared
than a frontal lobotomy.

[MODIFIED WITH MARCH 24, 2006, VERSION]

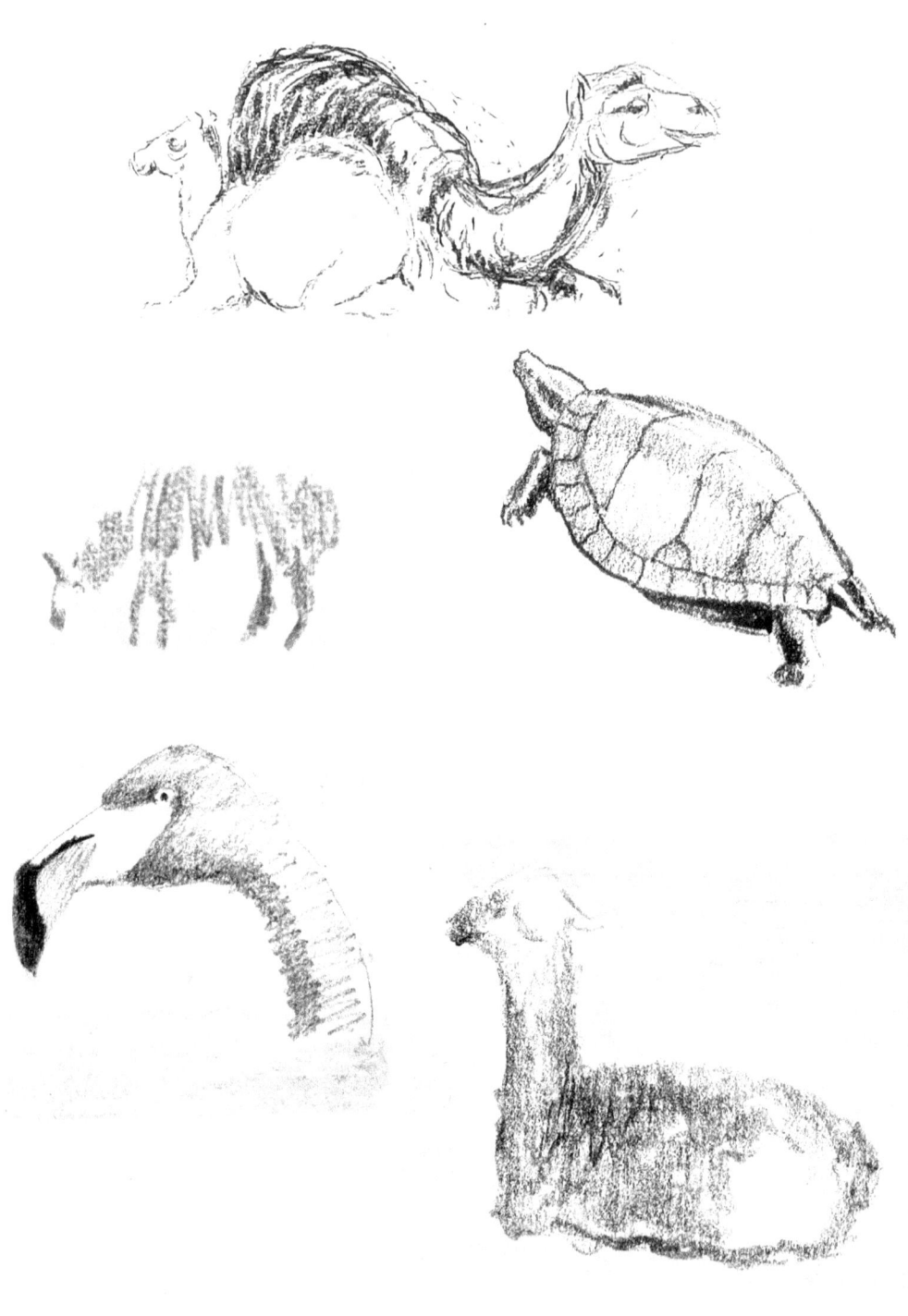

# Love

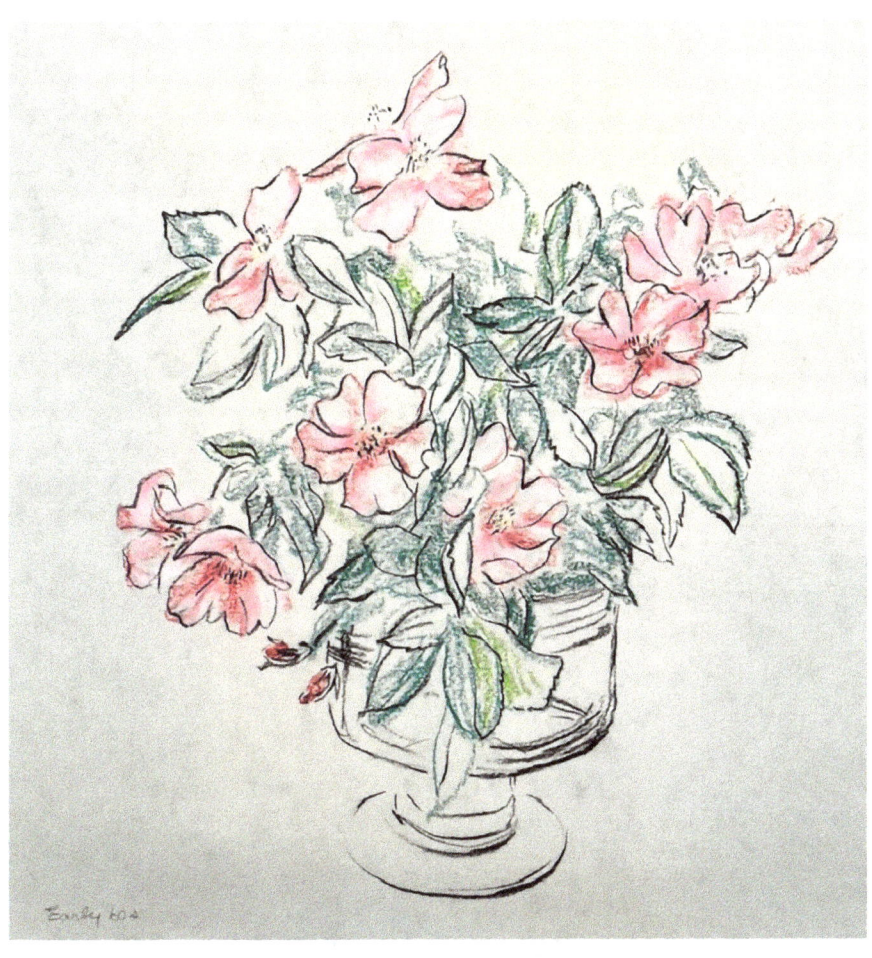

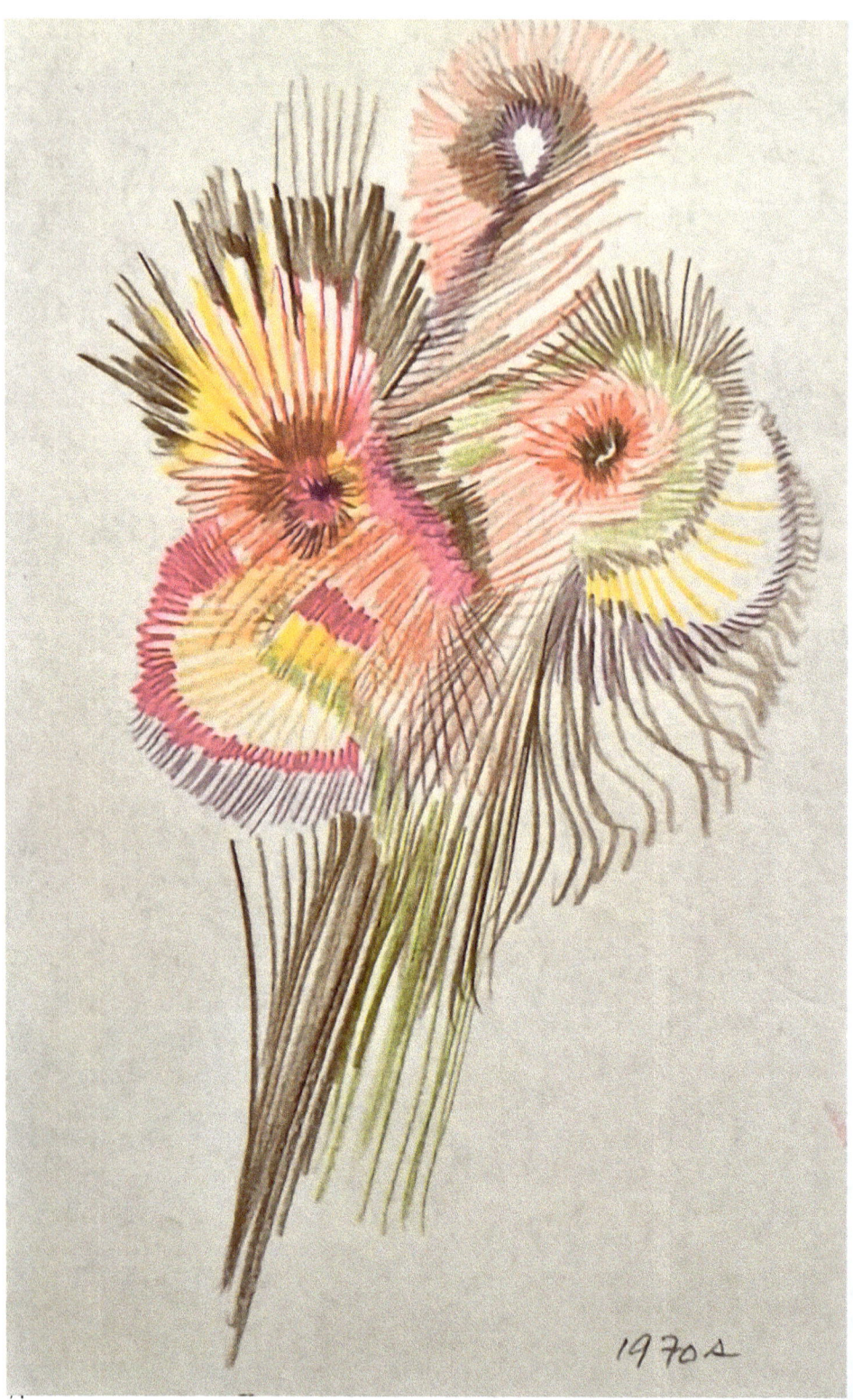

# Somewhere Between

Somewhere between
moon and earth
there is balance.

Somewhere between
yes and no,
is and was,
there is truth.


# Walking in Brilliance

Walking in brilliance
with you
after profligate snow
and the sun
conspire
to be-jewel the world
for a while.

# Future Imperfect

I dreamed
that you left
and there on the floor
by your chair was
half the blade of
a broken saw.

# Alone

Her absence is here.
Her wasness:
where she sat,
where we walked.

It won't go away
when I'm with her again;
it will marry
the isness.

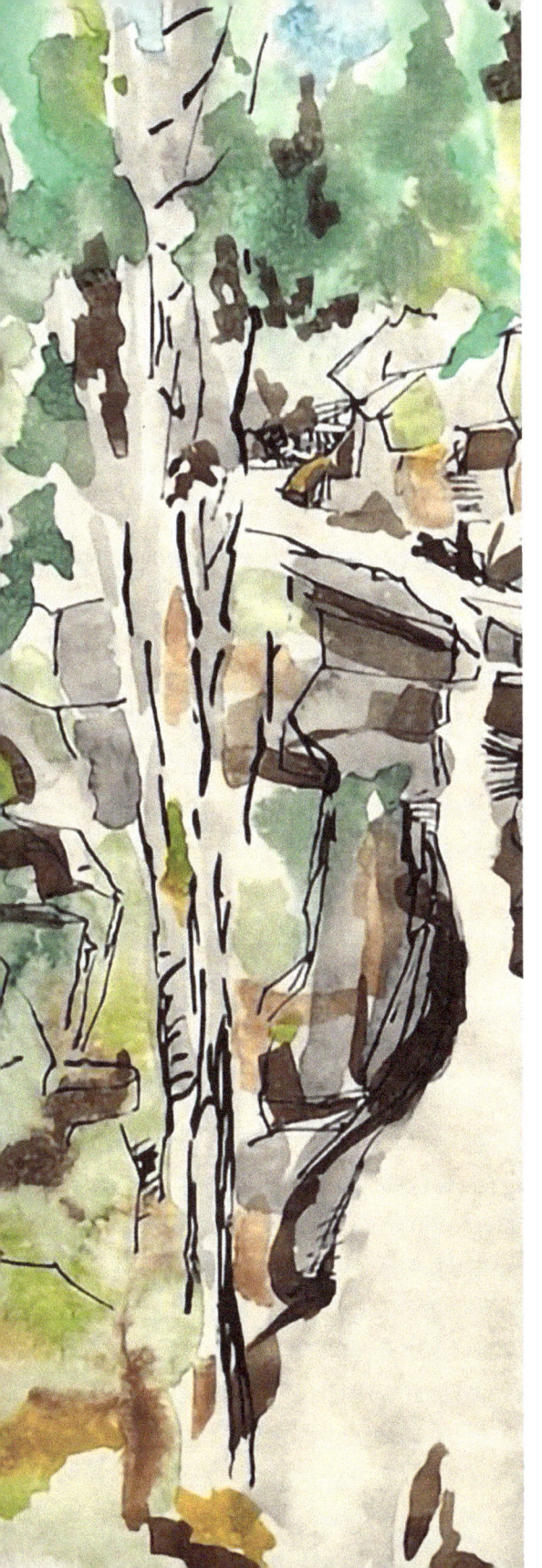

# August

The season is waning,
not yet abjectly,
but plainly.
The blooms are profuse
but the urgency's gone.

The bees have relaxed,
moving routinely from
sweetness to sweetness
more in the manner
of husbands than lovers.

Tomorrow we'll meet
and savour the moment,
and maybe agree
that autumn is near.

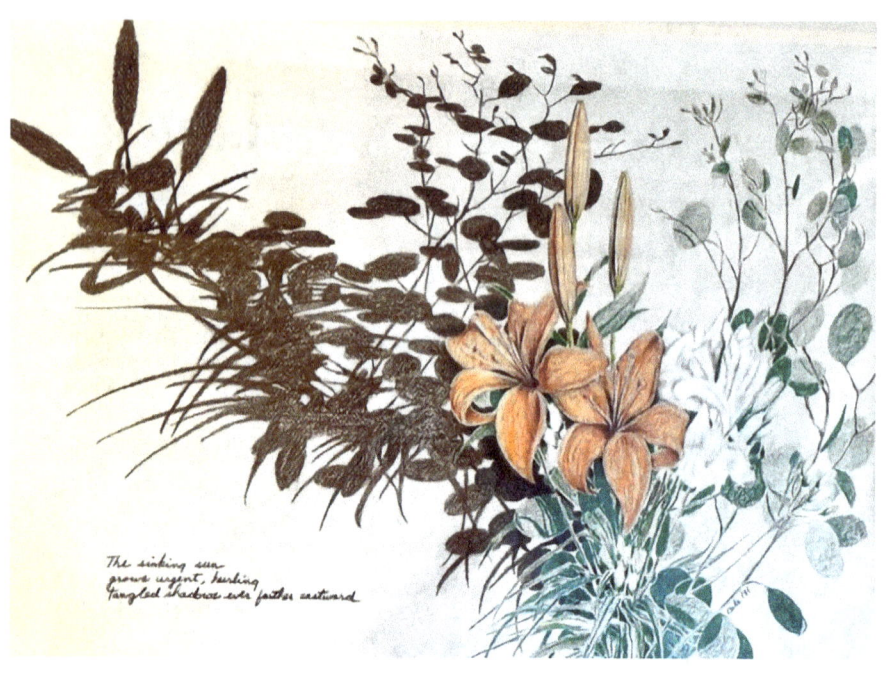

# Late Afternoon, Edmonton

The sinking sun
grows urgent,

hurling tangled shadows
ever further
eastward.

THIS IS SANDRA'S POEM FOR DALE

# Your Present Is...

Your present is
a prison
for the past,
a place
too small
to put
a future,
a fugue
too discordant
with the
symphony
beyond.

However attractive
my melody,
it remains
a stranger
to your past,
a siren call
to future
outside locked
prison walls.

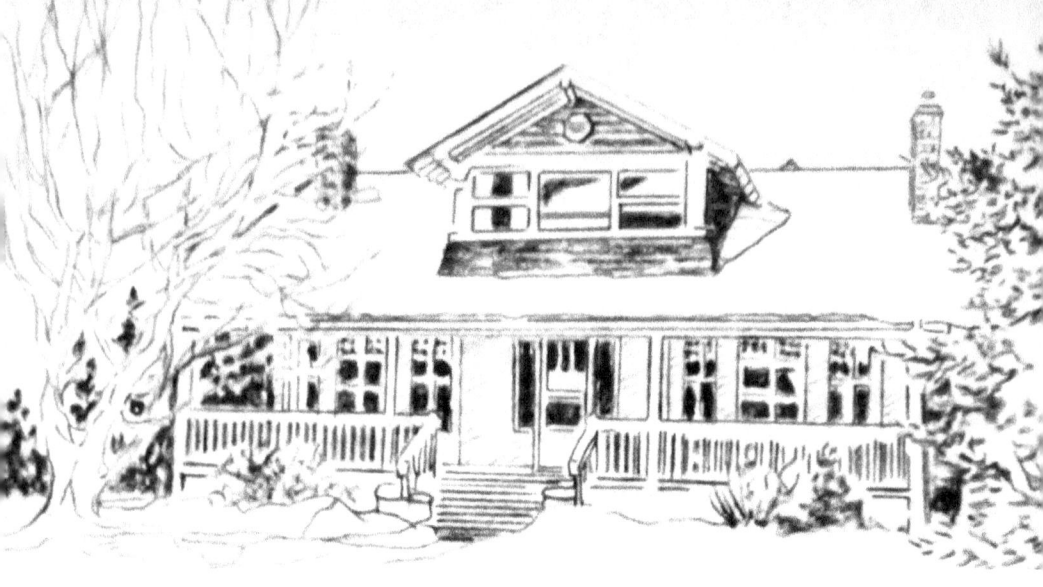

# Why Dress?

Why do you
put on clothing
when you know
I long to see
your splendid
mid-life body?

Why do you dress
your words in caution
when you know
I lust to see
your soul?

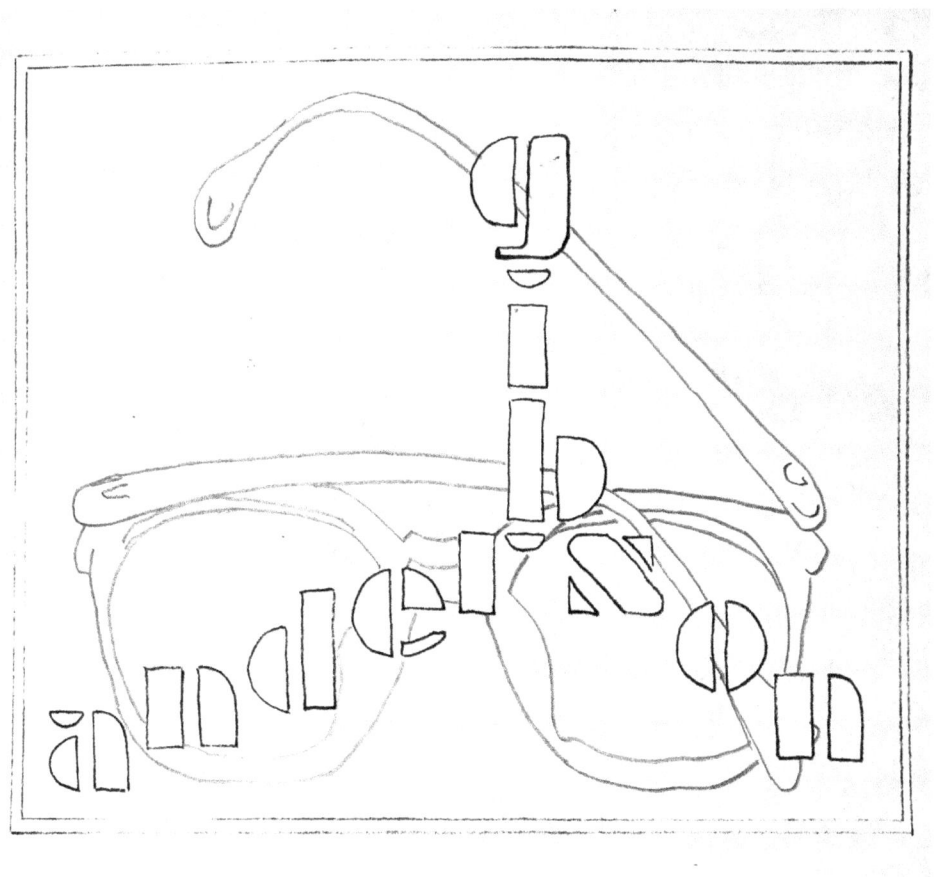

# Paleo – Love

"We have a history,"
you said, and seemed
surprisingly surprised.

Yes, a history,
and an archeology as well.

If we travelled
through our layered love
we'd come upon
a forgotten trove:
your mountain poem,
mine about the falls
that never freeze;
menus, boarding passes,
tram-car stubs;
record shards,
chipped and broken tumblers
which, when held against the ear,
resonate with boogie beats
and Ella singing Nearness
through the night.

Deeper down, we'd find
a paleontology:
the imprint of your breast,
your ribs, your hands
upon my chest,
pressed in unforgetting stone;
the patterns
of our dialogues,
also locked in rock,
each web of reasoning
and spine of fragile logic
made concrete,
every insight, every flaw,
exposed to time.

Our thens and nows and evers
are perpetual.

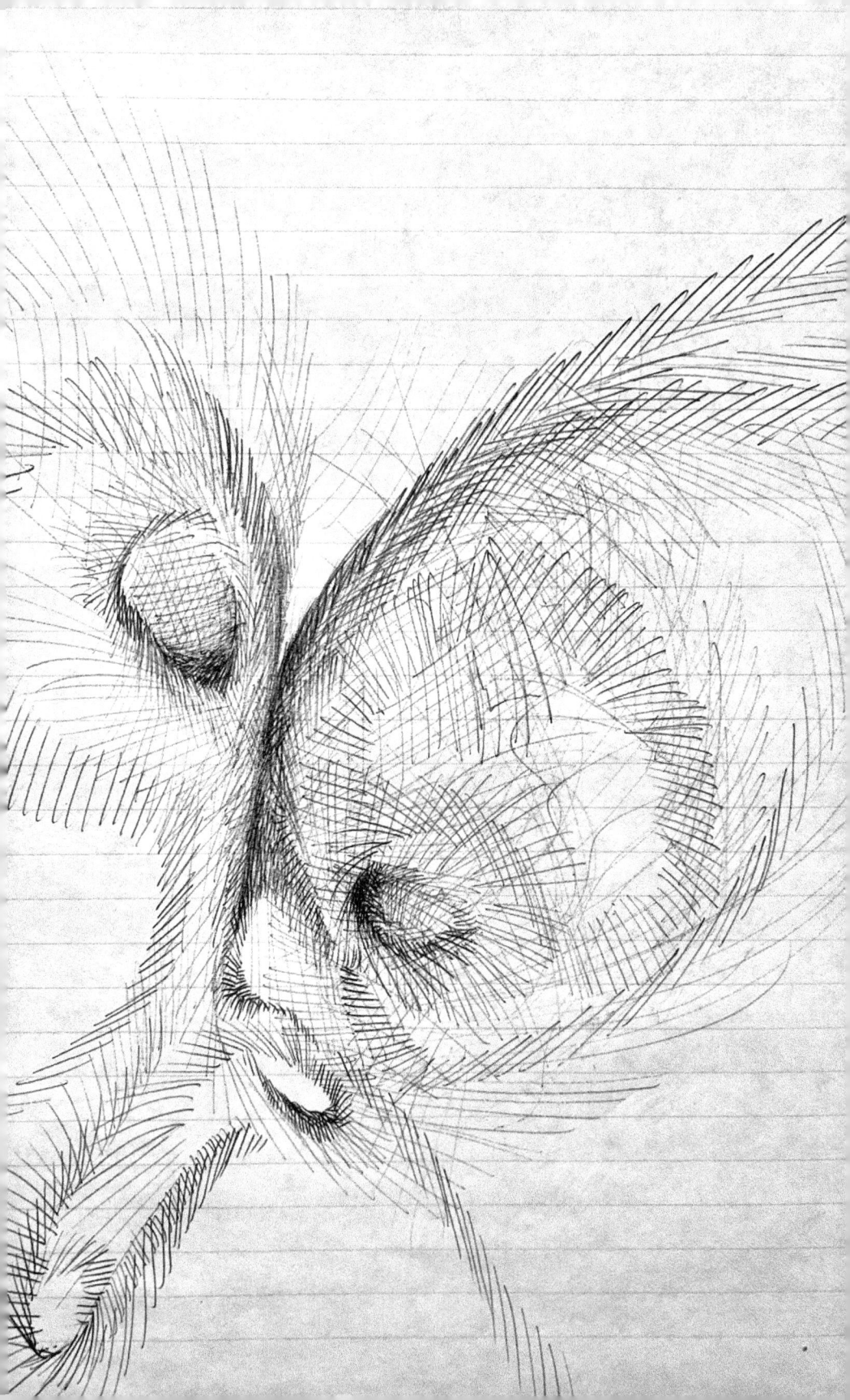

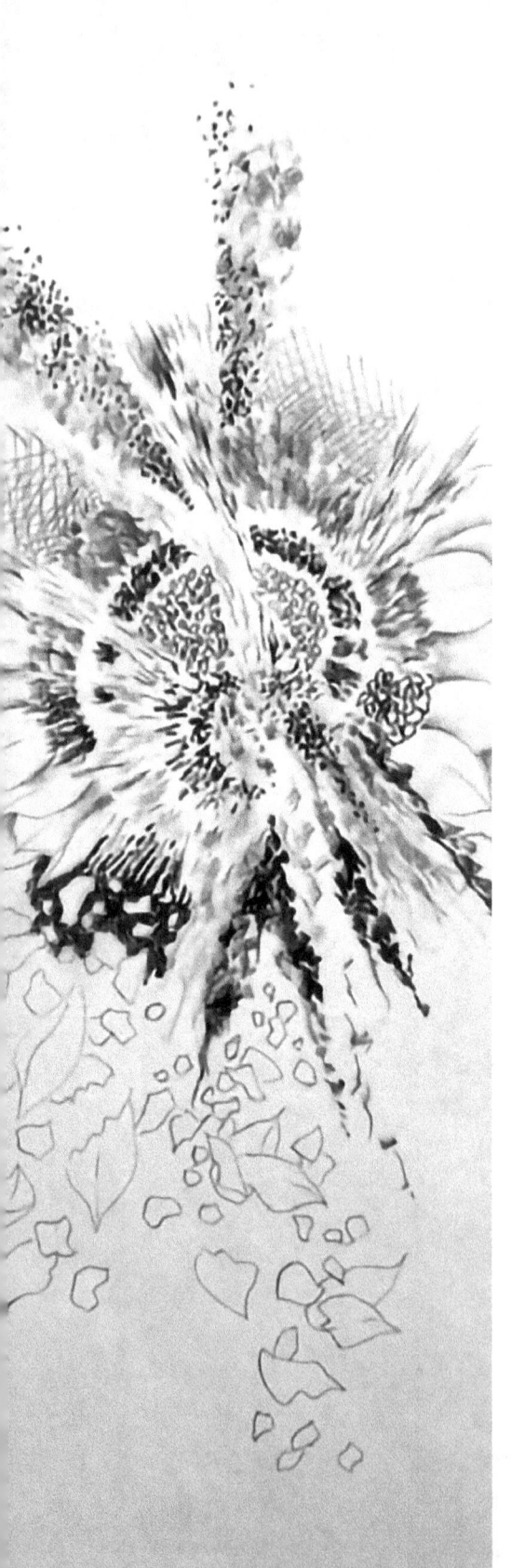

# My Dear Lady Swan

My dear Lady Swan
It has been much too long
since I have been gone
Centuries seem to have passed.

****

Dear Lady Swan
Since you've been gone,
you're gone too long.
Since Thursday last
another century has gone past

****

Dear Lady Swan
I lunched upon your gift
of 13th century song.

# The Magnets

They felt their
fields of force
invisibly
in touch.

but both
resisted contact,
veering off as
closeness grew,

until
they each rotated
half a turn
in opposite directions

and then
fell upon each other,
locked as though
in love.

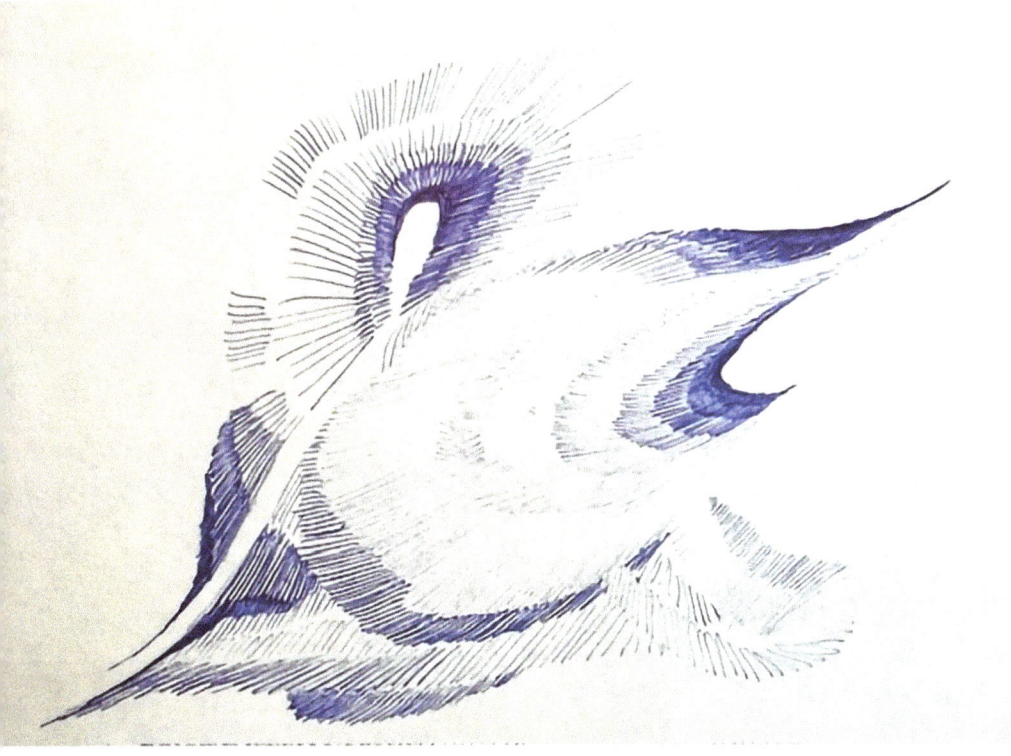

# The Foreigner

That I was made a foreigner
by a single act of treason
was to be expected.

What was weird was that
I couldn't
speak the language anymore.

And so I study other tongues.

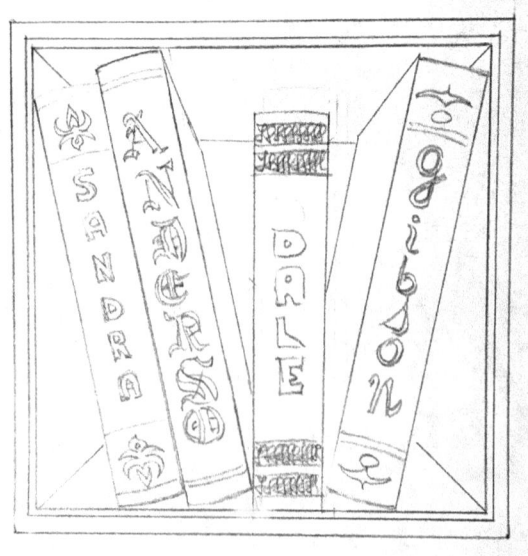

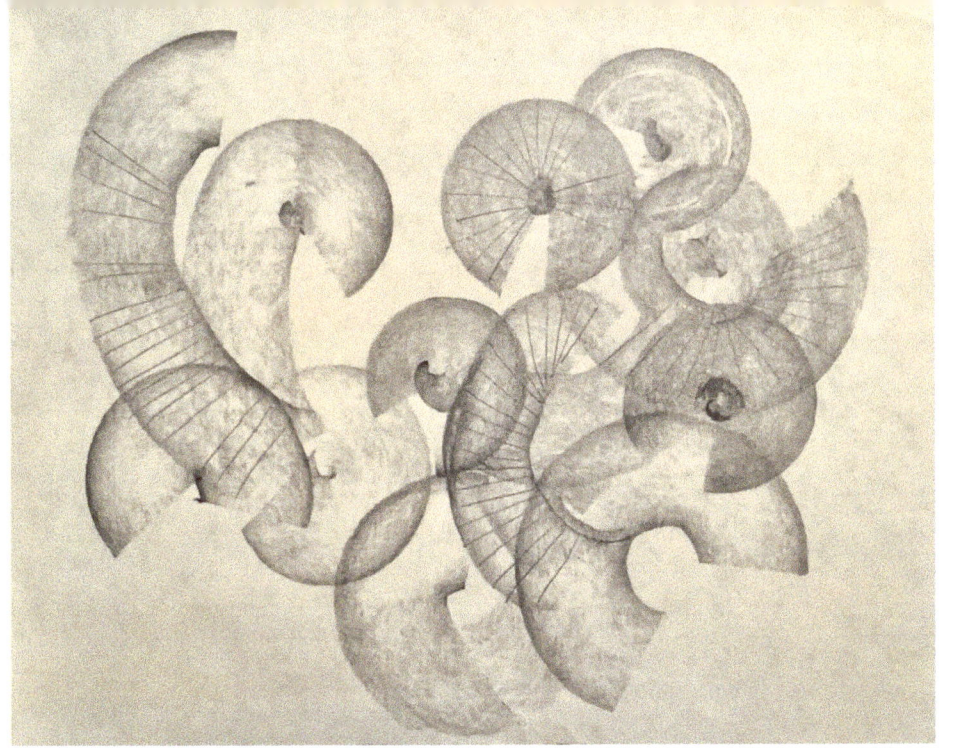

# You Sang For Me

You sang for me
a song few others ever heard.

You sang like some
familiar yet exotic bird.

You sang for me of joy,
you sang for me of love

You sang of things
I knew not of.

I spoke to you of things
I'd never told.

I danced for you,
suddenly, finally,
bold.

# April 14, 1991–April 14, 2001 Reprise

You take up temporal
beauties
and splash down
permanence
in your colours,
in your smile,
drawing flowers
across the table
from me
to float in sunlight
wherever
we may be.

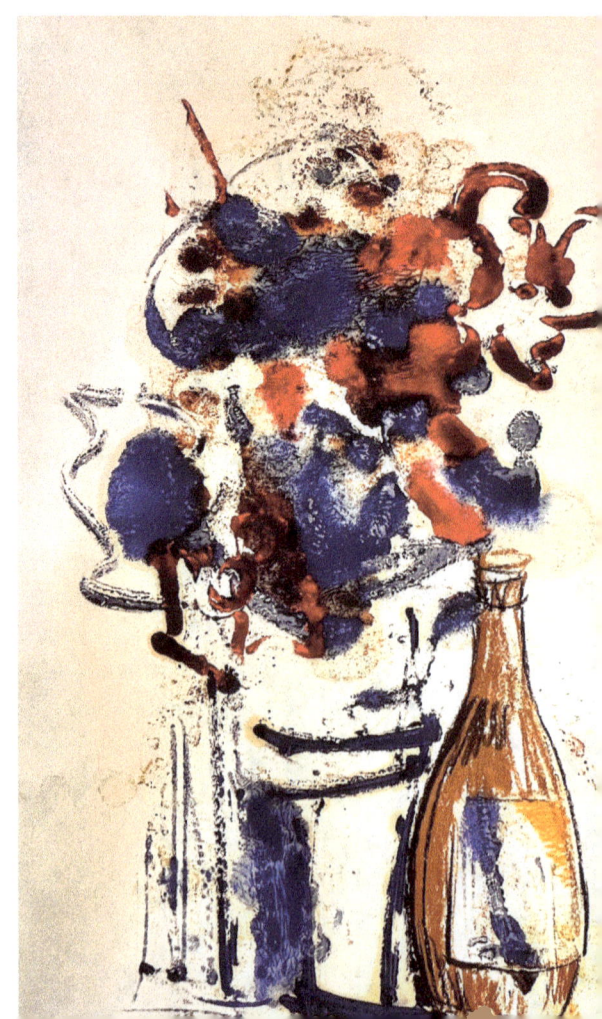

# Flowers became beads

Flowers became beads
of colour,
decade-deepened,
linking our lives.

We've worn them proudly
in public
since the flame
of self-immolent blame
died into embers
of acceptance
we see in others.

We see love,
however wary,
but always pale
reflection
of ours:

happy the space within us
where full love dwells.

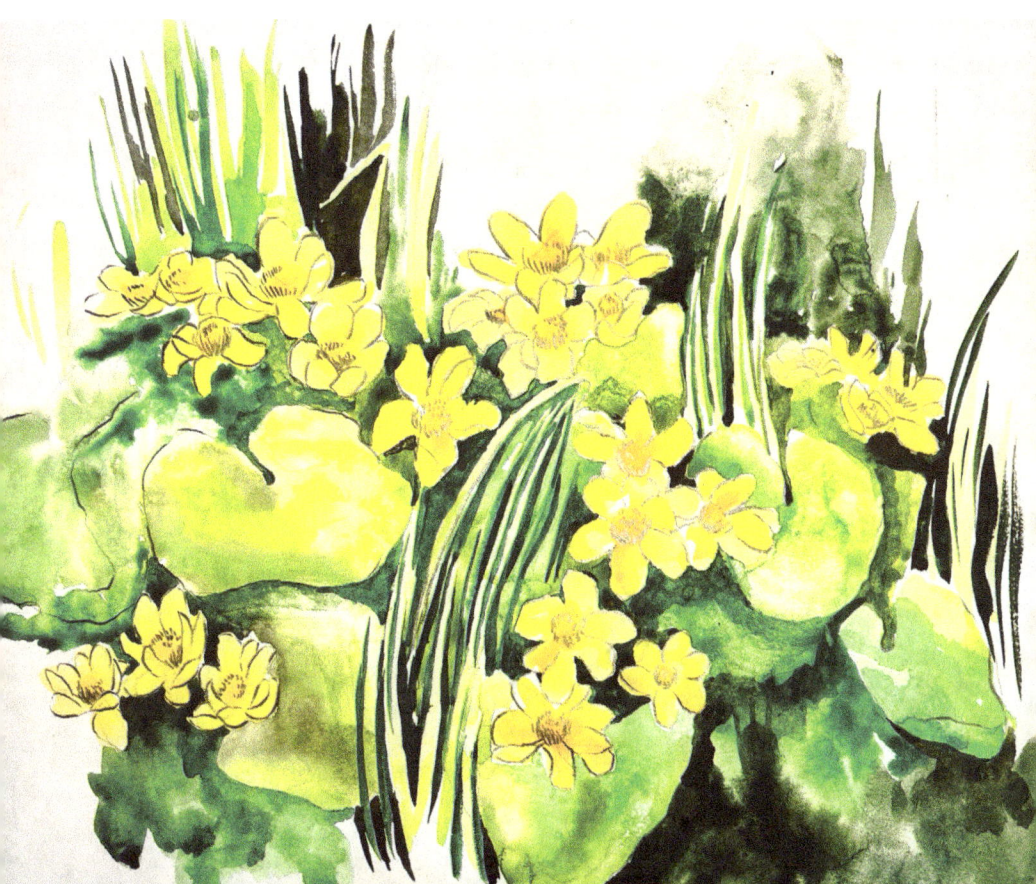

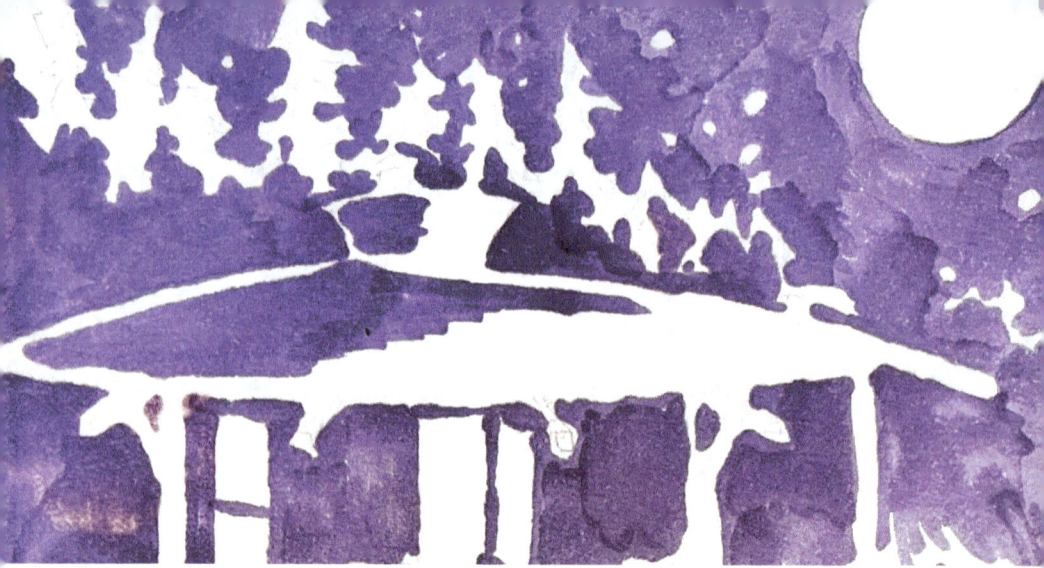

# Upon a Hill

Sandra stands upon a hill
with boundless vistas
and holds a cage
containing me

standing on a hill
with many vistas
holding up a cage
containing
her

Then I unlock
her cage
and she unlocks
mine

But neither chooses to leave.

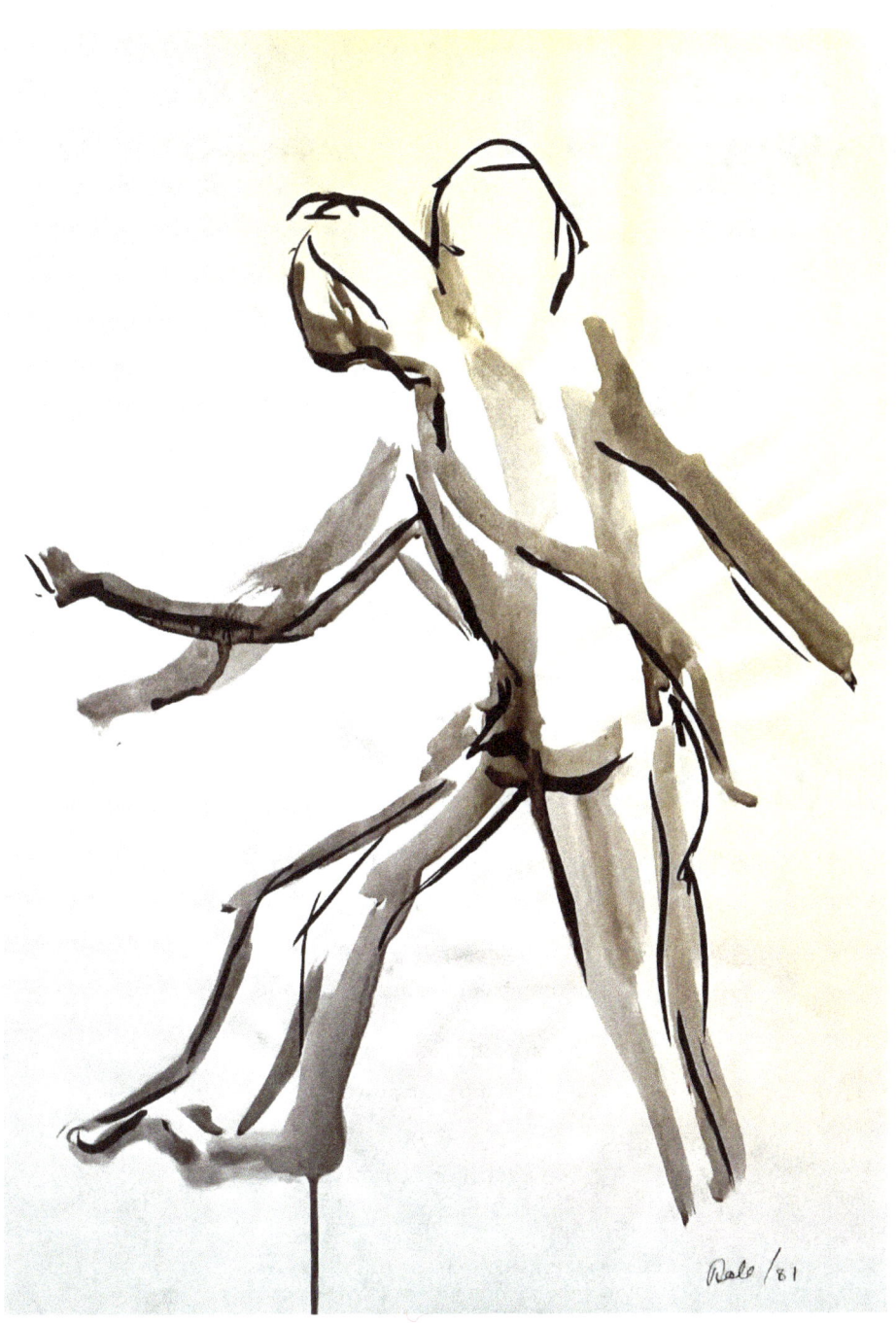

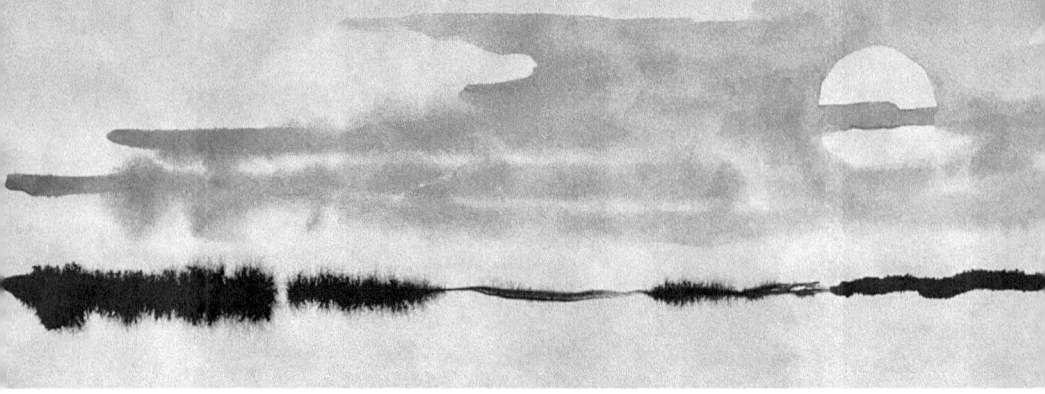

# Sandra By Moonlight

Only I can see
how this autumn moon
defines these evanescent hills.

# To Dale,
# With Profoundest Love, Sandra

The black storm clouds
hover no more than
distant on the horizon
like a wash of paint, drying.

You've thrown your line
and my boat sways
calmly
on a sea of contentment:
No longer need for crying.

**Response to the 1995 Valentine's card message:
"When you're around, there's not a cloud
in the sky! Except the one I'm floating on"**

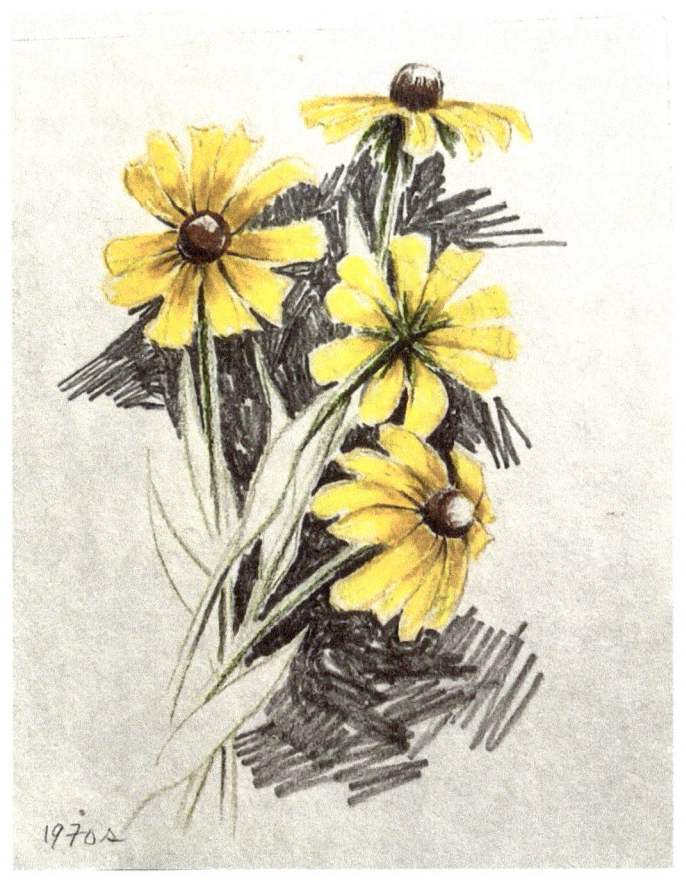

# Sandra My Love:

As sure as it is
that sunflowers are yellow,
our love grows more sweet
the more it grows mellow.

Thank you for being mine,
and for making me yours.

**Valentine's 2007**

# The Game

At first
it was only a game
a fantasy.

Some things
were certainly real,
but the big thing,
the awful thing,

was only a dream
for empty moments –
a figment to touch when alone
to toy with, caress,
a distraction.

# Guilt

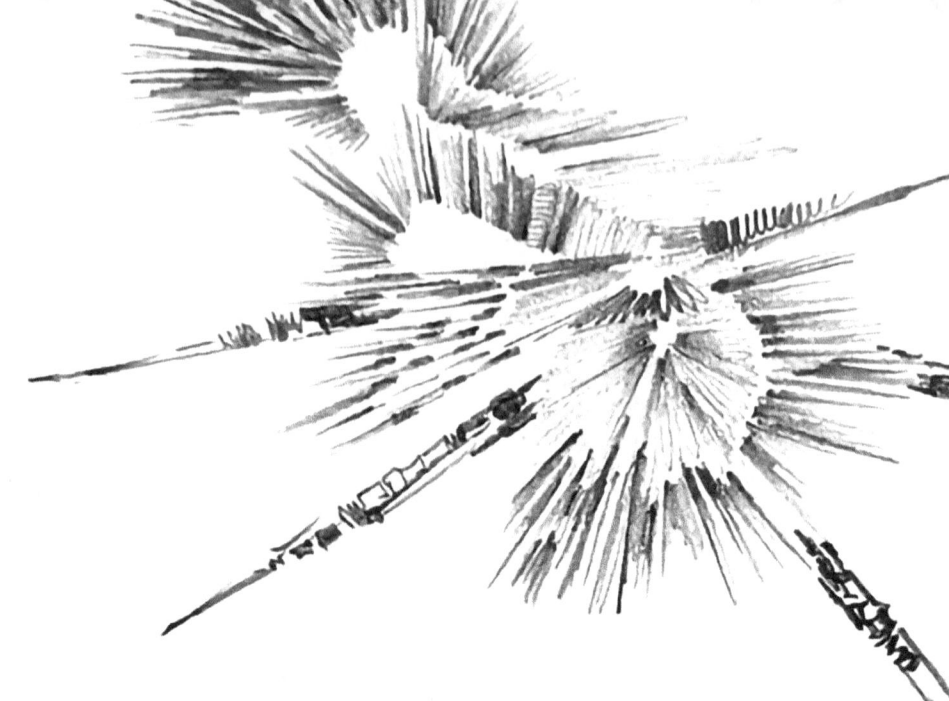

# The Rising Sun
# [or: Decision]

I ordered the sun
to set in the east,
rise in the west.

It refused,
so instead I
decided to re-write
my life

and I
edited decency out.

The rising sun
veiled at first,

bursts its shroud
and
shatters every window
of my home.

# Something Beside Me

MY MOOD WAS LOW MOST OF THE WEEK. TIREDNESS, CHIEFLY, & RENEWED PROXIMITY TO DAD, I GUESS, AND THE ENORMITY OF THE BUSY-WORK TO BE DONE BEFORE I CAN EVEN BEGIN TO TACKLE THE IMPOSSIBLE ARRAY OF REAL WORK I'VE COMMITTED MYSELF TO DO, AND....

(JOURNAL JUNE 5-12, 1990)

Something beside me
is absent.
is aching,
is tugging.
Something almost magnetic
- a vacuum, a danger -
is pulling.

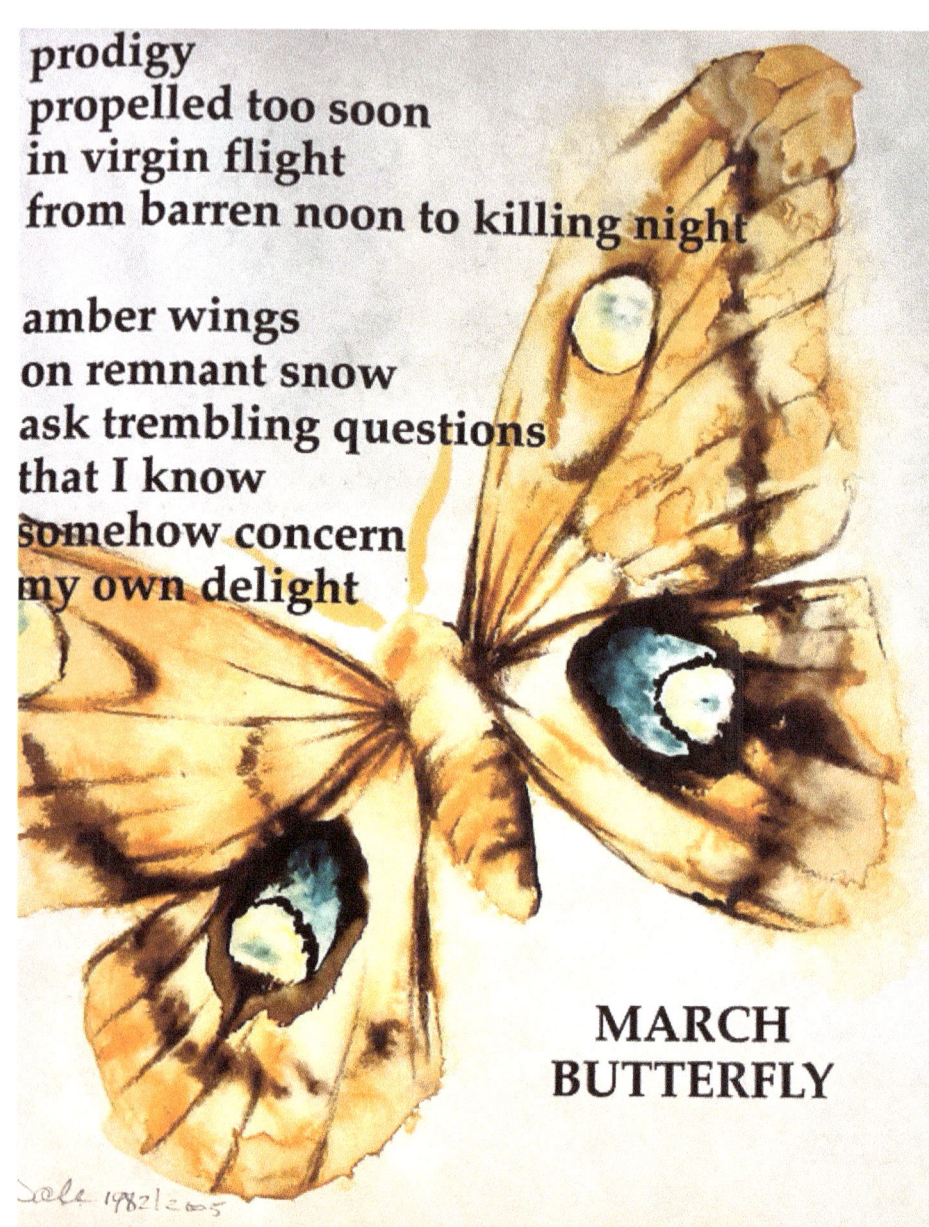

prodigy
propelled too soon
in virgin flight
from barren noon to killing night

amber wings
on remnant snow
ask trembling questions
that I know
somehow concern
my own delight

**MARCH BUTTERFLY**

# March Butterfly

Prodigy
propelled too soon
in virgin flight
from barren noon
to killing night.

Ochre wings on remnant snow
pose trembling questions
that I know
concern
delight.

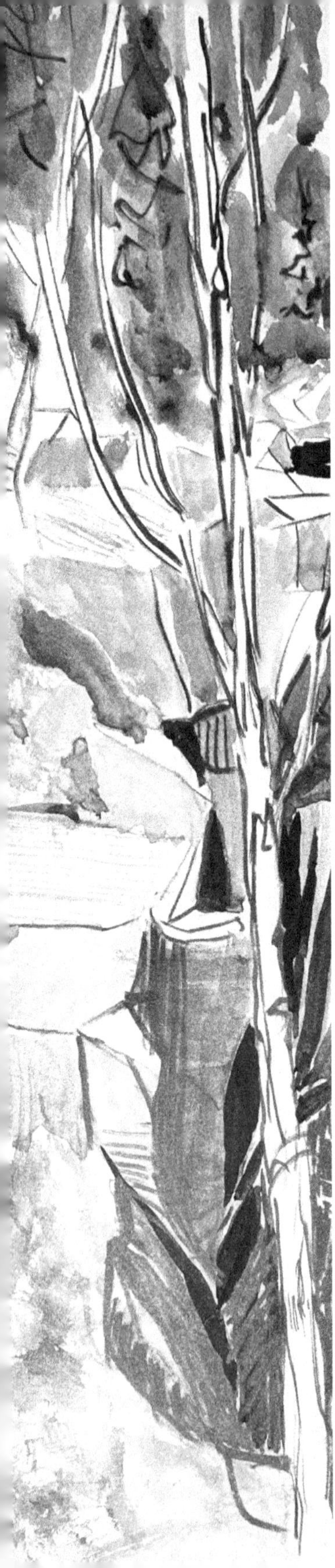

# Lake Agnes

Unseen
above the other world
snug
beside the precipice

this is not purity.
The lake's polluted
contaminated
by the stillness
(still as secrecy)
by the clarity
(clear as consequence)
and by
its own impatience
(restless undertow
pulling everything
toward the waterfall)

adulterated
by the lust
to fling itself
out into space
to tumble, sparkle
fly and frolic
down the mountain
for as long as
joy's
allowed.

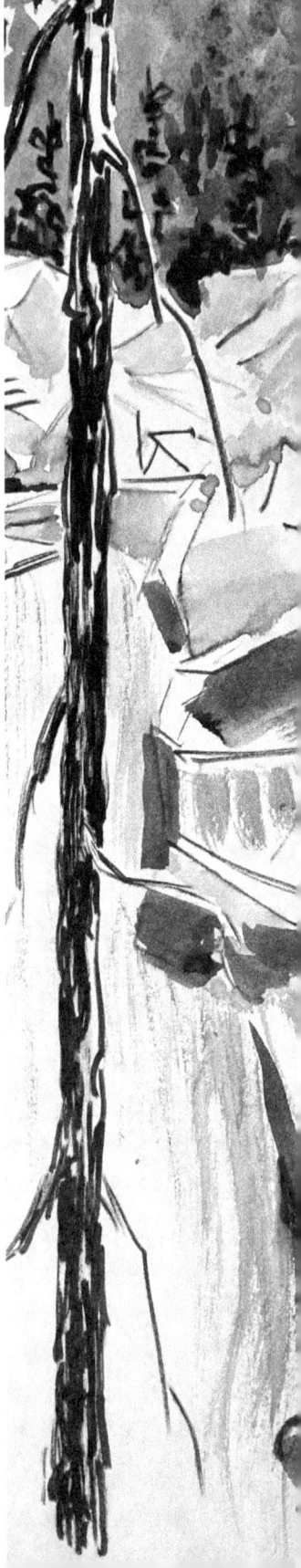

# Time Out

though they don't even
Take off their watches
time turns it back
then implodes
pulling them
after it
into a
void
so
intense
they cannot
endure it for
more than a century
or two at a time before
minds decompress and they
notice their watches ticking

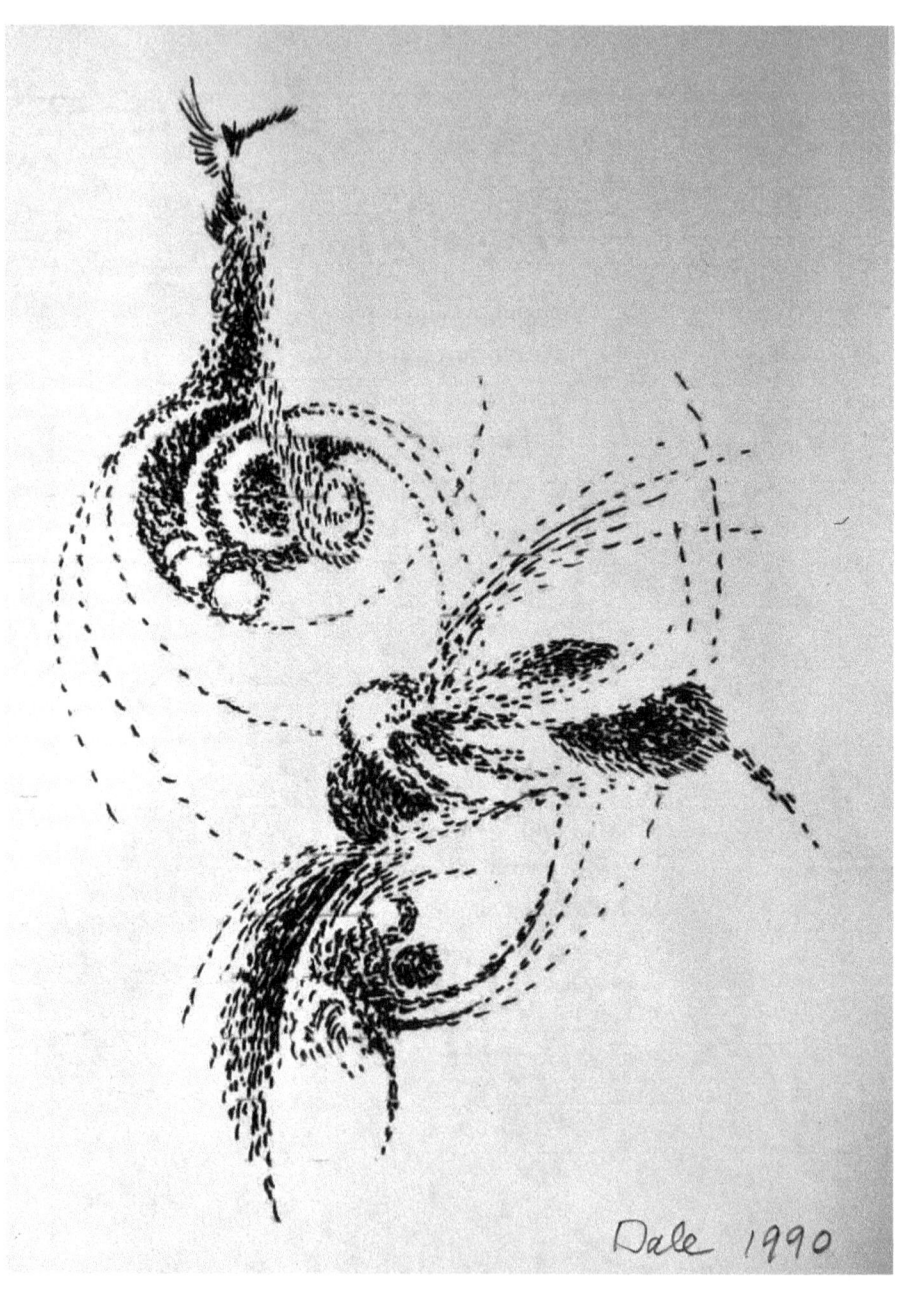

# Peace River Road

The ice
on the Peace River Road
is worst where
the hills are the highest.

A truck pirouettes
behind us, and several others
lie on their sides in the ditch,
bottoms exposed.

Ahead, and behind us,
drivers who've managed to stop
at the edge of the road
to put chains on their wheels
skitter and slither
like spatters of water,
or oil on a grill
trying to return to their cabs

while we,
caught without chains,
are not able to stop
but drive on in dread,
not even sure
it's a journey
we want to complete.

# Walking Into a Glass Door

The way seemed clear
and I strode right ahead

until I was struck
in the face
and knocked to the floor
by something unseen

and I knelt
on the carpet, watching
my blood fall in drops
and seeing my object
waiting there
just past the glass.

# Crossroads

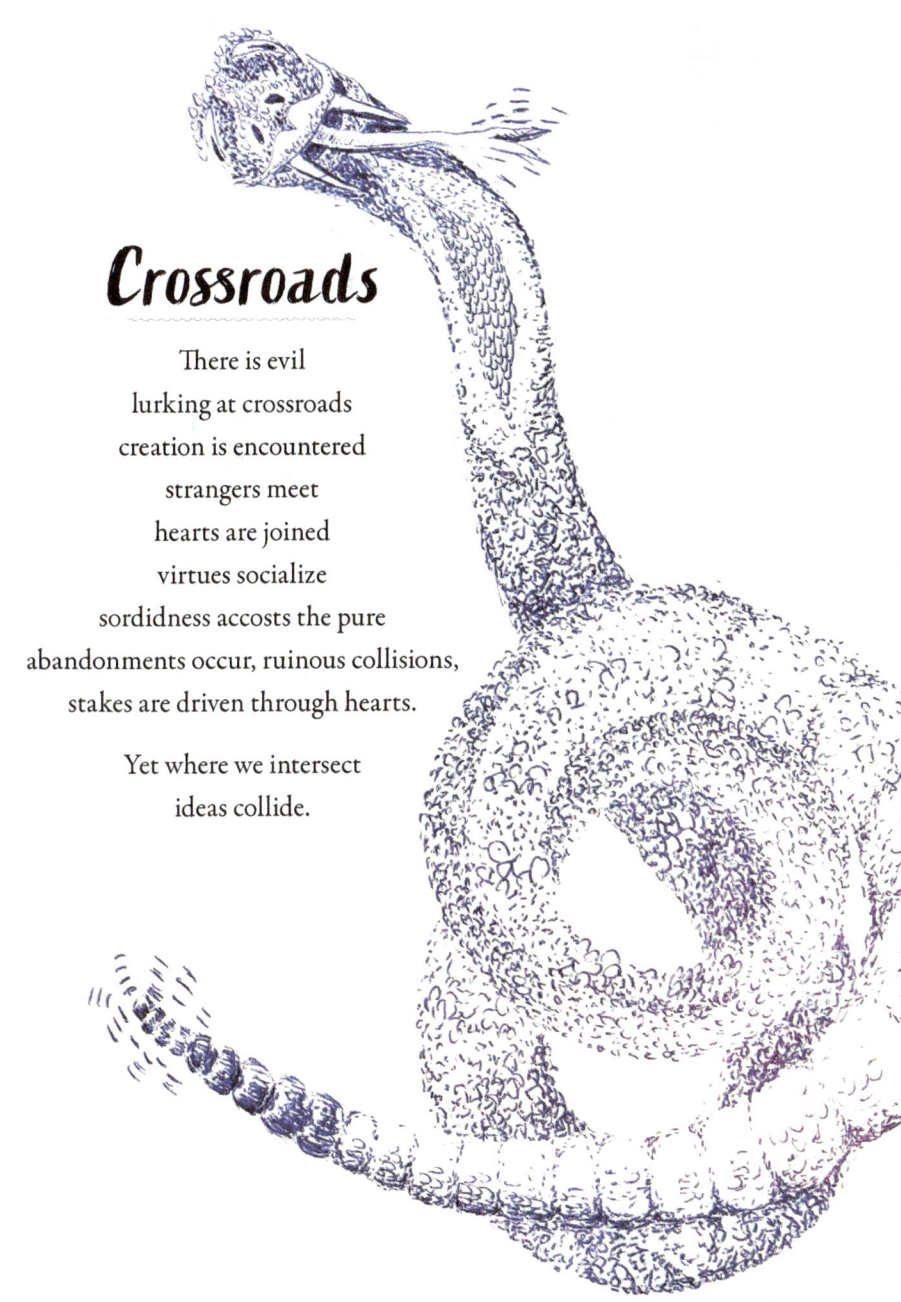

There is evil
lurking at crossroads
creation is encountered
strangers meet
hearts are joined
virtues socialize
sordidness accosts the pure
abandonments occur, ruinous collisions,
stakes are driven through hearts.

Yet where we intersect
ideas collide.

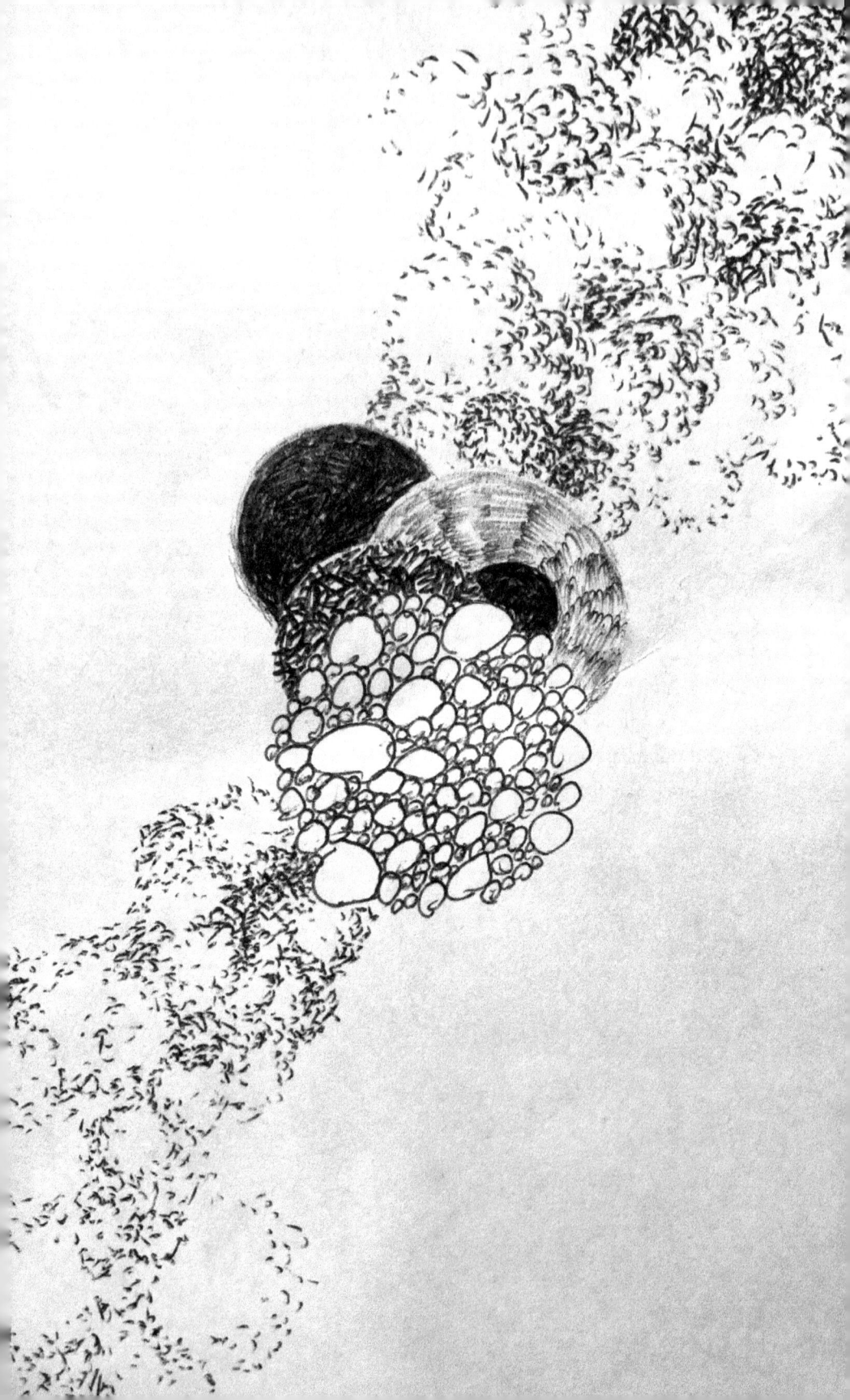

# Atoms [or: Decision]

I'm thinking
of atoms
glancing off others
like balls in a game of
three-dimensional billiards
with
preordained but
unpredictable
consequences.

# Collision Course

One is hurtling at me
from the left;
the other
from the right,

big as trucks.

They're sure to crash,
here,
where I stand
transfixed
by information.

# Near where

Near where
we lived at first
in sweet surreal seclusion
adjusting to self-hatred
were (perhaps still are)
some mutated magpies
ravenous as the normal kind but
grey as whisky jacks.

# Genuine Pariahs

"Pariah" came to mind
as we entered,
and we later wondered
(if pariahs are allowed to wonder)
what its origins
might be.

It's a Tamil word
the English stole
like so much else
but never fully understood.

In English it means
"outcast"
but in Tamil
it's a member of a caste
looked down upon
but never
altogether execrated.

Thankfully
we encountered only
genuine pariahhood.

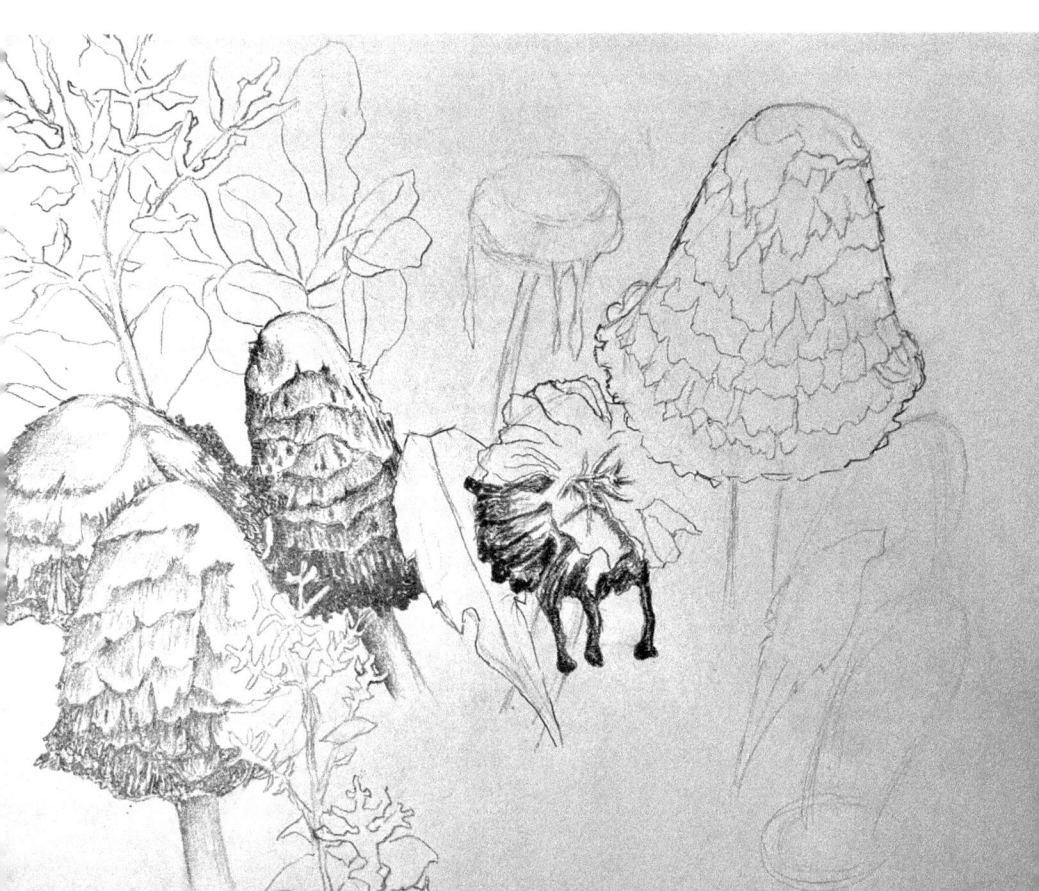

# Richard the Turd

He did an evil act or two,
no doubt, and was deemed an evil man,
deformed by reputation,
demonized by history.

His soundnesses,
his decencies, his boons
were drowned in notoriety.

I think I know a little
how he felt.

But don't regard him virtueless:
iniquity often has often greater value
than philanthropy.

Richard's wrongs
have served the world well
as education
or, at least, as entertainment:
a school in which, a stage on which
to sin vicariously,
without a loss of worth,
indeed, with gained esteem.

Perhaps I, too, will prove to be
a better lesson than a teacher.

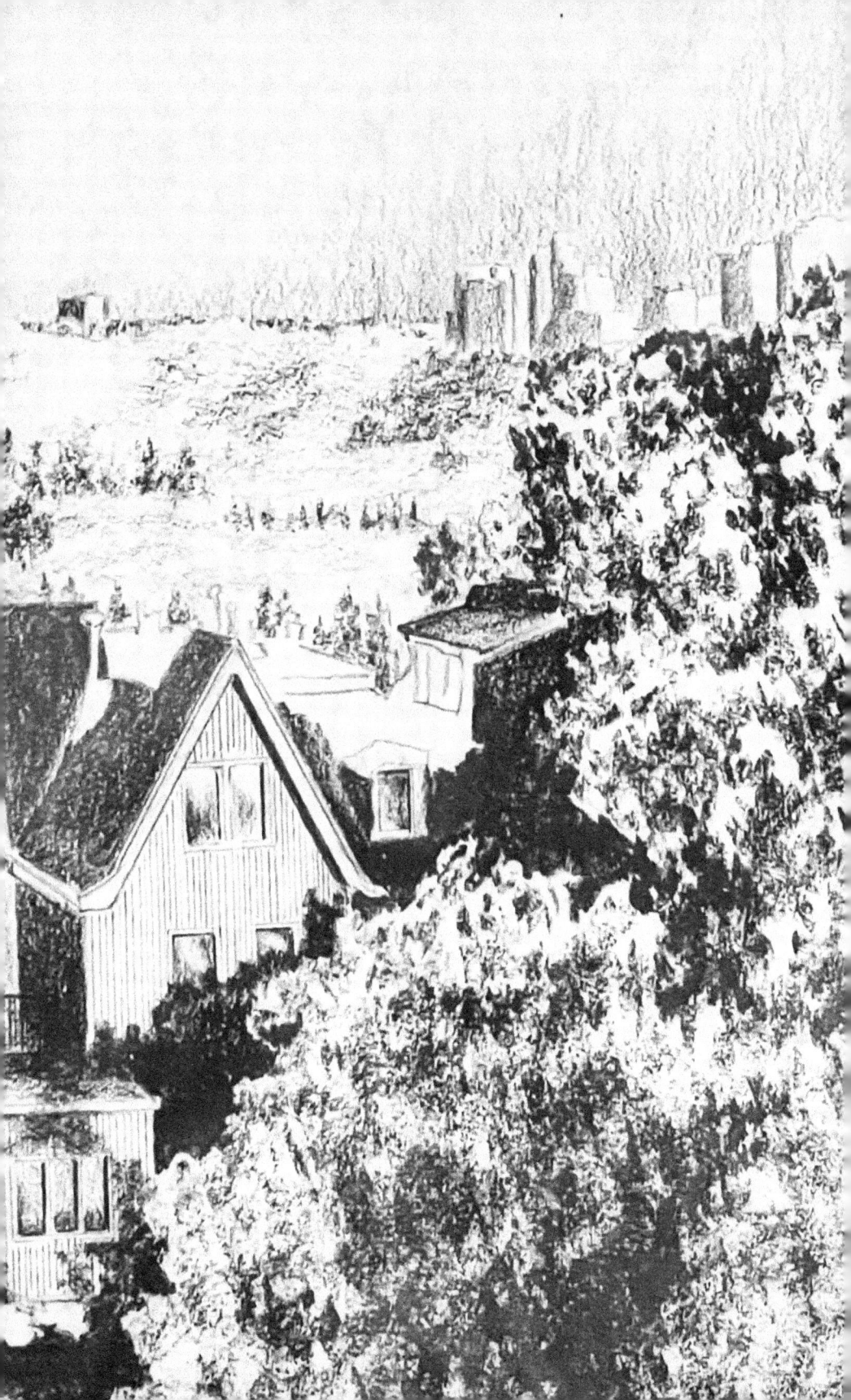

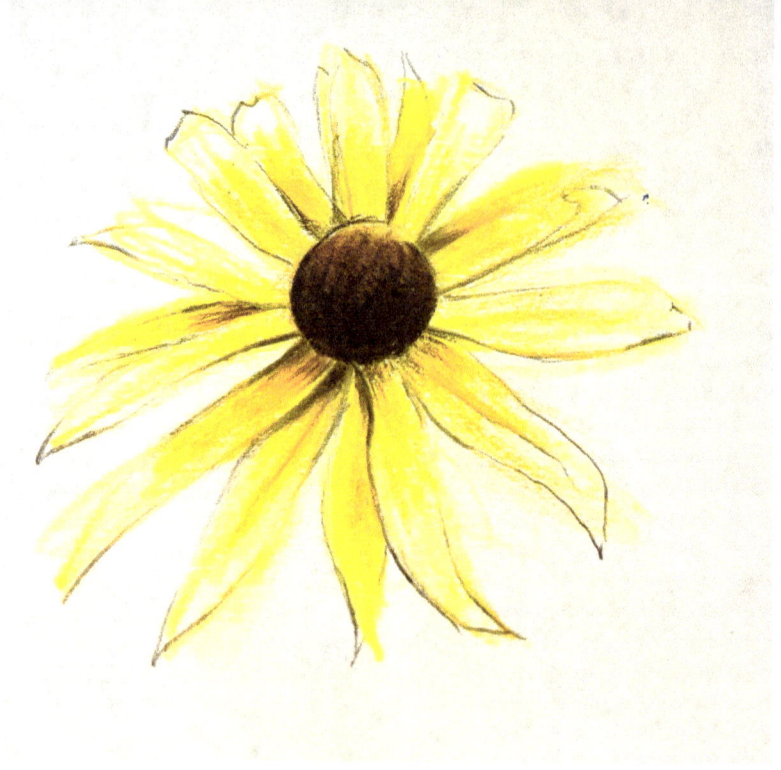

# Omelettes

It's not entirely true
that makers of omelettes
must be breakers of eggs.

Sometimes an excellent omelette
can be made from eggs
previously broken.

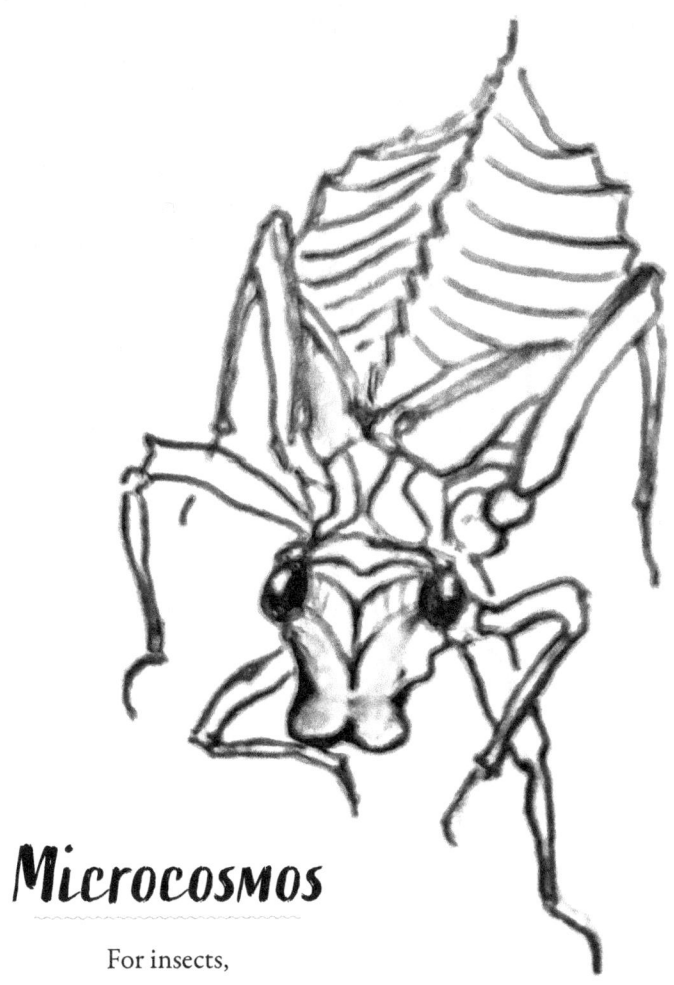

# Microcosmos

    For insects,
      walking on water
   with swift nervous strides
   that dimple the surface,
    (like kids on a mattress)
     requires no Christ.

       But
   raindrops are bombs,
   exploding like geysers
in lake-size puddles and ponds
    and hurtling to smash
      the unsheltered,
stunning even the armoured.

        I,
   suddenly shrunk,
knew this was true when
knocked to the ground and
      scalded by
her (your) falling tears.

# Shards

An ugly candy dish
hand-painted by my
mother's mother,
a snowplow drawing by my
daughter's son,
some poems I
can't accept aren't publishable,
diplomas, letters, books,
divorce decree.

A clash
of furniture, mingled
photographs of mutual strangers,
several once-new things
worn comfortable
by exile.

These fragments
I can find.
What's harder is
to know what
forces
smashed them,
and what powers
now arrange
and re-arrange the shards
with kaleidoscopic
restlessness, beauty and
illusion.

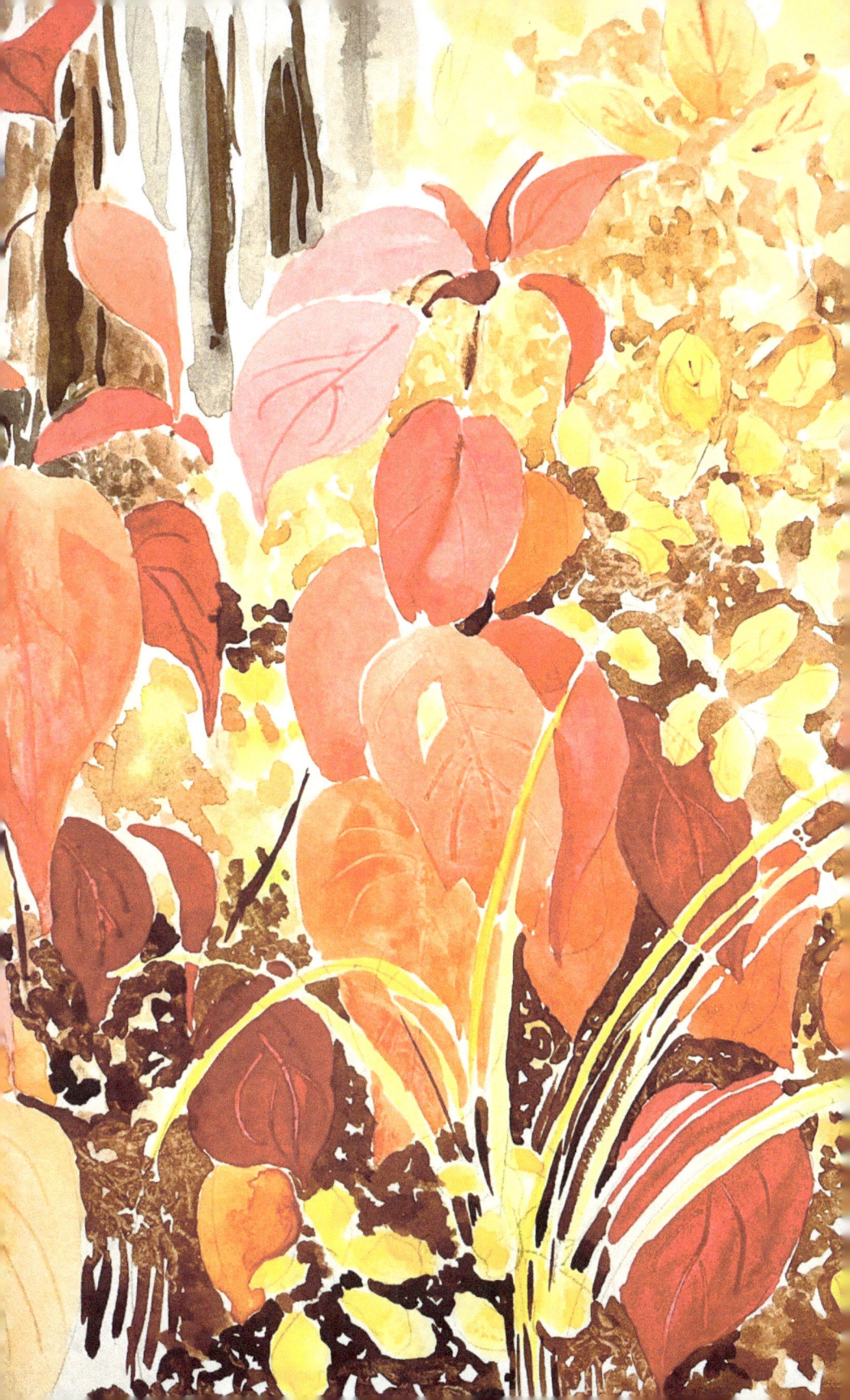

# It's In Me

It's in me
a parasite
lurking like a mugger
scuttling away from the light
whenever I open my mouth
when I'm by myself
slinking back.

I can't explain why the decency
isn't a parasite too.

# Autokleptia

I dreamt the other night
That I was caught stealing things
From myself.

By whom, then
Can I be trusted?

# Dilemma

To forgive myself
would be to acknowledge
the lowness of my standards.

Not to do so
would be to deny
my humanity.

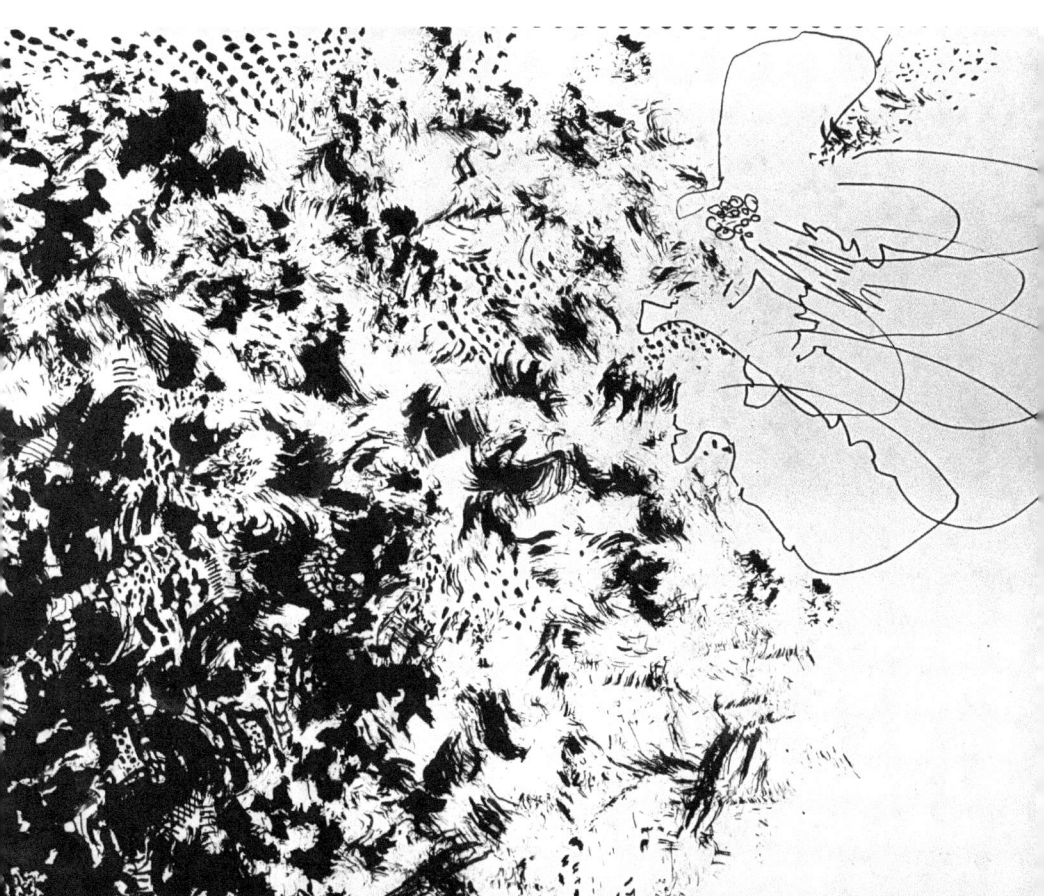

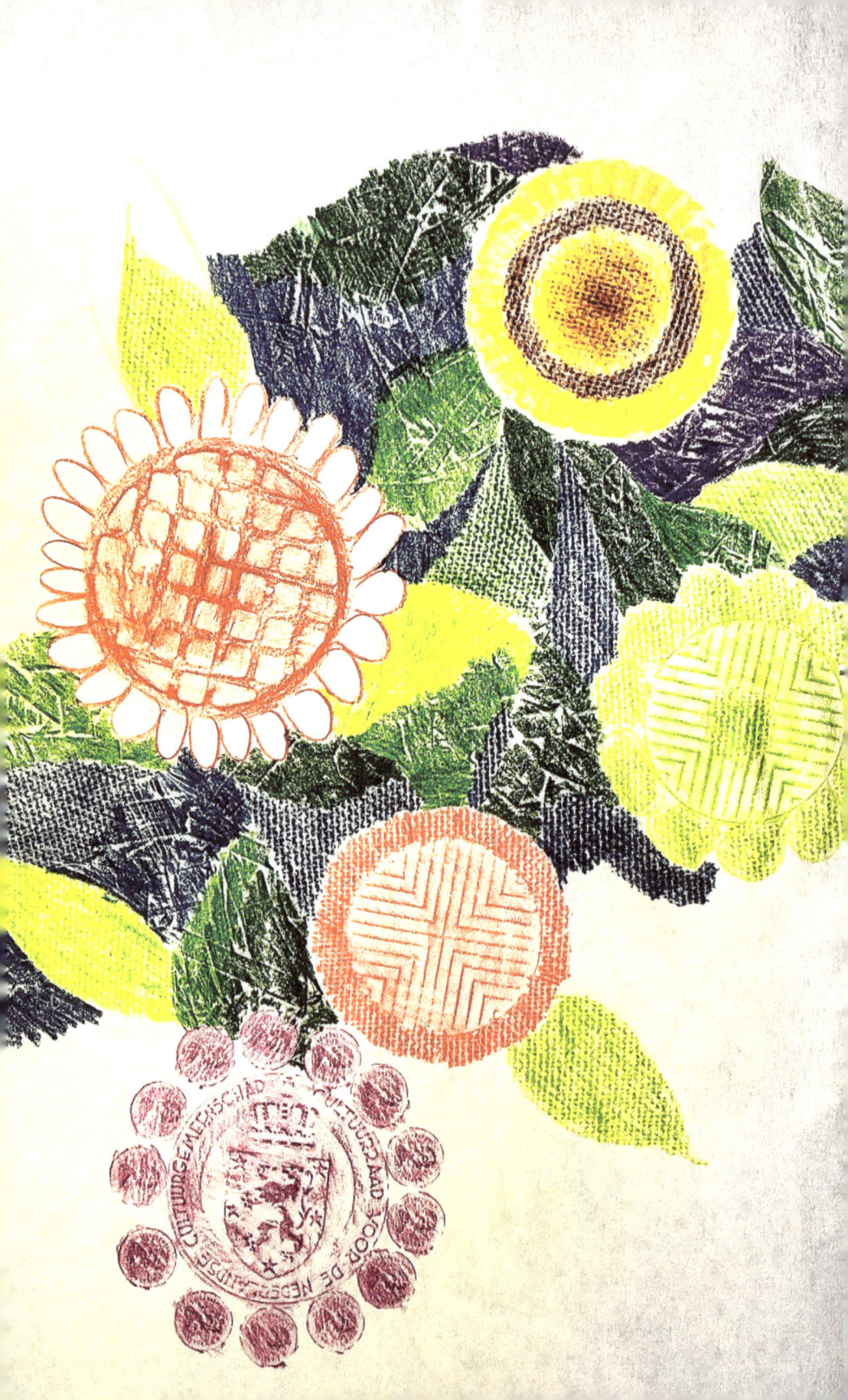

# April in Ottawa

It's the middle of April,
2002,
Crocuses
sweetly violate lawns
here in Ottawa.

Back in Edmonton
lawns can't even be seen for snow.
I don't know what it's like
in Winnipeg.

Everywhere it's the twentieth anniversary
of the Charter of Rights

the eleventh anniversary of
a primal scream in a Winnipeg garage
when the civil libertarian
hacked his marriage in half.

There's a Charter conference.
Politicians and lawyers and civil servants
and political scientists, statisticians, judges and journalists
attend a celebration.

Someone at the back of the room
notes parenthetically
that the poor have
no power at all.

They argue:
some say the judges have too much power,
others that they don't have enough.
And when it's over,
I go to the Gallery.

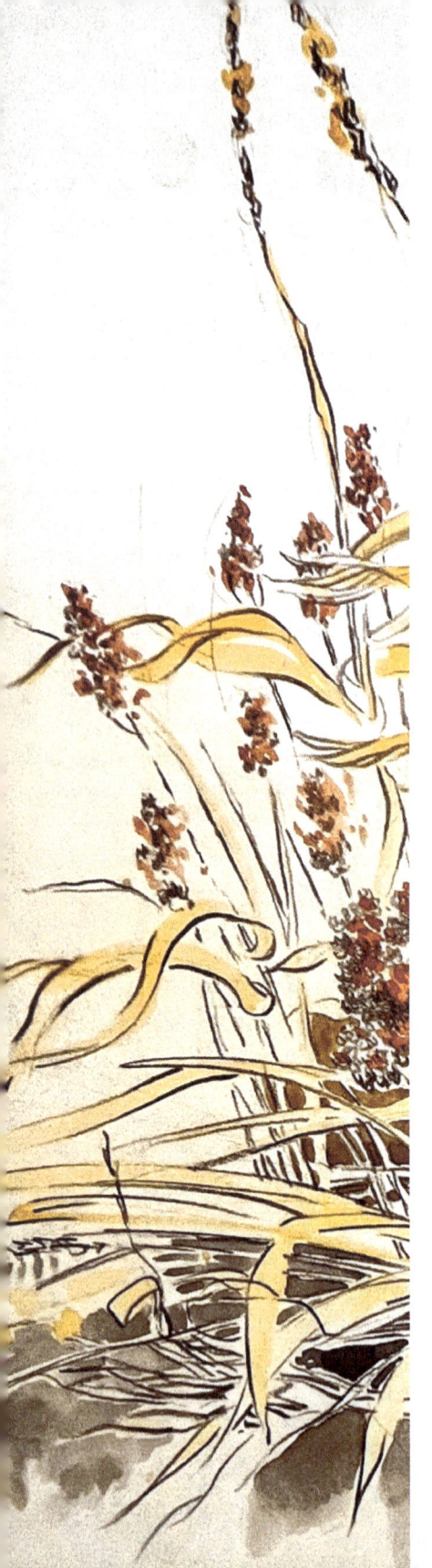

# The Birds

I read Poe's
"Raven" again
and confirmed
just how bad it is.

A hundred haunted gothic lines
mourning for the lost Lenore
in ballroom rhythms,
desperate rhymes,
anthologized for ever more.

But still, through murky films and layers
of rotting memory's soil and silt
that acid raven image stares,
a symbol of our grief and guilt.

There were ravens
in the place I fled
but fewer here.

Here, however, there are magpies,
ever present magpies,
nagging magpies evermore,

Gorgeous magpies,
birds black and white and iridescent
all at once.

Taunting magpies
swooping close, and hopping near,
fleeing when you
pay them heed.

Thieving magpies, stealing
what was long enough
to be a life.

Stealing
what is left.

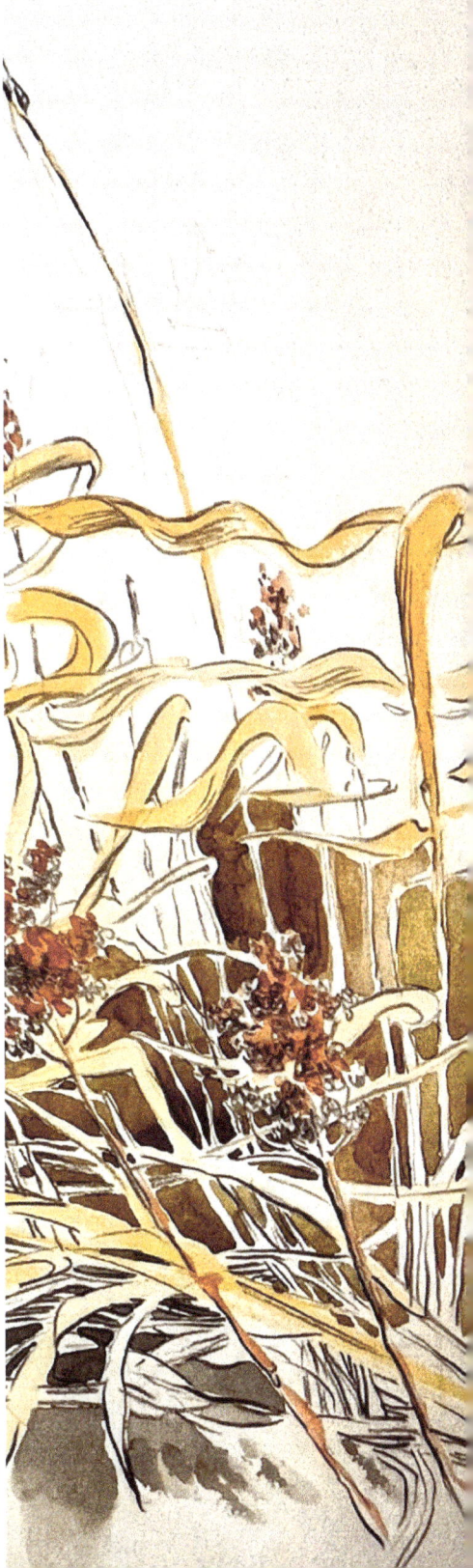

# Friends, Others

# Farewell to Former Friends

We went to another country
to honour the memory
of a cultured
long-time friend

The country
had once seemed friendly
and
moderately cultured
also

but this time we knew
before we left
and confirmed that
there were two
friendships to mourn

While in the U. S. for a dear friend's 2017 memorial service held in Connecticut

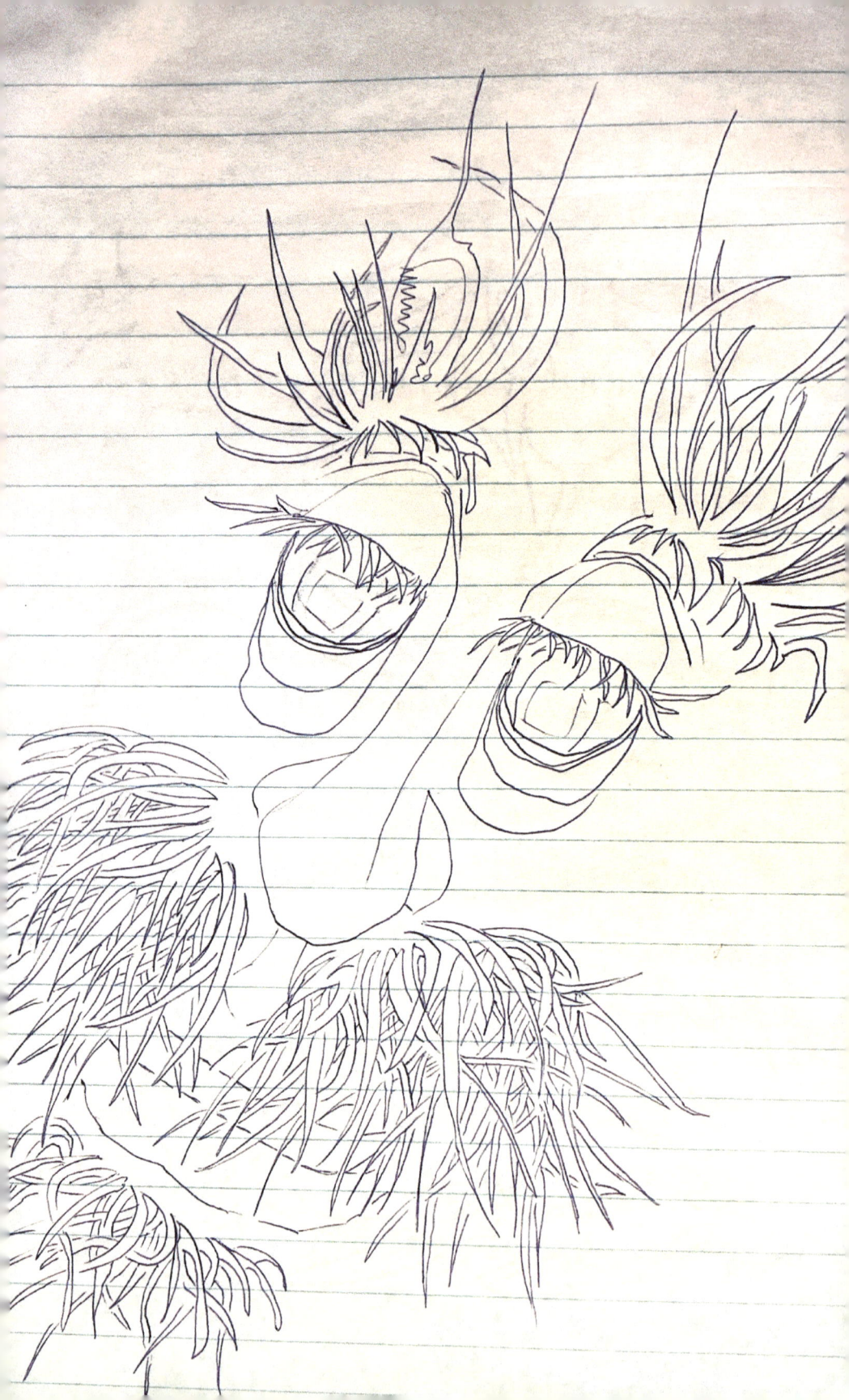

# Mrs. C's Ashes

You should have been there
Mrs. C.
showing your family
the right way
to spread you around
our front yard.

It was, of course, your yard
much longer
than it was ours.

Yours for twenty-five summers;
ice on the lake
when you came every spring
and gold on the ground
when you left.

Your white and red pines
(five needles for white,
was that what you said?
and three for the red?)
brought back from the forest as infants
from picnic excursions with W--,
who had the next cabin,
and carried the shovel and lunch,
and held your feet firm
while you stretched down into
a rocky crevasse
to recover that driftwood
you asked us not to destroy
when you sold us the place.

"Mr. W--" you called him
never his first name.
As a matter of fact
you never said much
on the subject of W--,

except that he wasn't a lout
like Pete the repairman,
who frightened you once
with a kiss
on the path to the dock.

No words,
just his lips,
cracked by the sun,
clamped to your mouth
by oil-stained hands on your back,
his surprisingly close-shaven chin
and tooth-pasty breath.

Though too much a lady
to say so, I think that
you probably kneed him.

In any event,
though he still kept
your boat and your pump
in good order,
I bet that he never
showed up at your cottage
so well-groomed again.

Mr. W--
was different.
He took no advantage, for instance,
the time at Sand Lake,
after swimming,
a bad-tempered turtle
waddled between
your clothing and you.

So you brought back
and planted the pines,
and they played
with the sun and the wind,
in your garden,
like children.

The garden's now gone,
except for the flowering weeds,
and plants that thrive on neglect,
but the family recalled how it was:
with blossoms cascading
from cottage to lake,
nourished by soil
Mr. W-- and you
carried in bags
from the woods.

The pines are now adults,
towering over the cottage,
shading the yard,
repeating the stories
remembering your summers
after the rest of your family
have gone.

# Relatives

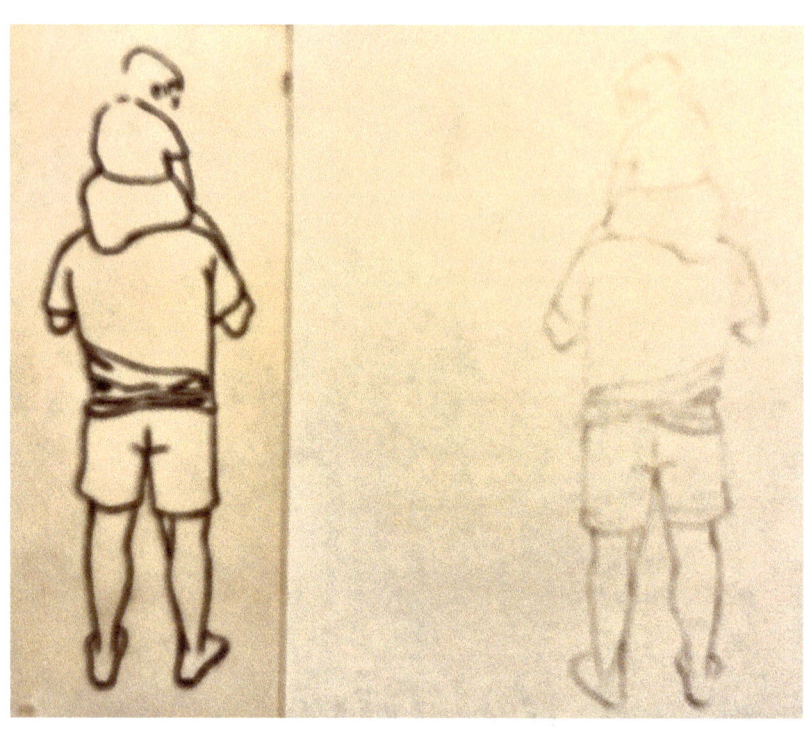

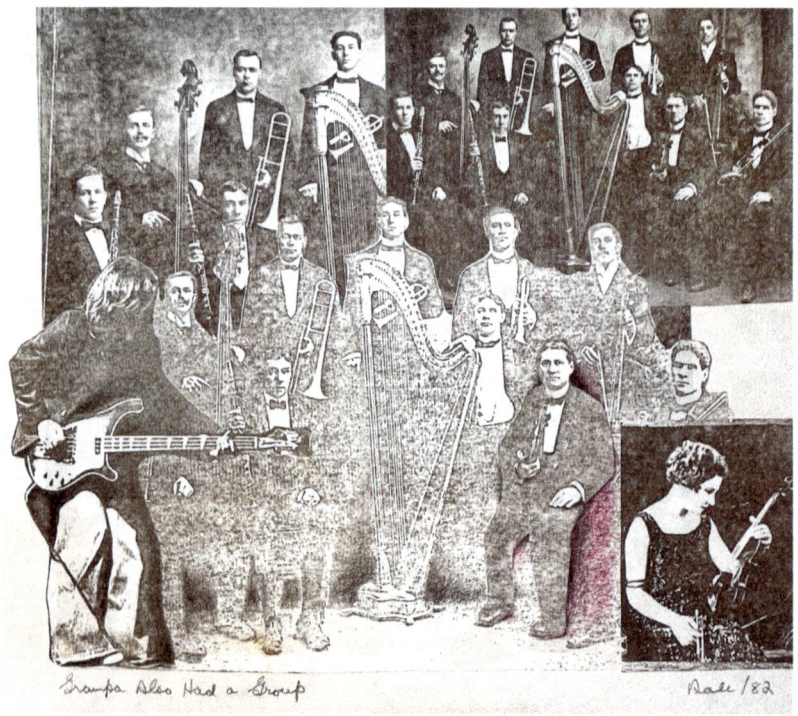

# Eiffel Tower

It
seemed
appropriate
to see
it with
my son
with whom
I'd built
Meccano
models of
increasingly complex design
but when
we reached
the observation deck
I realized
outgrown
he had his dad

# The Symbolism

The symbolism
was too overwhelming
for a poem.

Mother
and the others
condescended budgies
in the lounge
and wrapped their cages
up with bath towels
every night.

And
at the far end
of the corridor
my mother's room
looked west
across the churchyard
to the river
and the sunsets.

But
like the colour snapshots
on the notice board
and hobby paintings
in the lounge
actuality conveyed too little
with too much.

If less is more
in art
more is also often less
in life.

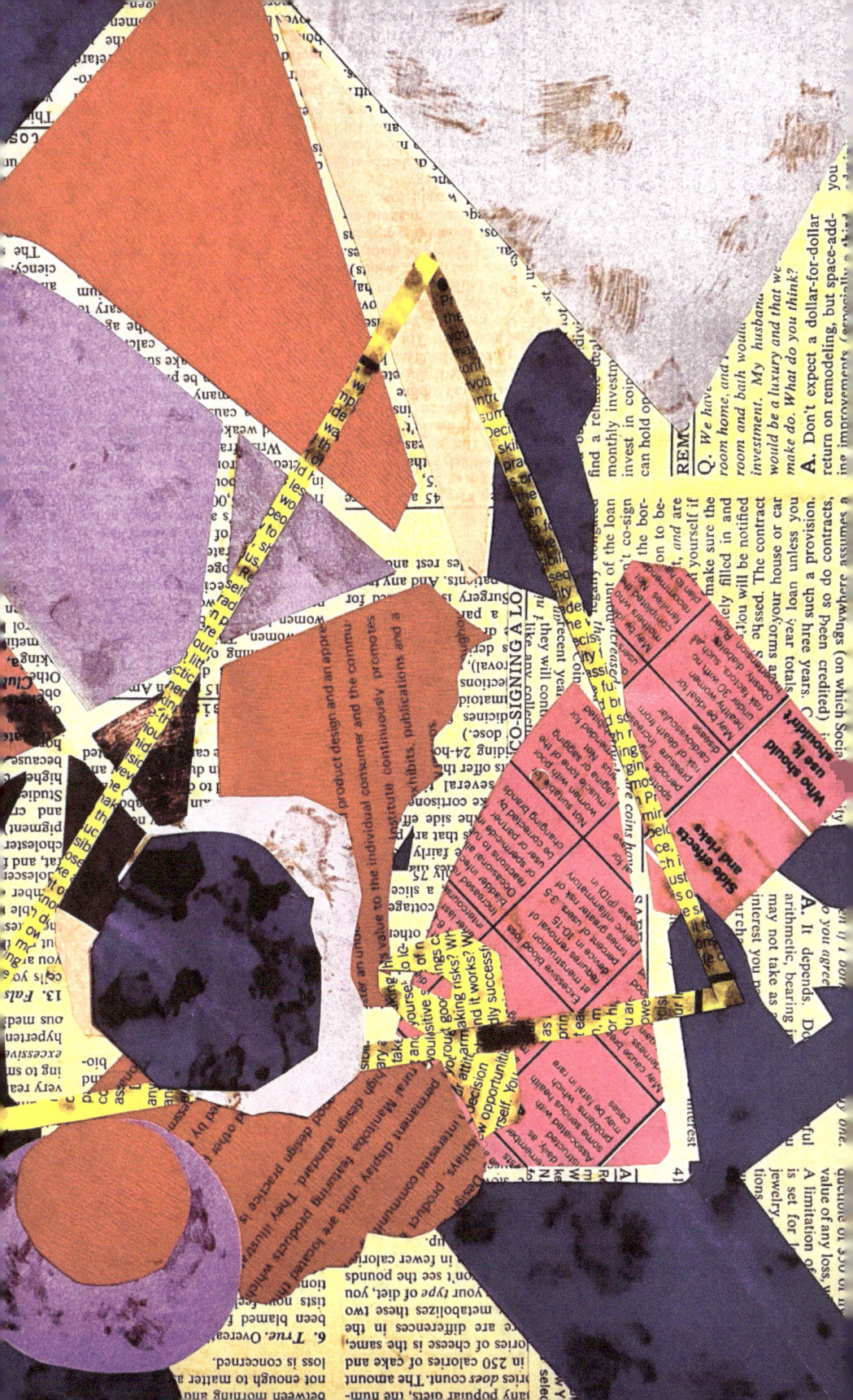

# Can't Be Sure

For Mo

The rain is cold
lamenting something lost
preparing something new

He is warm
and comfortable
we think
but can't be sure

There is singing by his bed
words are said,
love expressed

He understands, we think
but can't be sure.

\*\*\*

The sun is shining
when he dies.

What does that mean?

That life goes on?
That nature is indifferent
to individuals?
That symbolism's meaningless?
Perhaps

We can't be sure

That he leaves
a legacy of light and warmth?
Of that we're sure.

Read by Dale at the memorial
for his father-in-law, Mo Mosher, Jun 28/03

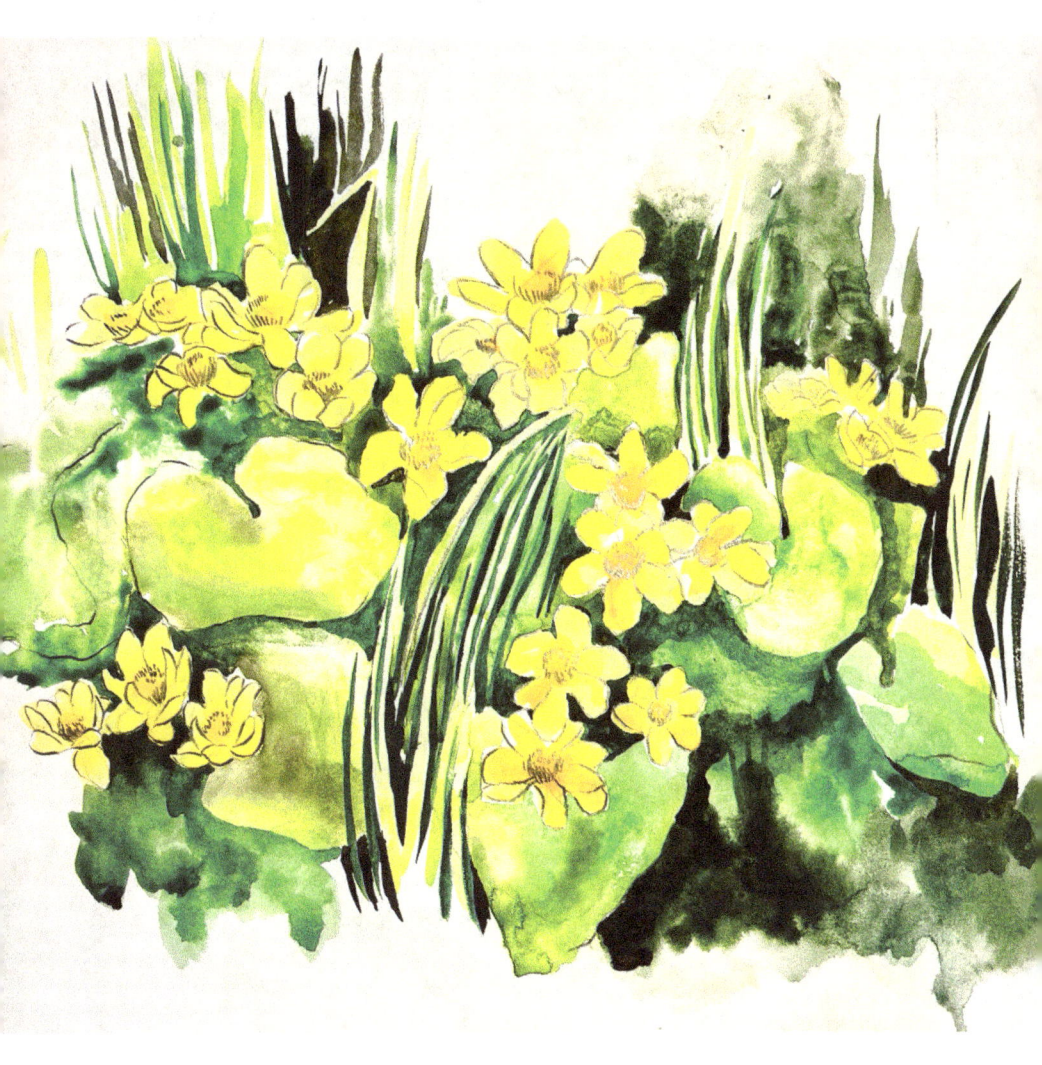

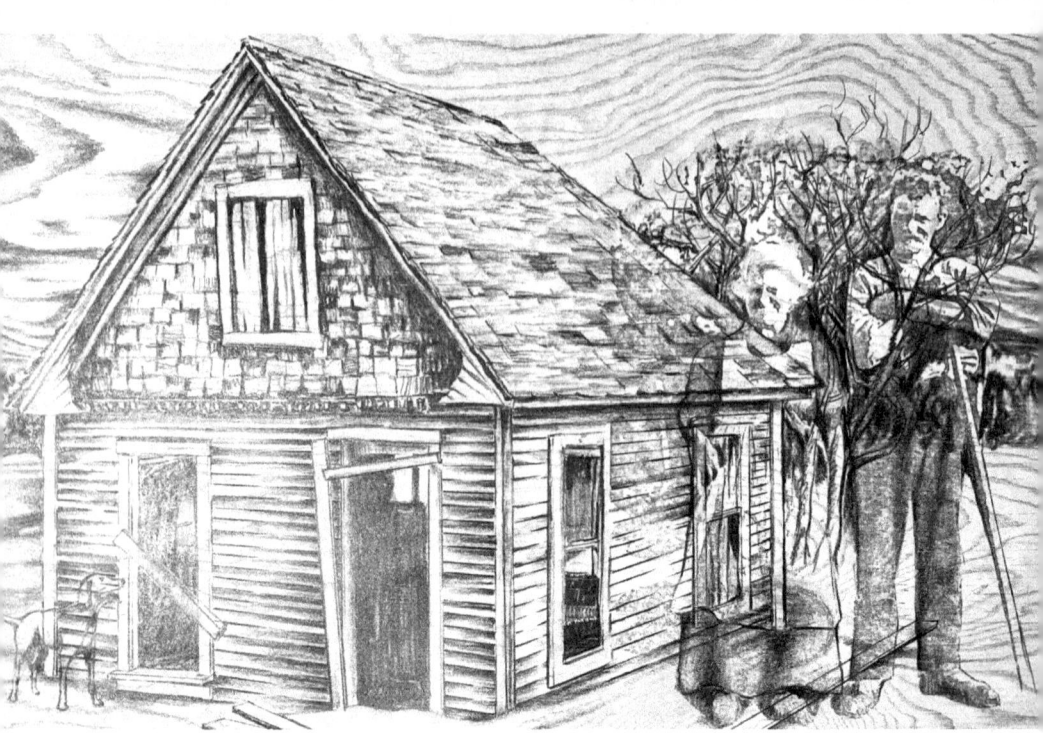

# Fires of Iceland

The fires of Iceland
drove them away
erupting under their futures,
dusting their fields and their dreams
with acidic ash,
fueling their flight,
heating their immigrant huts.

I flew over Iceland
one time at dawn
the clouds below were ablaze,
torched by a re-kindled sun,

and I wondered
about my mother's
Icelandic father
whom I never met,
nor was told much about.

I know
that he came from Iceland
about the turn of the century,
with only a wife and a fiddle,
that his wife gave him seven Canadians,
and his fiddle supported them all.

Was there fire
within him? Who knows?
The face in his photo
cratered, volcanic,
- north wind whether igneous or sedimentary
I can't tell – your dad
is stoic, like his name:
Thorstein.

Did he know about
Iceland's Alberta poet,
Stephan Stephansson,
author of homesteads by day,
grower of verse by night?
Well, perhaps he did
Was there an Icelander didn't?

But his children knew no Icelandic,
since he'd altered their name
from Johanesson to Johnston,
and he'd punished them
for speaking Icelandic.

Gramma survived him, but
she too had little to tell.

# Baskets

The basket
that her parents gave her
held a lot, especially on her father's side
intelligence, determination, and loyalty
and from her mother – trust.

Mine left me less.

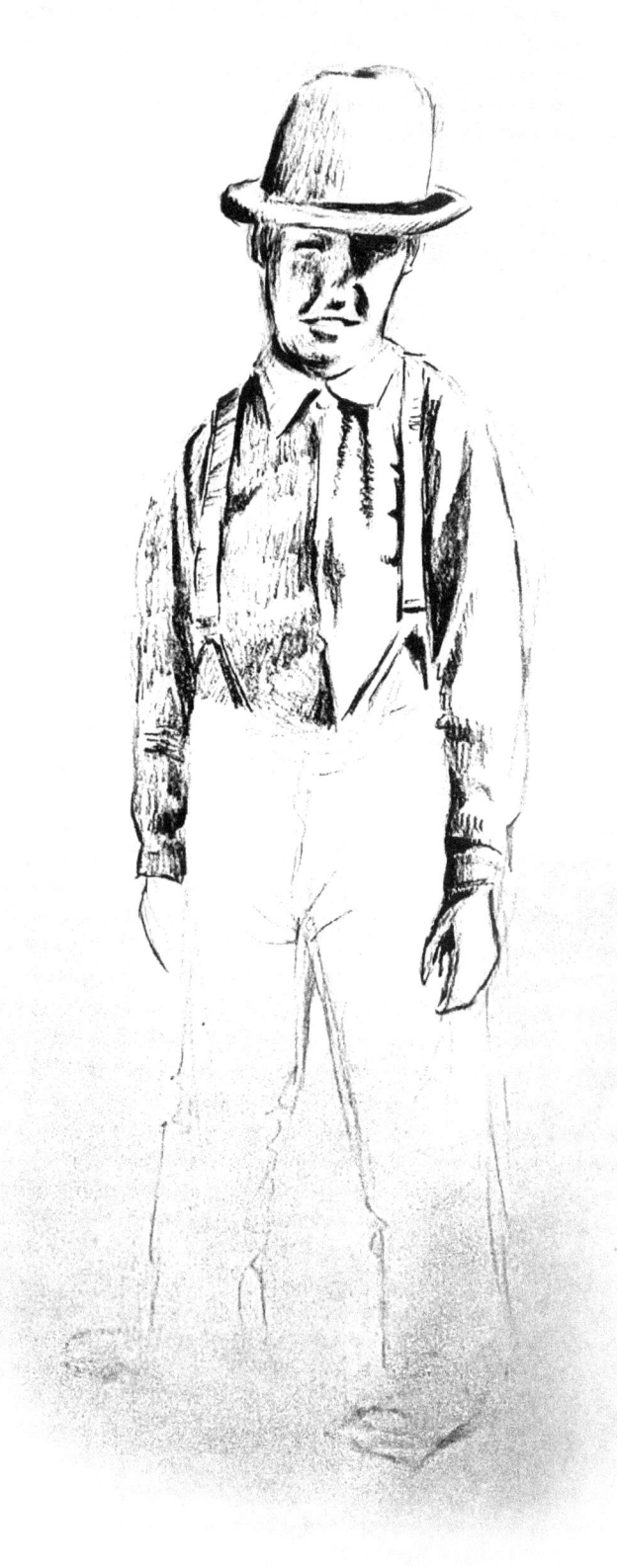

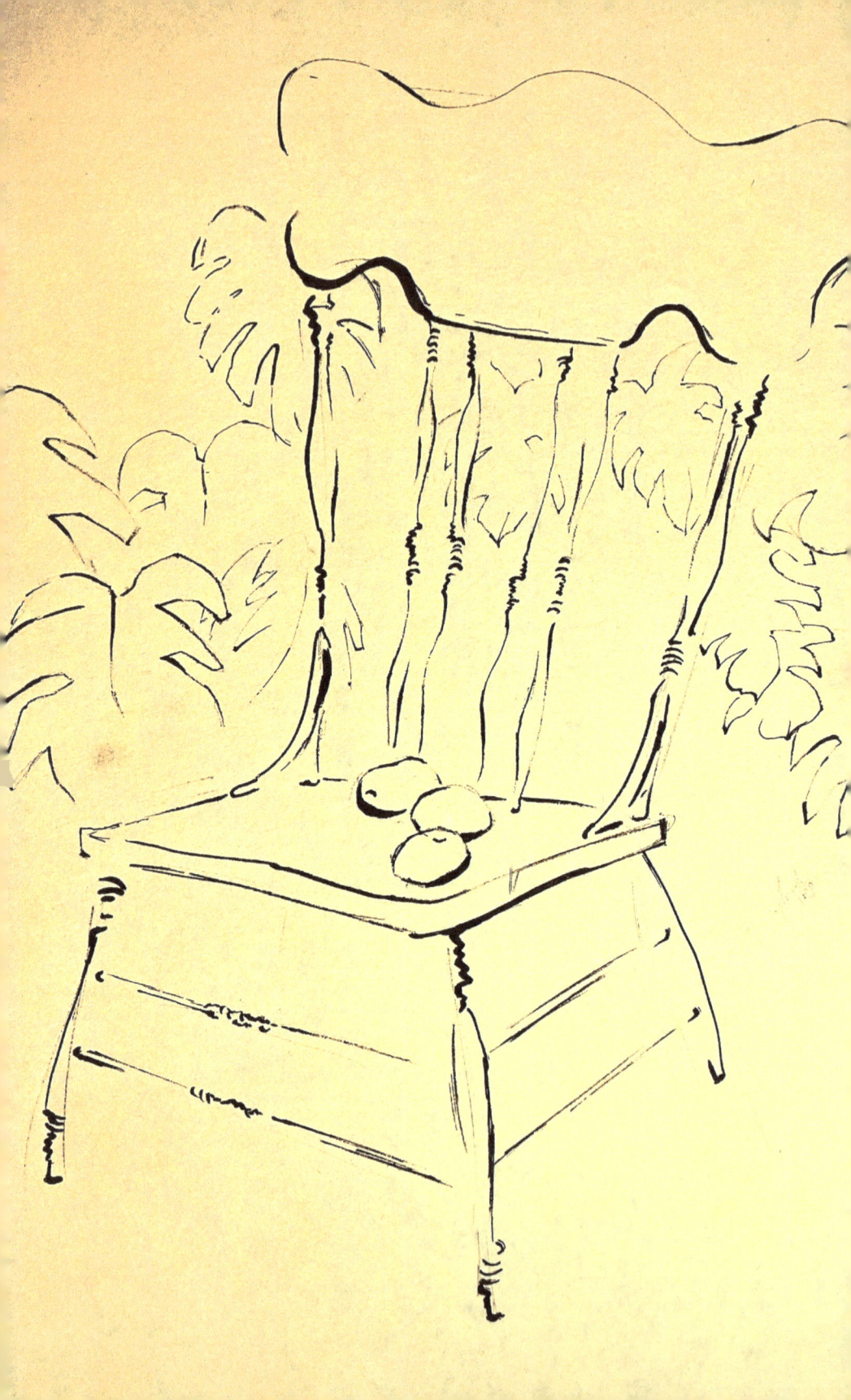

# Winter is Finished

Winter is finished
but for some patches
of grit-encrusted snow
hard to distinguish
from alkali.

At the other edge
of this scarified prairie
my father sits
in his threadbare chair
with his bottle of rye
and his TV remote
and waits.

# Generational

"Love you"
said my sister to my father
as usual
before her ringing off

After a pause
my usually unresponsive father
replied
"You think that I don't too?"

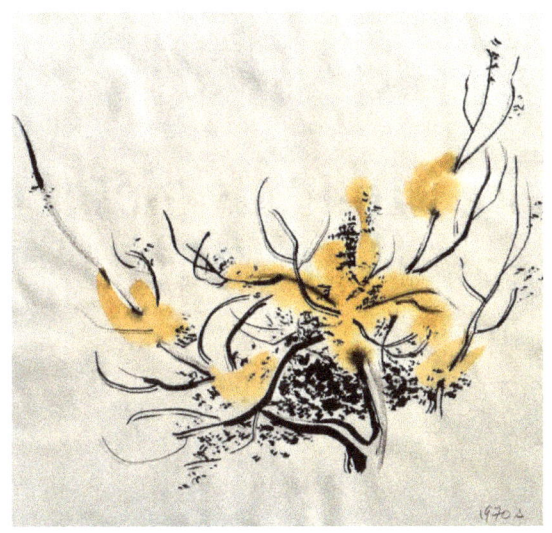

# Ann's Funeral

He hadn't ever been
trusted much with decisions
and when this one had to be made
he was drunk.

So we opted, on his behalf
for fire rather than rot
which, it later turned out
he would certainly have not

He had not had the guts
to tell her good-bye in person
and now he could only demand of us all

Where's Ann?

insistently, drunkenly, guiltily, lovingly, endlessly
Where's Ann?
Where's Ann?
Where's Ann?

# The Night My Mother Didn't Die

"She won't last the night"
I was told,

and I looked for a poem
in the night,
a message in entrails.

The stars weren't quite
where they should be,
misarranged, though
certainly infinite enough.
Where was
the Dipper, for instance?
(Not that she'd ever
notice the difference)

and –
honestly –
a meteor fell.

Too trite to be used,
though I thought of my father
shooting me –
part of me –
into her
limited
infinity.

(Not good, because
meteors fall out of,
not into, the infinite,
but maybe not bad,
since I really did think it,
and what's this about?)

Meanwhile, my mother
refused
(once again)
to do what they said,
refused
her own wish to die,
refused
to be poetry.

# 249 Ottawa Ave.

The final time
I saw the place,
empty, pending sale,
stark as January,

what it brought to mind,
by contrast chiefly,
was a snapshot taken
some time in May or June
of 1936, not long before
my sister's birth.

It might have been occasioned
by my own third birthday,
since I'm right there
in the foreground,
up against a caragana hedge,
wincing at the sun,
and somewhat better dressed
than usual.

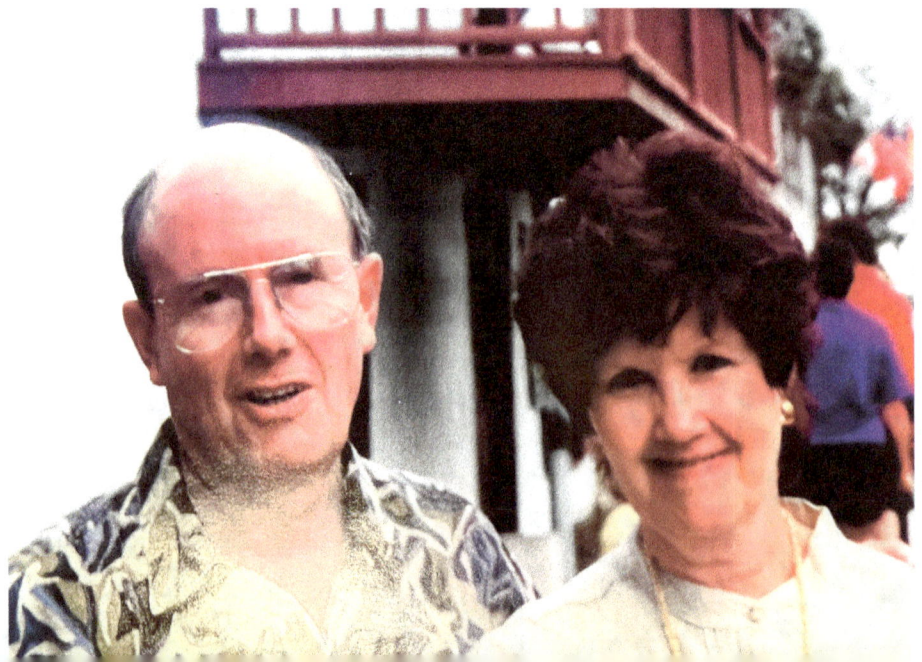

Behind the hedge
my mother hides her pregnancy.

The front entrance to the house
is also out of view,
behind a bursting lilac bush.

And Dad's behind the lens of course.

Most of what was hidden
then is in the open now.

My sister was the first revealed.
She grew straightforwardly to be a forthright
little girl, and then
a candid, over-trusting woman

who, like me,
escaped as soon as possible,
and hid in matrimony.

The hedge had been removed
by that time, and the
twisted lilac bush
would soon follow.

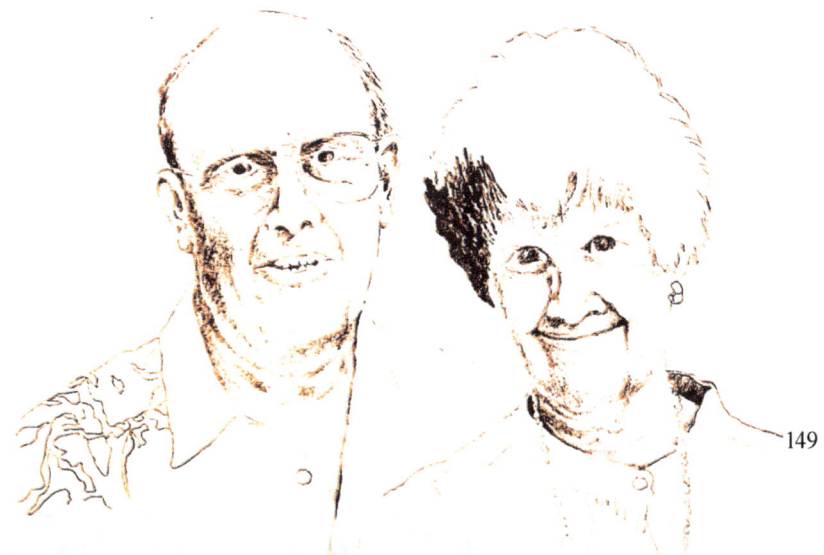

Mom then hid herself
in sipping wine
and Dad in glove advertisements
and sordid thoughts.

Now Mom is dead
and Dad is under scrutiny.
My sister's life's open
for Jehovah and his Witnesses
to use.

And so the only secrets left
are those that crouch
behind the little boy's
squinting, unrevealing eyes.

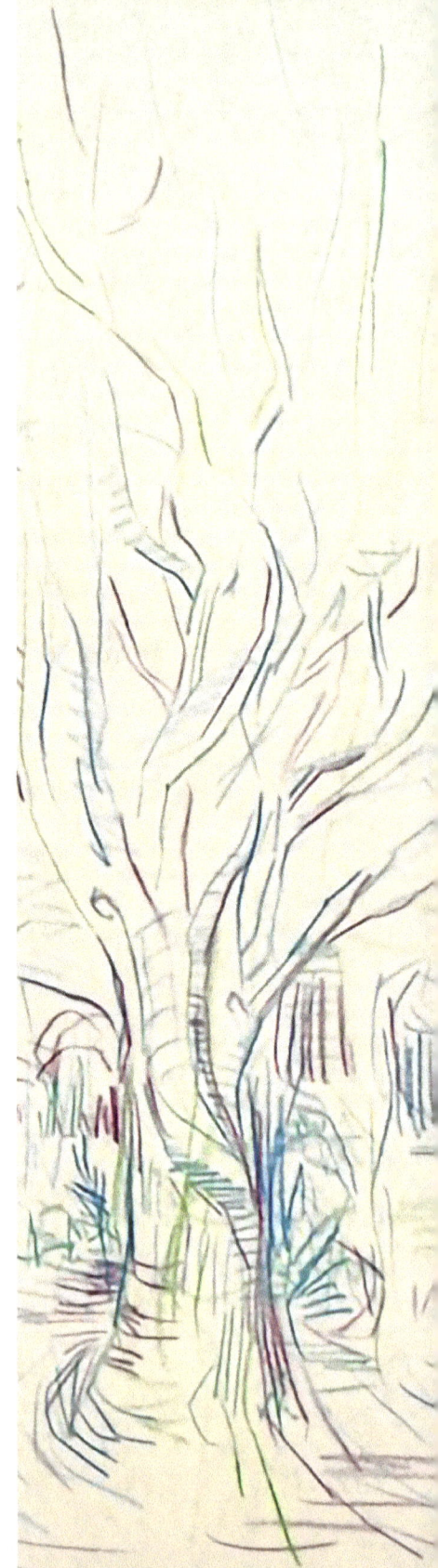

# The Prairies

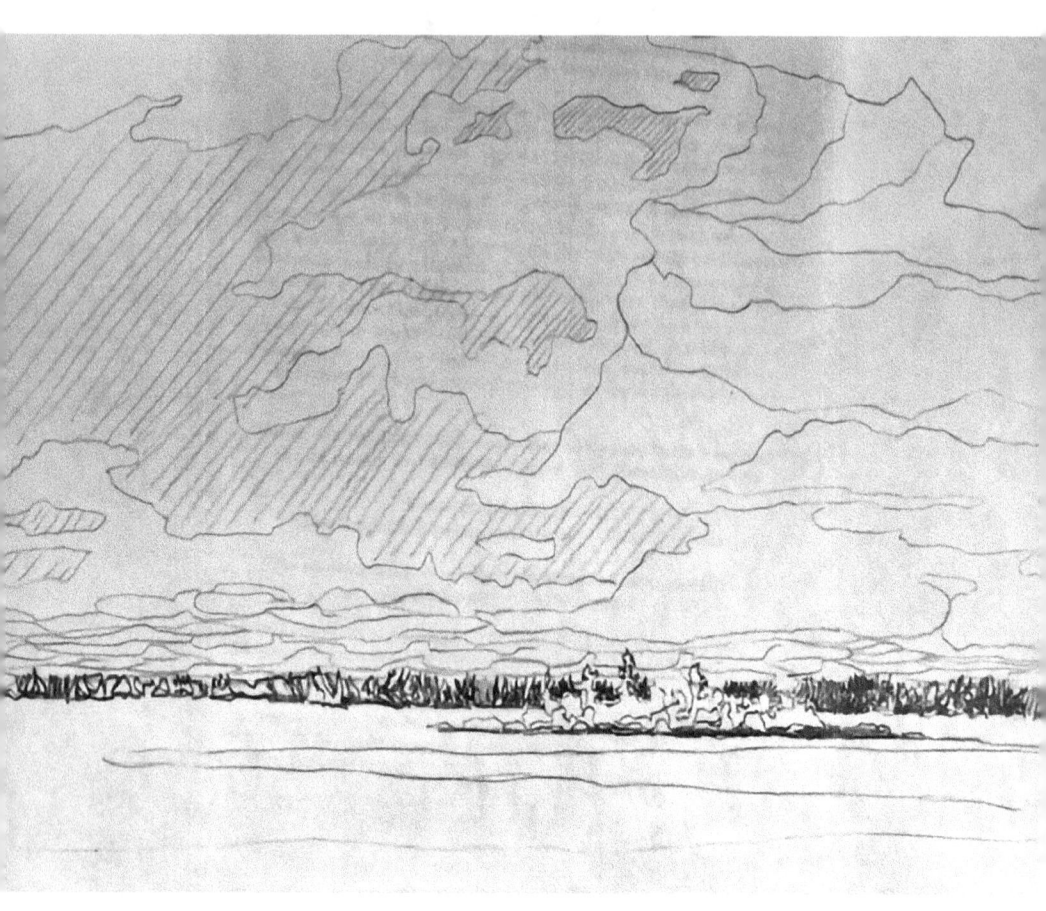

# Winnipeg International Airport

The prarie sky
puts landscape in place,

contains a dozen droning lights
trapped within a bowl
of unimaginable dimentions

# Prairie Dragon

Winter flight to Winnipeg.

Below
a prairie river dragon,
whiter etched on white,
claws at winter,
thrashing its
thousand-kilometer tail
and snorting frozen fire.

Once it roamed
with dinosaurs
and cruised
the inland sea.

Ojibway travellers called it
Mishipizhiw
and paid it ransom
of tobacco and berries
for a guarantee of
uneventful passage.

Engines droned.
I listen for irregularities
and vow
to leave a little something
at Regina
for the dragon.

# The Library

The library
looks like a turtle,
giant tortoise of Dundas Ave.,
periscope head alert,
reconnoitering for external dangers.

Prepared to withdraw
and live on itself for a while
like its monastic ancestors
insuming the hoards
of their provident forbears.

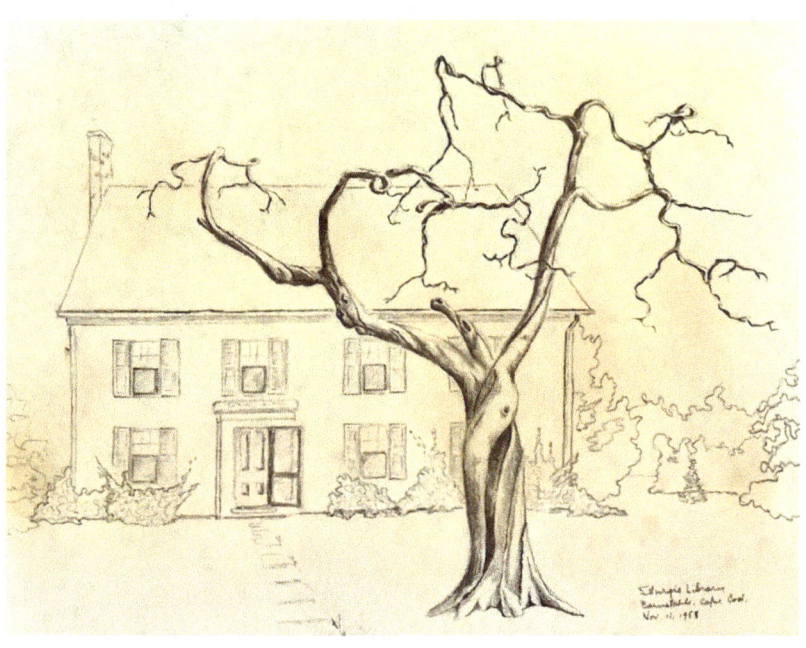

# Winnipeggers are Masochists

Winter seared my earlobes
carved my forehead
probed my lungs with shafts of icy steel

which so satisfied me
that I wrote a poem about it.

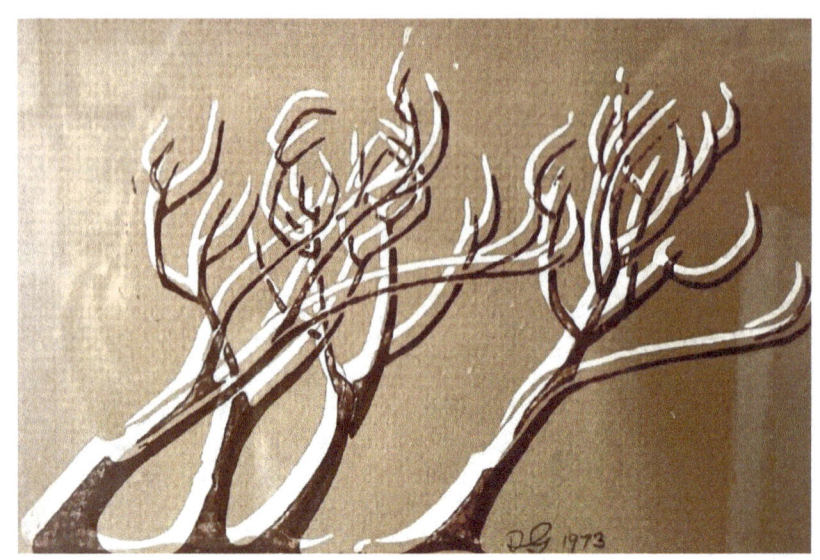

# Winnipeg Blizzard

By evening all the streets were blocked.
Theatres and restaurants closed,
and almost everyone stayed home, well insulated from the storm.

Responding to some elemental urge,
I tramped the churning streets on snow-shoes,
pummeled by the dehumanizing wind
which snatched even thoughts away
and sent them spinning through vortexing snow
and bouncing down abandoned boulevards,
crashing into trees and snowdrifted cars.

Wellington Crescent:
the street-lamps howled like coyotes.

Wellington Crescent:
should at least be Lagimodière Blvd!

Dare I, two blocks from home,
flanked by picture windows,
speak of him
who walked, snowshod, 2000 empty miles to Montreal alone
in 1815-16 with the stale news
(the best since Wellington subdued the French at Waterloo
some months the year before, but false)
that the storm in Ruperts Land was over
(it had just begun, in fact)?

Returning home,
I noticed that my outbound tracks
had been obliterated by the wind
.

But never those of Lagimodière.

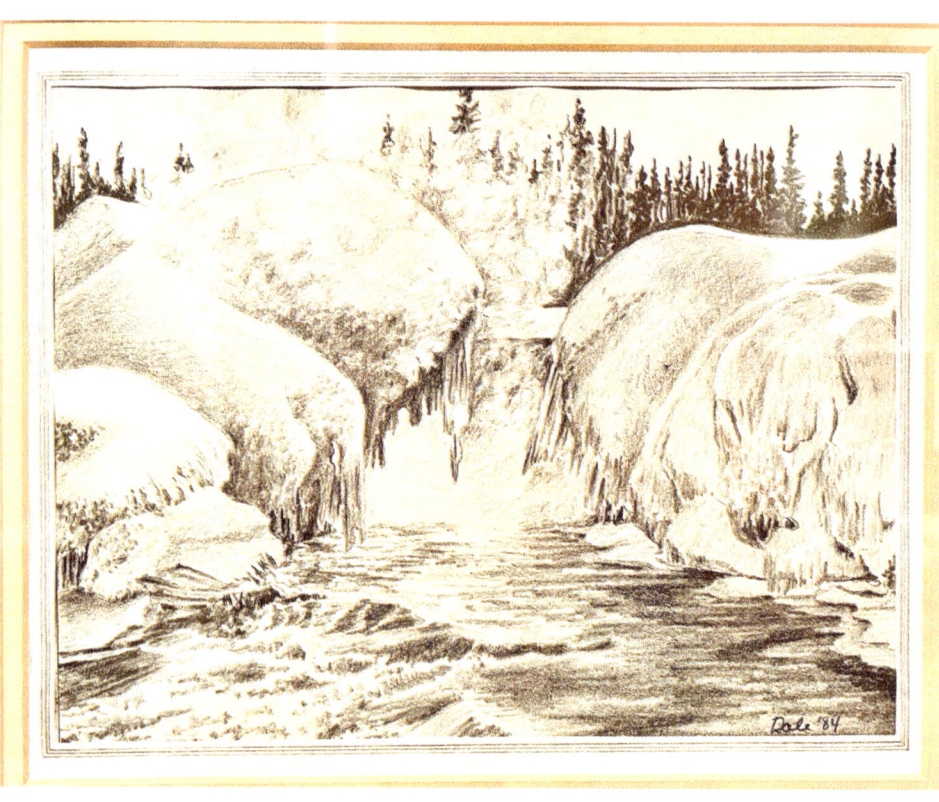

# Pisew Falls in Winter

I'm walking on an icy path
beside a frozen stream

where stillness parts
and winter opens
like a lover's robe.

Torrents roil
and spume and steam,
turn trees to sculpture,
shrubs to wedding cakes,
toss diamonds in the sun,

and draw me to
the icy edge.

# Ecocracy [August Styles]

Tiger lilies roar
by the water

Hare bells chime
by the door

Fireweed blazes
in various places

Queen Anne's Lace
crochets the shore.

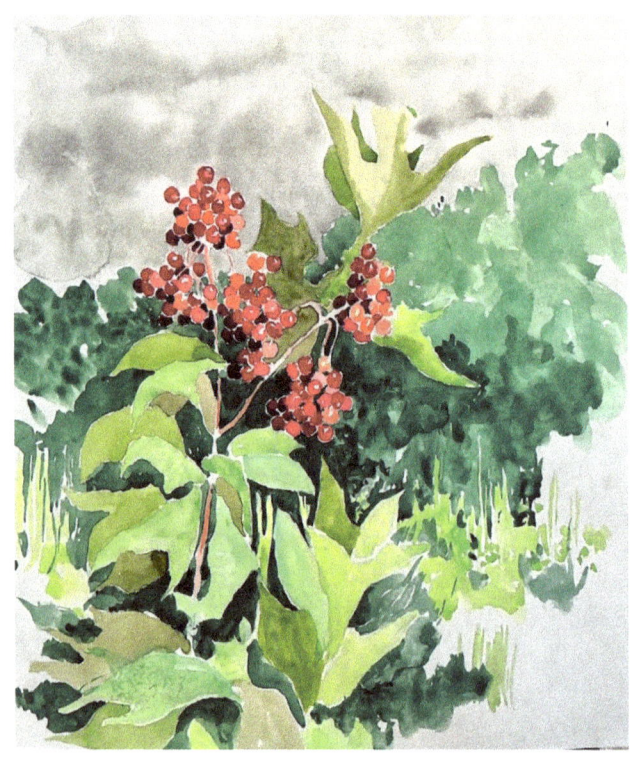

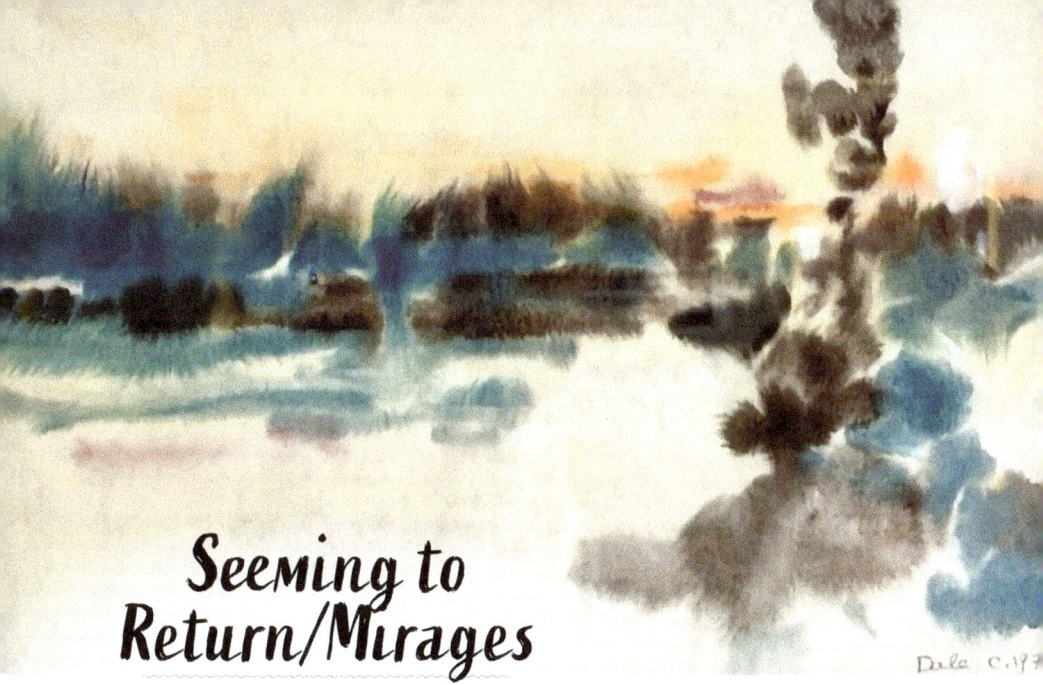

# Seeming to Return/Mirages

Distant shimmers of blue

on the road back home
are
not prairie lakes
but
flowering flax in arid fields.

Soaring teddy bears, floating pussy-cats
are transient thunderheads.

Silhouette dinosaurs
looming at dusk
are fossilized threshing machines.

The rubicund moon
which seemed at first
as close as family

grows smaller
and paler

as I
approach.

# Before the Flowers

(Written for Kris while crossing
the prairies again in early spring)

Again
spring winds
have torn the blankets off
and

secrets shiver
in the prairie ditches

open to the

wheeling hawks
and
warming sun.

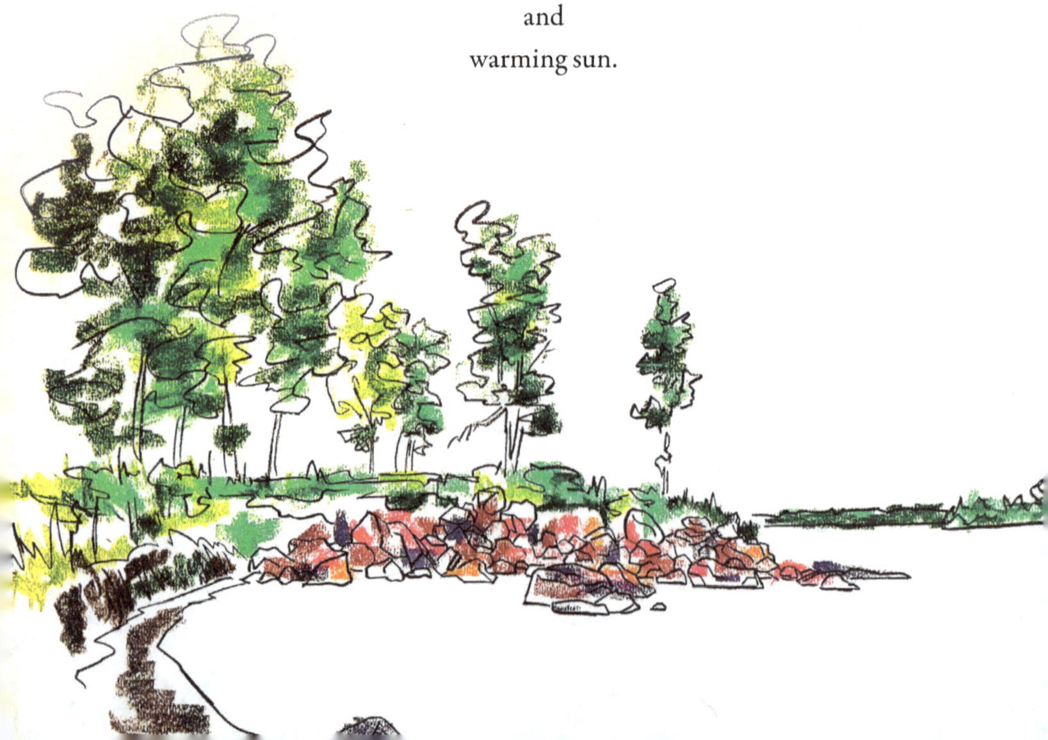

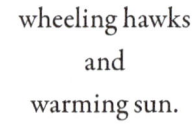

# West of Saskatoon

Modest greens, and
early hour pastels,
undulating buffs and almonds.

The concrete curves
of Borden Bridge
peach at sunrise
arching the river
with feminine strength.
A modern span serves routinely,
indifferent as a husband.

Ripened fields of wheat,
proud as adolescents
coming home at dawn,
flaunt their adulthood
beside their neighbors'
mottled immaturity.

Above a brasher field of rape,
a goshawk rises, glides,
relaxed but garnet-eyed,
dark wings lifting
golden body, taut
with prairie wealth.

And further to the west
pumps rise and fall,
fucking slowly, sorrowfully,
like sinners damned
to wallow in their crimes.

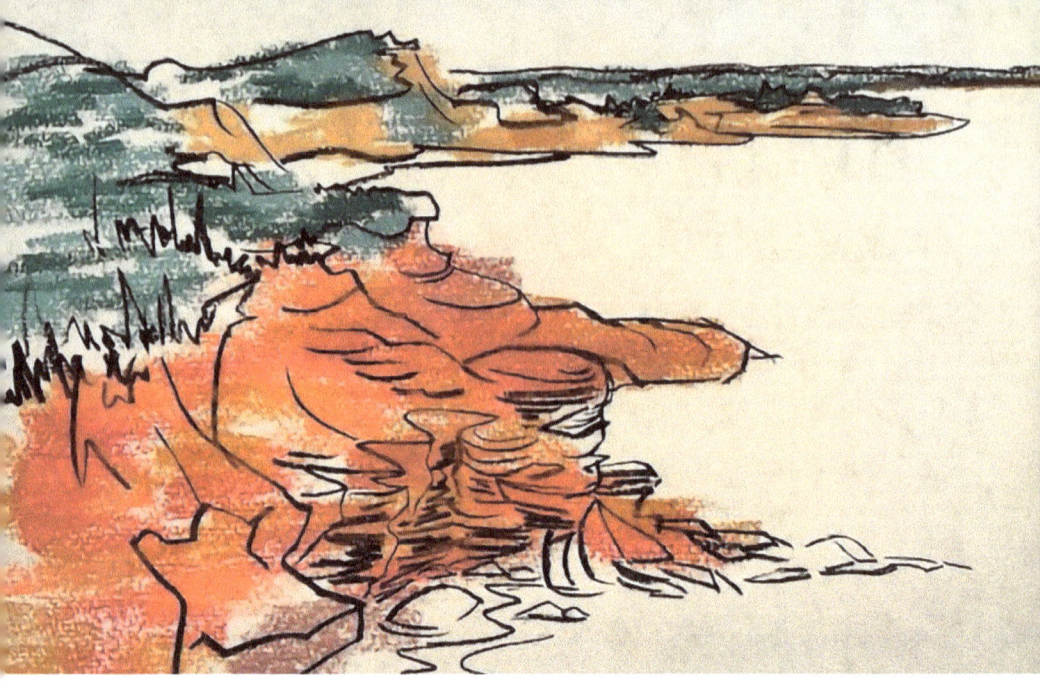

# Unsure Weather

Unsure whether
its war with winter
is finally over
the prairie wears khaki
with
combat ribbons of
russet, burnt orange, and ochre

And cold spring sunshine
glints off potholes like
bayonets

I DROVE TO WINNIPEG ON THURSDAY - 13 HOURS TOTAL ELAPSED TIME - ON A GORGEOUSLY SUNNY DAY THAT SHOWED THE PRAIRIE'S WONDERFULLY SUBTLE NOT-QUITE-SPRING COLOURS TO BEST ADVANTAGE. CLOUDS OF GEESE - BOTH CANADA AND SNOW GEESE - WERE FREQUENT.
JOURNAL, APRIL 11, 2015

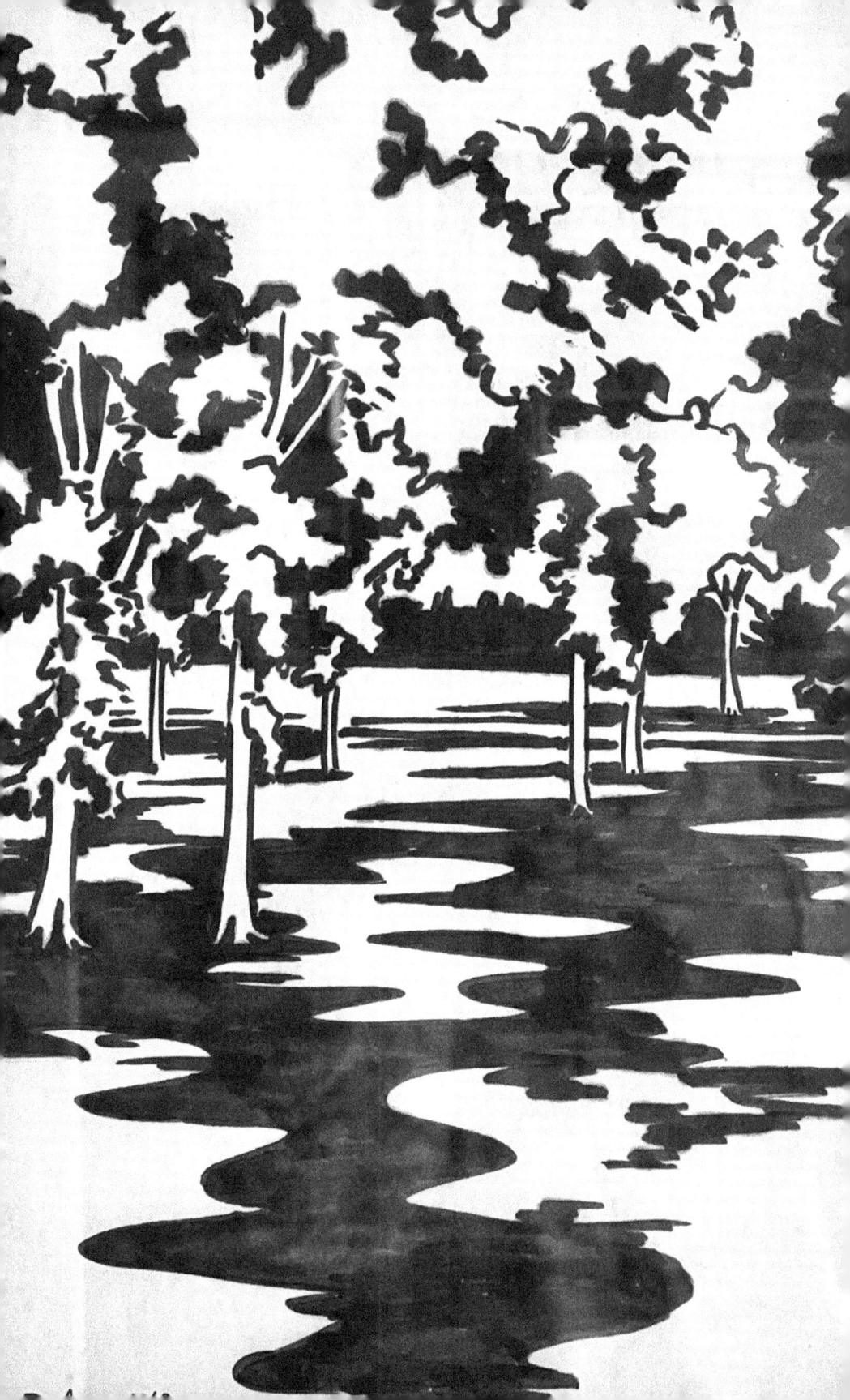

# The Free Enterprise Pussy-Willow

I was
skiing
with a friend
in Riding Mountain Park

The temperature was warm for February,
though the snow was deep
and many winds
ambushed us
at the clearings

Just beyond the wire
at the boundary of the park
a pussy-willow bush,
well-sheltered from the wind
but open to the sun,
had prematurely burst
its buds.

On our side of the fence
the shrubs were less ambitious.

"See how public ownership
inhibits growth!" my friend declaimed
(Our friendship stops at politics.)

"If winter hasn't killed them in a week,"
I snarled
"Some huckster will be selling
and arranging guided tours!"

Returning
to the scene
a few days later,
not a blossom could be found.

But judging from the tracks
nearby,
the culprit wasn't either
frost or enterprise.

Apparently,
a hungry elk
had leaned across
the boundary fence
and nipped
our controversy
in the bud.

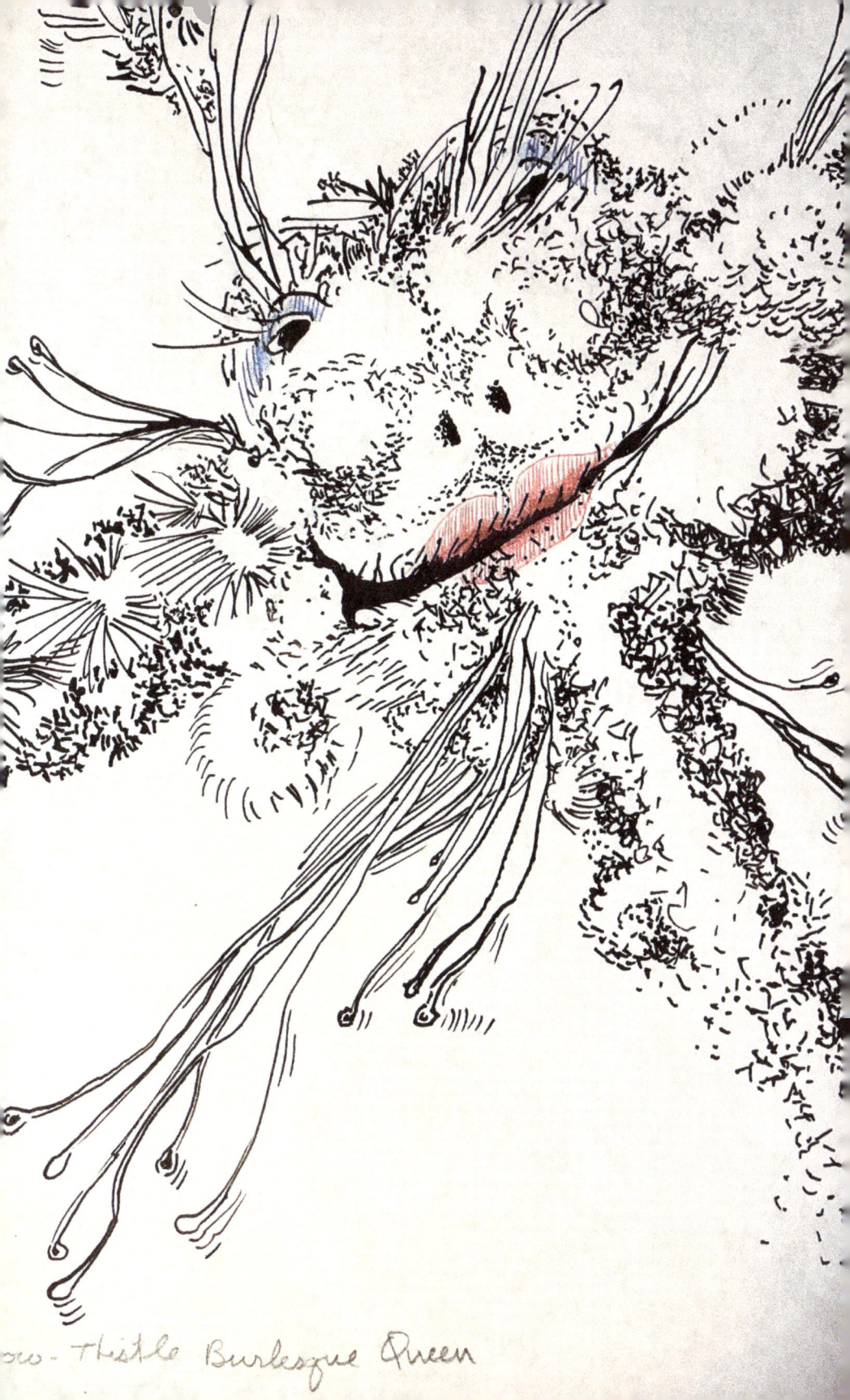

Sow-Thistle Burlesque Queen

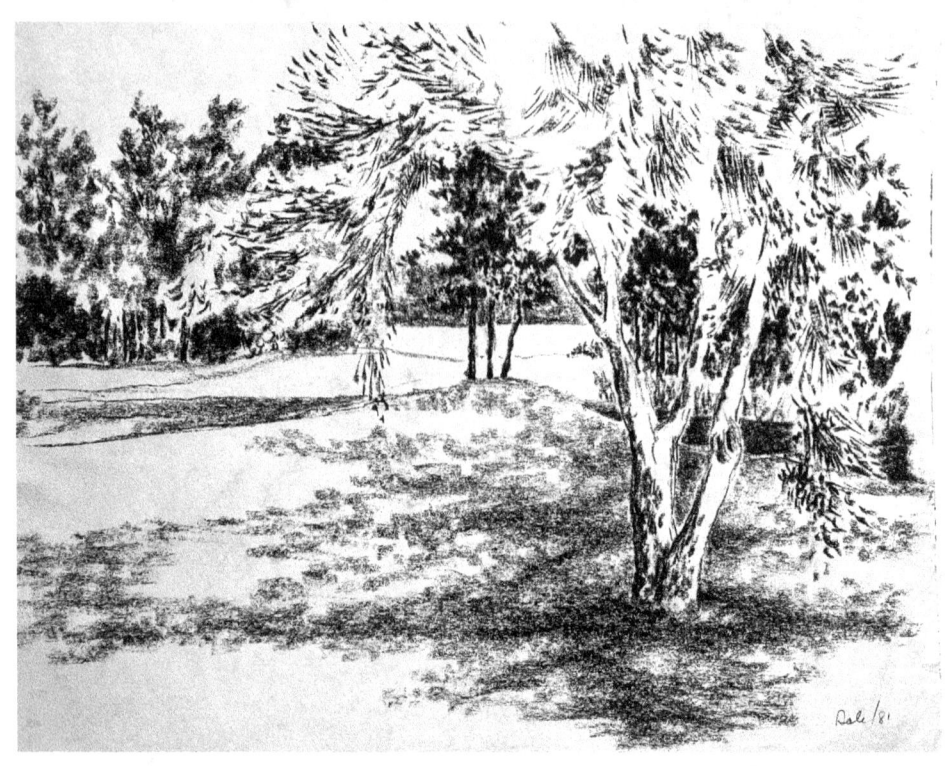

# Homecoming Away From Home

I have done well
since leaving Winnipeg
and
so has Winnipeg

Perhaps
it was a parting
fated to occur

Taras Shevchenko sits
stolid, atop his marble toilet still.

The fog is unfamiliar – and
the absence of snow in March -
but not even Winnipeg
escapes global warming.

The Archives – well,
you wouldn't expect Archives to change much
and they haven't – except that
they're less patronized and
less fully funded than ever before
but that's always been so.

There are several new buildings
some of them tasteful
but
they converted Eatons to a hockey arena
and the Bay's on life support.
They tell me the U of M Faculty Club
has closed.

My new family is here
the old one isn't really.

The reason you can never go back
is that it's no longer there.

On the other hand
if it isn't
there's no reason not to.

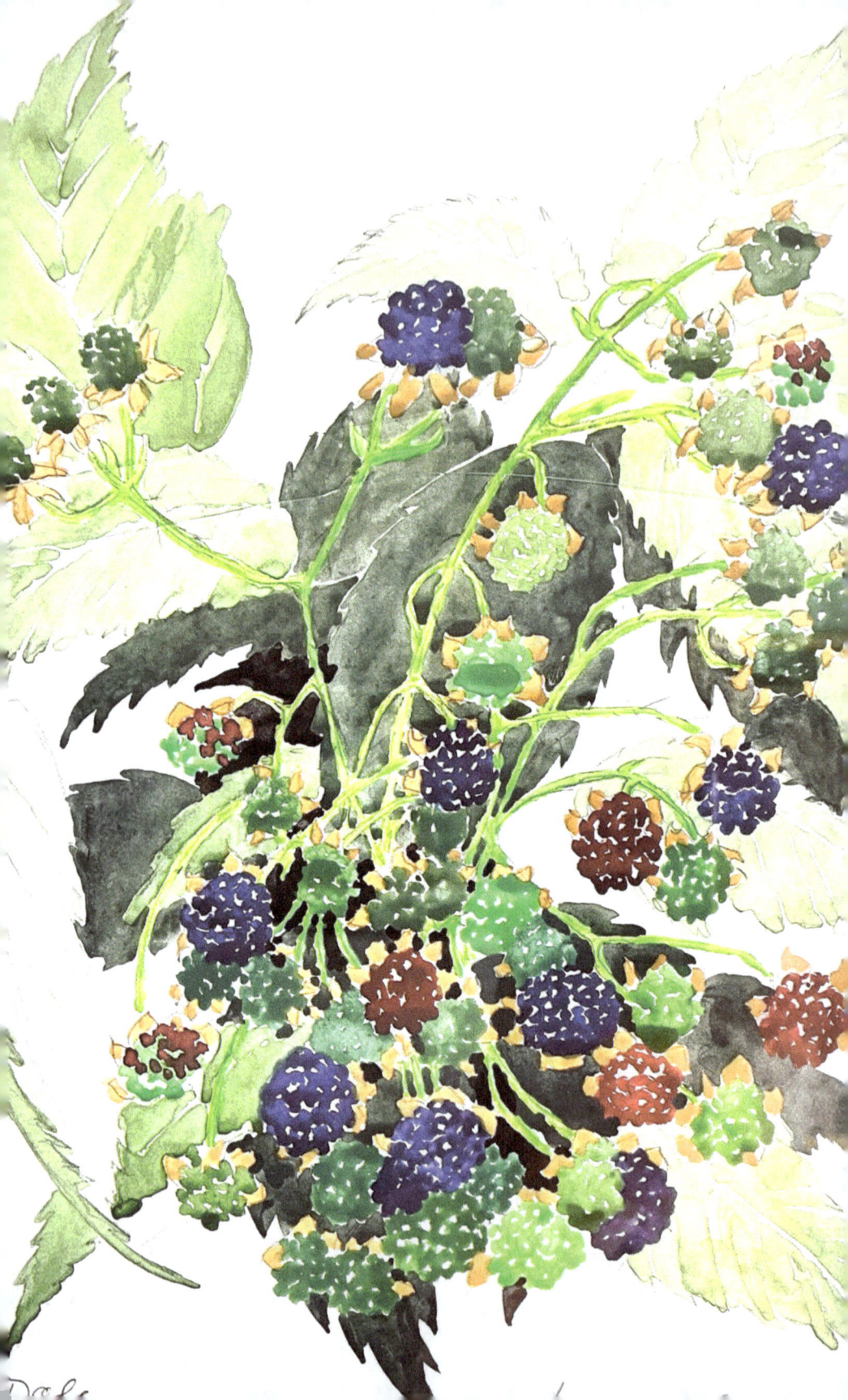

# Other Places

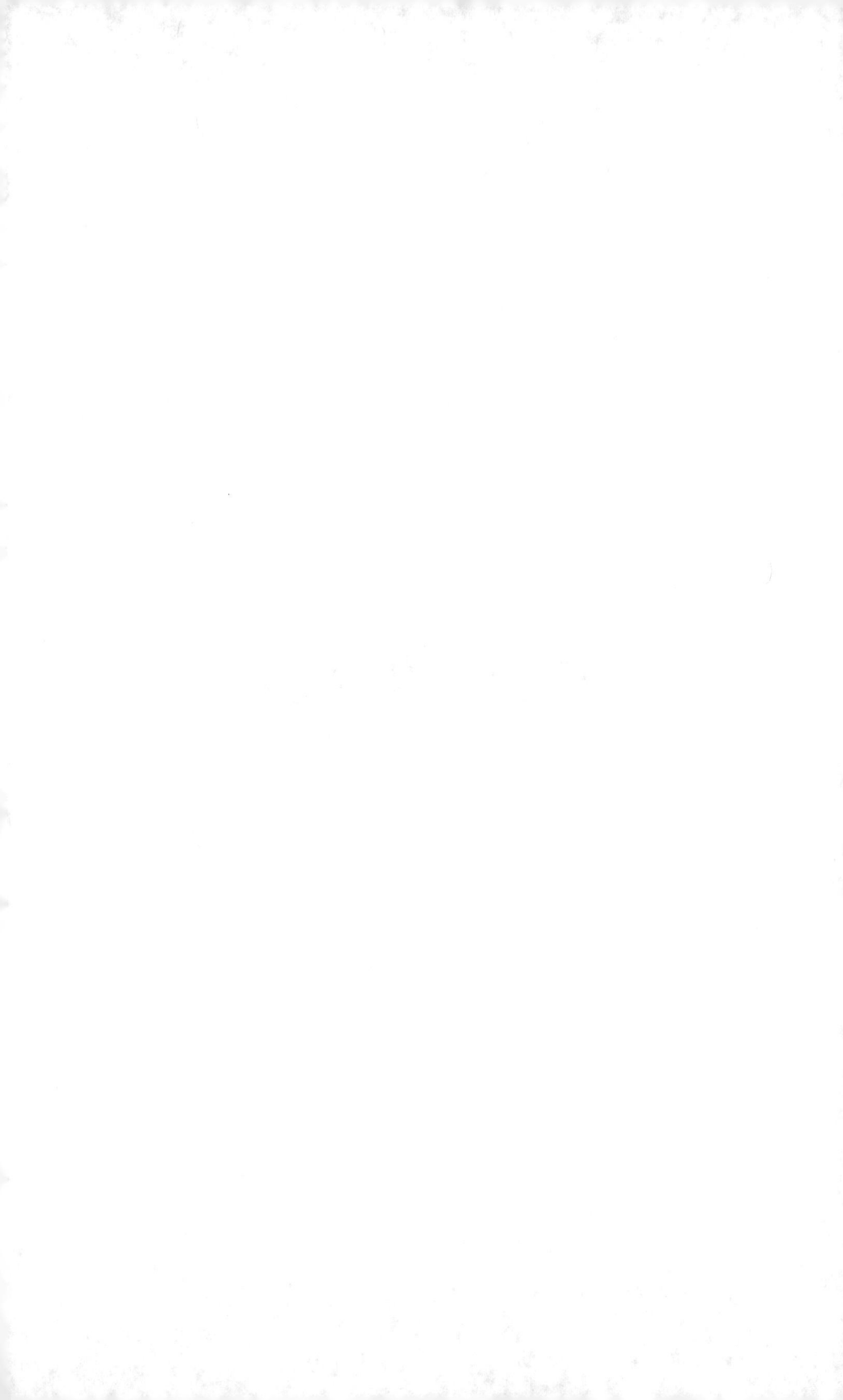

# Other Places – Canada

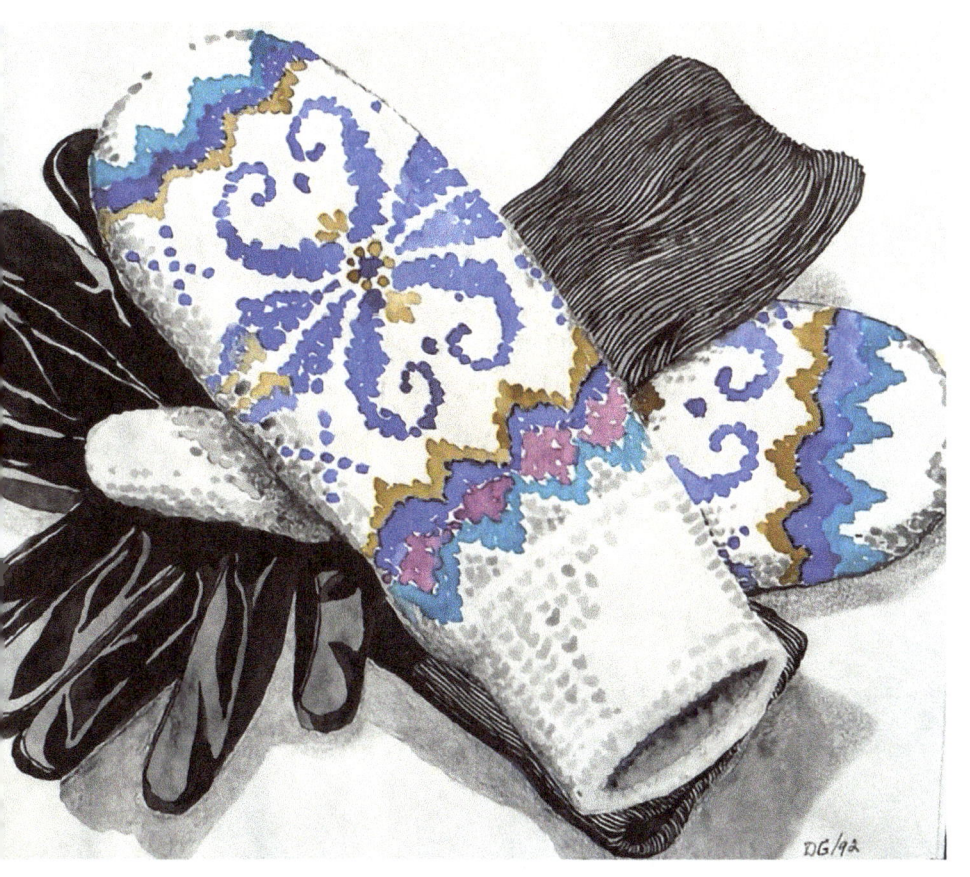

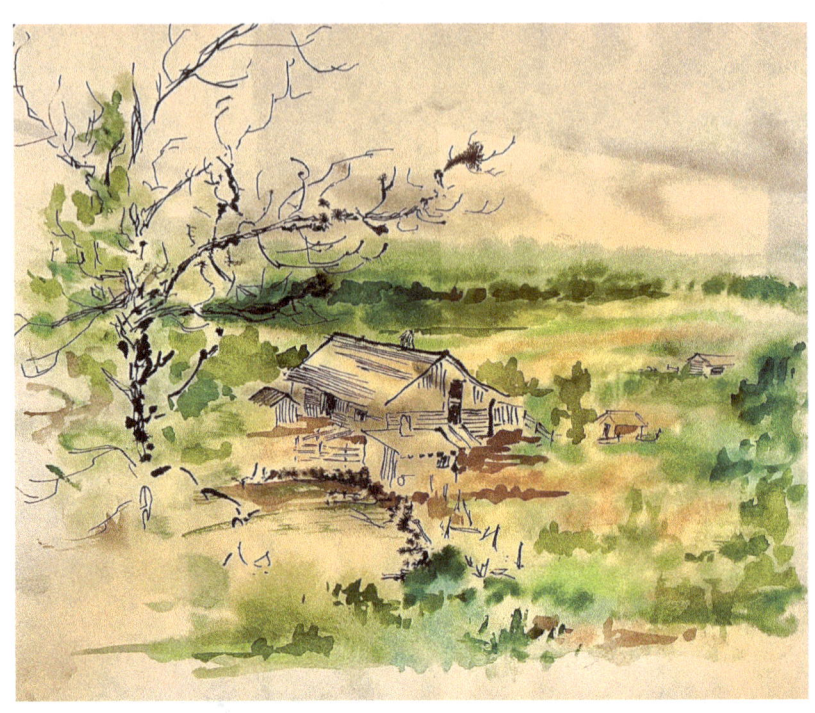

# Squaring the Great Circle

The midnight sun was turning
melting tundra lakes to purest turquoise
under us
when snuffed
by orders from the captain to lower window blinds
and concentrate
on our empty little screens.

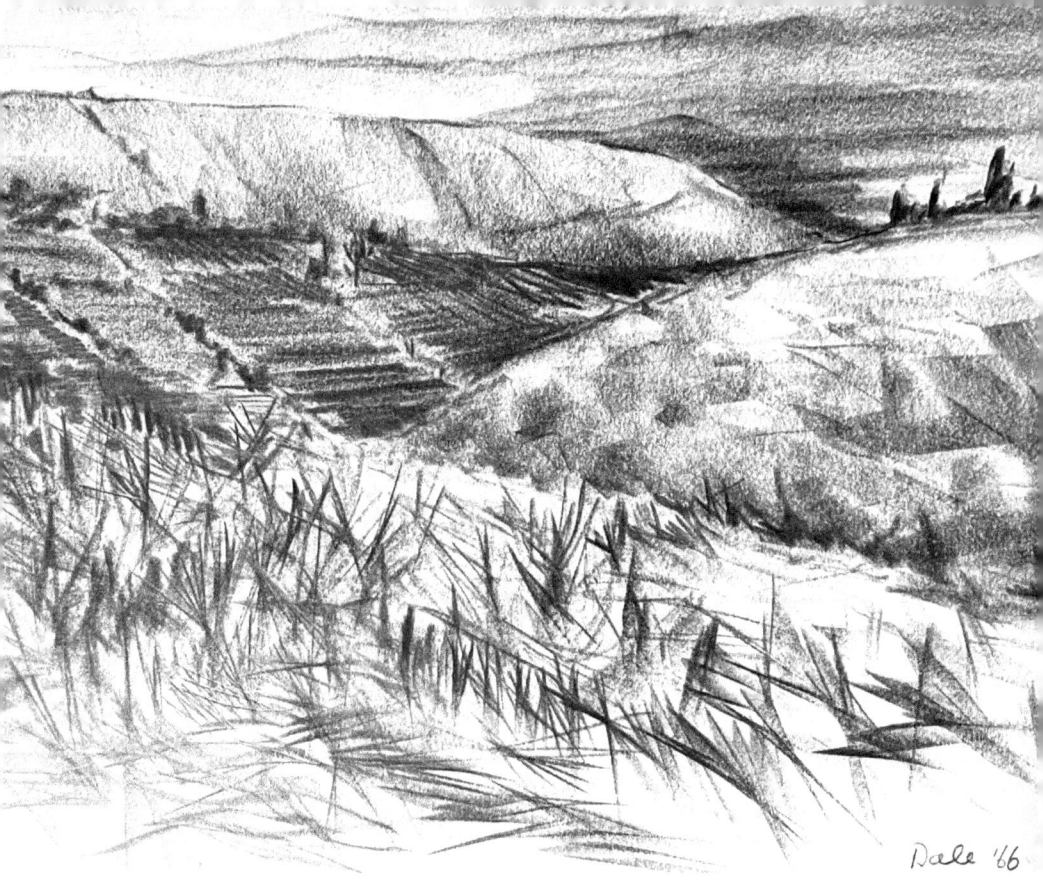

# High Art

From thirty thousand feet
snow-dusted fields
are art.

Endless Shadbolt images unfold
de-peopled cities could be
Harold Towns.

Patterns unobserved on earth
are obvious:
the truths that facts obscure.

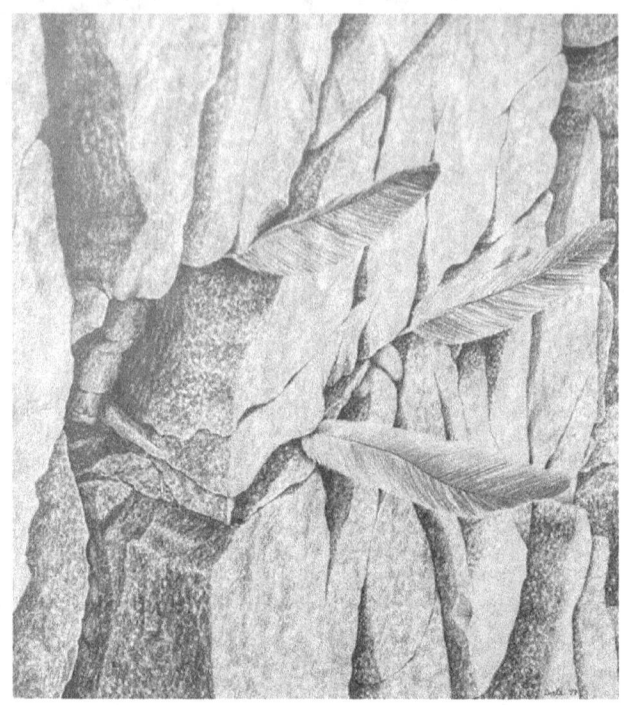

# Stone and Feathers

About the middle
of the north shore of Lake Superior
there's a
perpendicular cliff
rising
fifty feet or more
above the waves

and
a narrow granite ledge
inches only above the water,
just wide enough to walk
and contemplate.

Long before I was,
the Great Whoever
shattered the cliff face,
leaving
scores of gaping
splits resembling letter boxes
wherefrom protruded
eagle feathers, real or presumed,
and
pouches of tobacco
in case the Great Whoever
should be a smoking man.

When I visited the site
almost a lifetime from now,
I, a non-believer, was awestruck
by the power, for good or evil,
of belief.

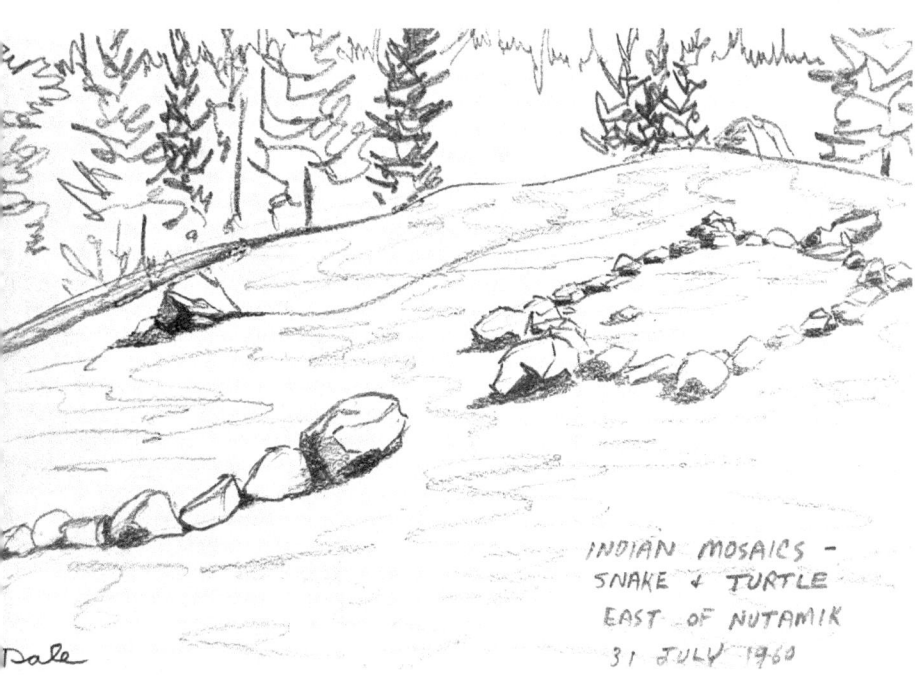

# Spirit Sands: Spruce Woods Provincial Park

Waves of wind
make visual music
with these sands

arrange and re-arrange
the
light and space

in fugal patterns
never quite alike

\*\*\*

Fingerprints of time
destroyed by human footprints,
trademark treads by
Nike, General Shoe, Adidas,
scuff and trample
scores the wind composed,

jackboots stomping Debussy

\*\*\*

Tomorrow, though, next month,
the wind will triumph

undulating staves and unheard harmonies
will sing the tracks away,
re-purify the sands

\*\*\*

I once was sure this cycle
was the world's way

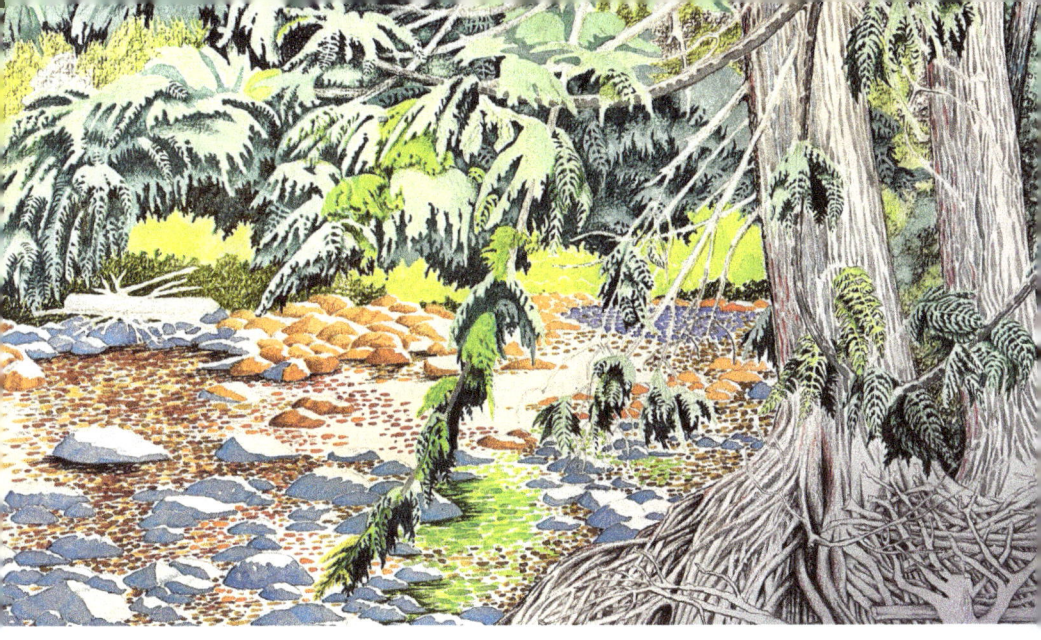

# Red River Saga

There's little accord
about the beginning:
Benevolence of a loving creator?
Cruel prank of a beast?
A circularity with no start or finish?

The Cree claim
But then they weren't there either.

For me, a big bang will do.
Our own molten splash
caught in the force web of others
whirled itself spherical
gradually cooled and encrusted
glacialated and melted and flooded
and was drained
               hereabouts
by the inland sea
eventually claimed by Hudson

for England
by Radisson
for France
(and later on for England too)

Neither troubling to ask
the lawful heir
of original immigrants
which immigrants
or their descendants
crossed the vast former lakebed
and glacier-scoured shores

arriving here
where two rivers intersect
trivial remnants
of primordial forests.

Here their gods gave them
fish and berries and game
and taught them to grow corn and tobacco.

And then they prospered until
the children of other gods
attempted to steal what they had;
flood replaced plenty.

That was the cyclical Red River pattern
til long after sails broke the northern horizon
and Montrealers set out
for a rendezvous in the west they knew nothing about.

At the shores of the Bay
in the forests and plains
on the banks of the Red
countless encounters occurred
and the peoples of Gods
traded their furs, their pemmican,
their knowledge, and themselves
to the people of God.

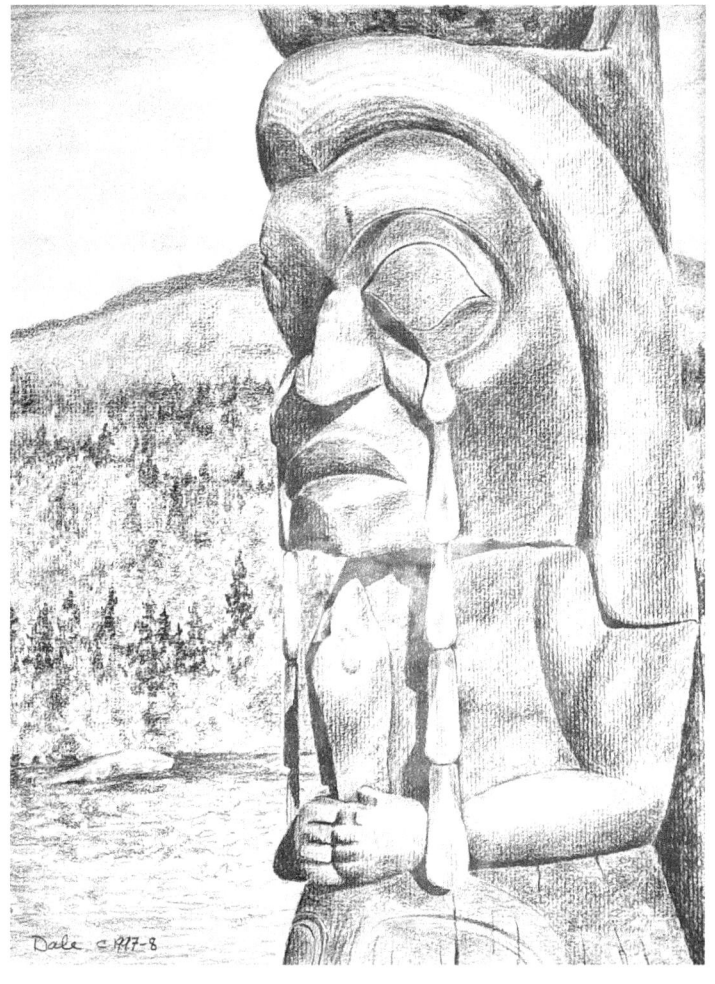

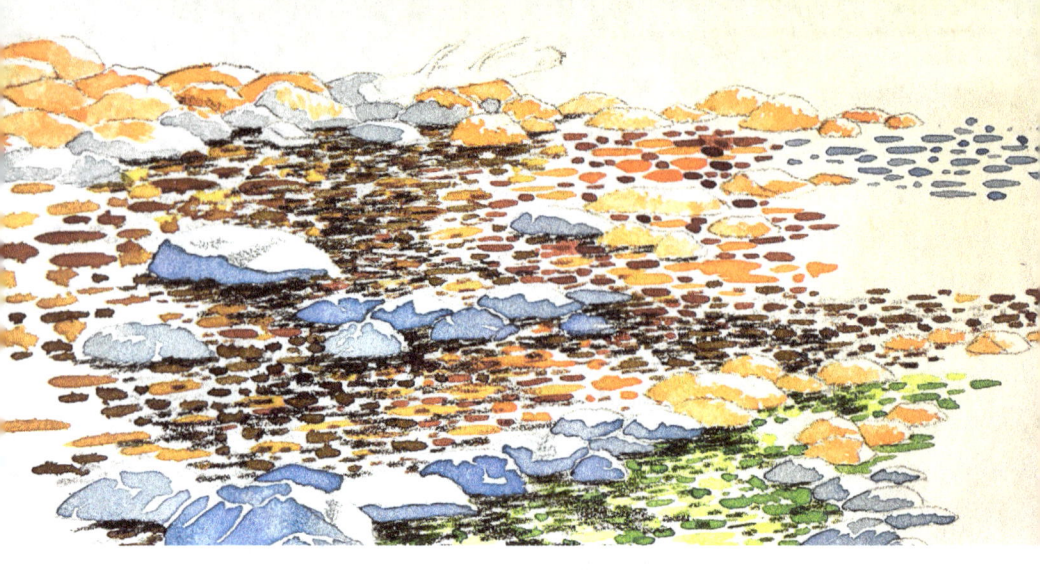

# Swimming Stones: Quadra Island

According to the photograph
there was a village here
where sea and sky and forest meet.

The people
held the elements
in equilibrium
dug-out boats bridged land and sea
and totem poles supported heaven

Through the people
deities communed.
Axes freed the timber gods
water wraiths rode boats ashore
wind sprites shinnied up the poles

The goddesses and gods
assembled every equinox
for portraits
by the village carvers

Afterwards
they climbed the poles
for potlach celebrations
in the sky

and threw down
every kind of gift
to show the villagers
their gratitude:
water-fowl and loganberries
salmon, hare, and deer
porpoises and myth

Then generosity
was made a crime
Potlach was prohibited
poles were taken down
carvings seized
boats abandoned

on this stony beach
where now there's
just a lighthouse
sullen trees
and shitting gulls

or so it seems
until the ebbing tide
reveals survivors sunning
where the mud's too deep
for bureaucratic feet

gods
pretending to be rocks
their totems
turned from shore

resting
from a romp with whales
sunning
waiting.

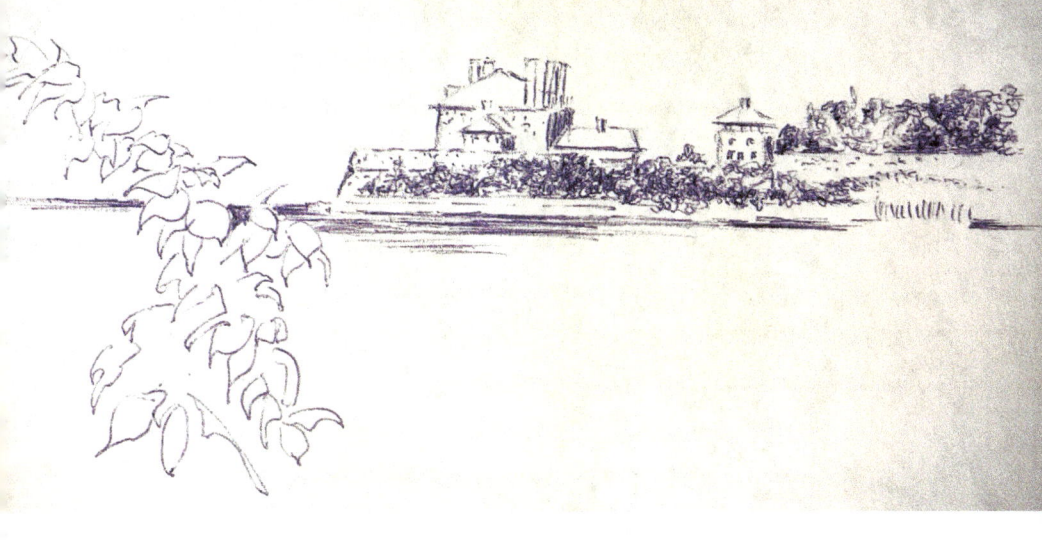

# Spring in the Vineyard

Tethered vines
are
dancing
writhing
in the April sun
gnarled
from
wringing
sweetness
out of circumstance.

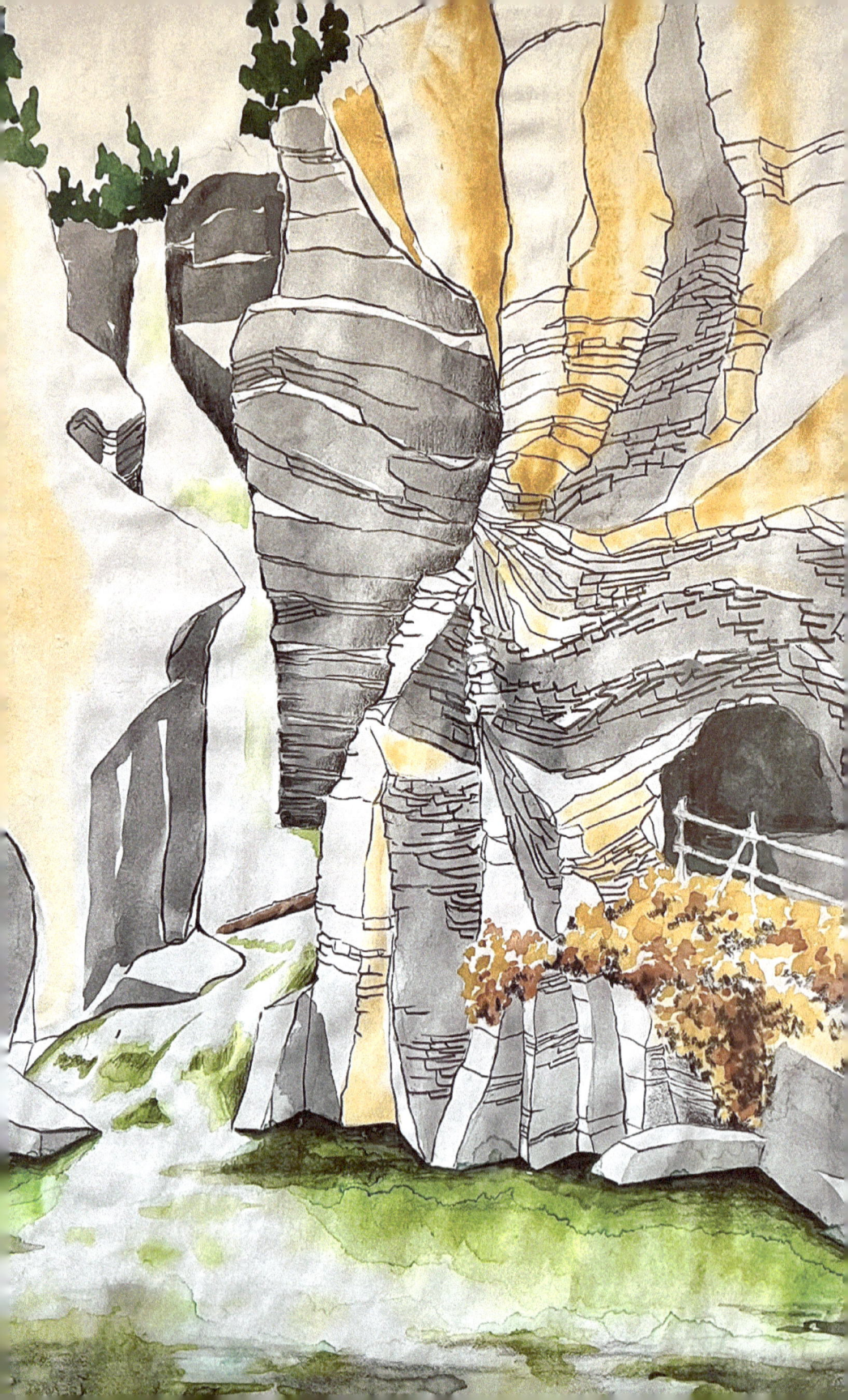

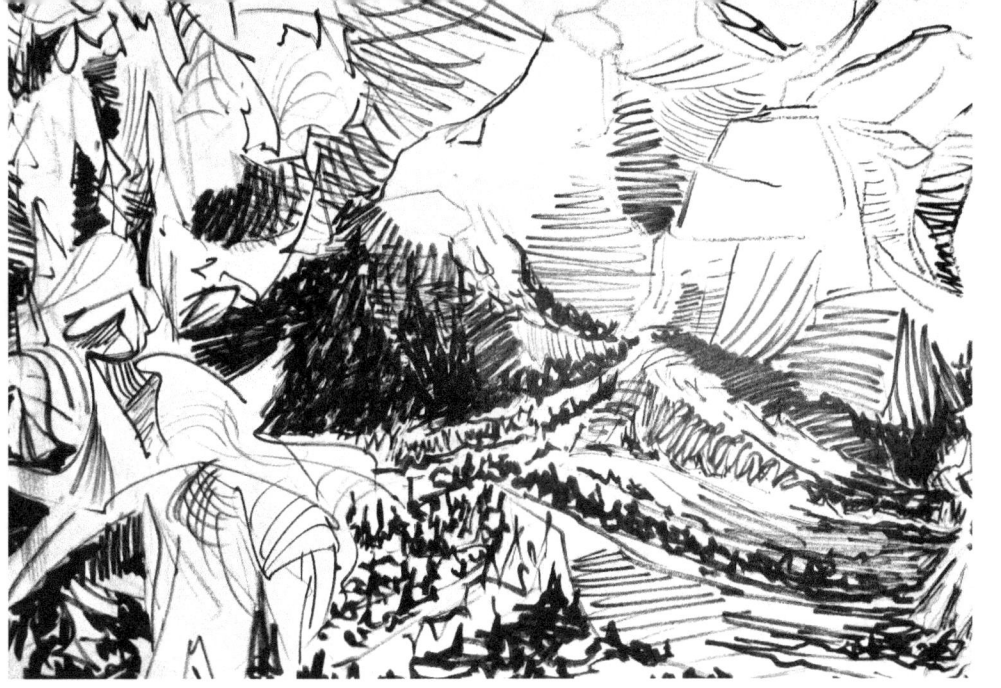

# Lower Bankhead

Jagged glacial peaks
surround
a several acre clearing
not so clear of growth
as a century ago.

Several
century-old foundations
of once massive structures
now form walls
of sunken gardens
shielding feral trees and shrubs.

Beyond
the building ruins
mounds of slag-black mining offal
support patches of scrofulous grass.

# Devon Dawn I

Hairline fracture
in the dark
pink with promise

lengthening, broadening

bringing consciousness
of you

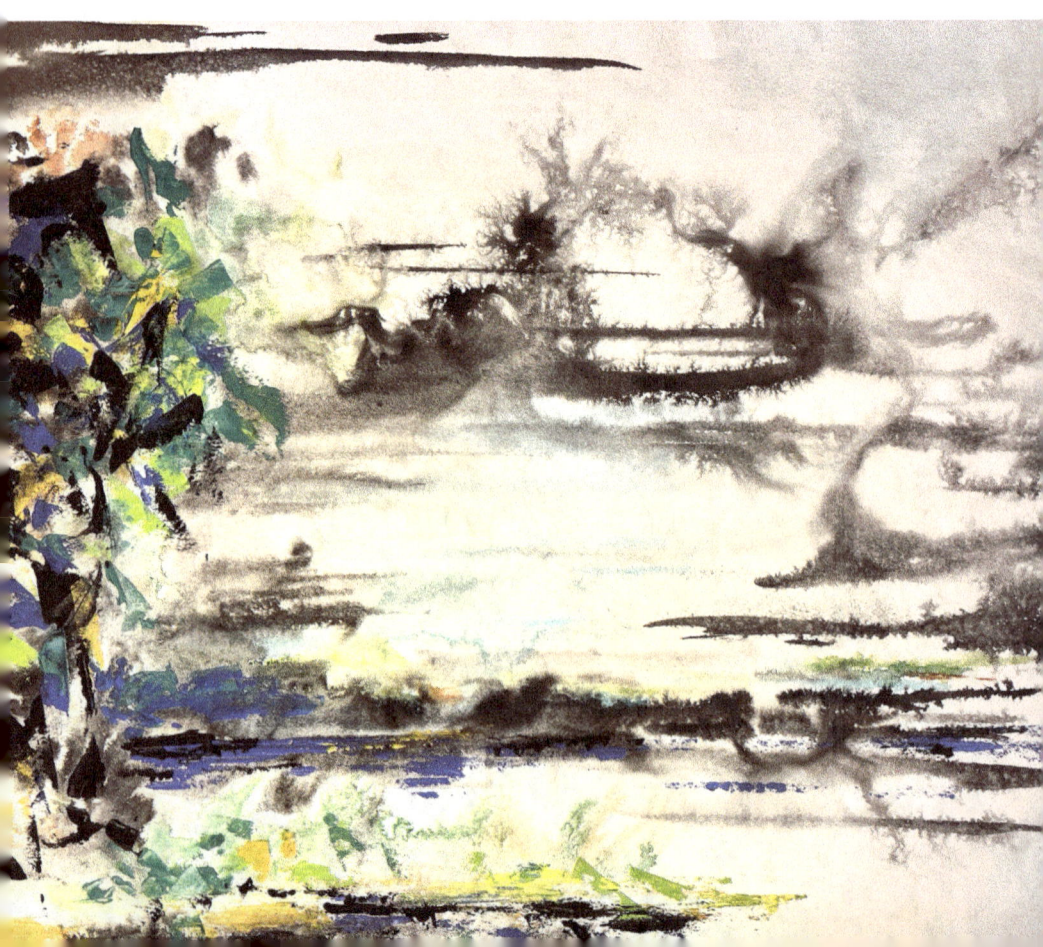

# Devon Dawn II

All the components of day
assemble naked
weather permitting
for an aerobic dance
before they dress for work.

They'll gather again before dark
for dancing less chaste.

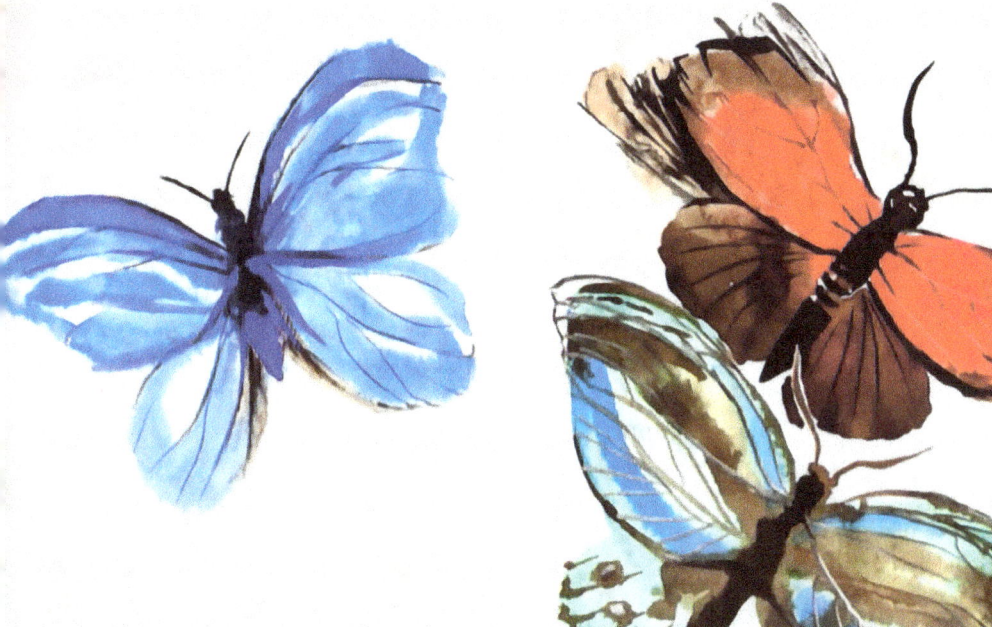

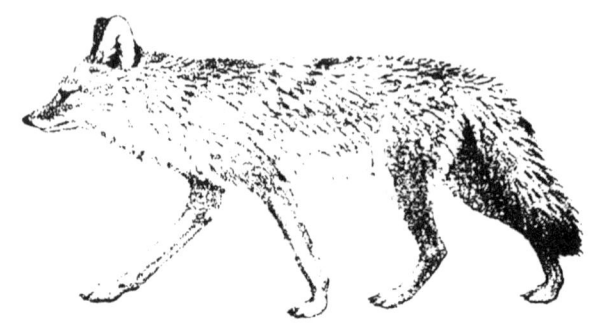

# Devon Dawn III
# (Howl(s))

Howls like this
were never heard
by Alan Ginsberg.

Bellowing
and
yowls and yelps and yips
worsened much by mist
violate the valley
early in the morning.

Is this sexual ecstasy?
Is it rage?
Is it agony of birth? or death?

Or is the valley giving
human violators warning?

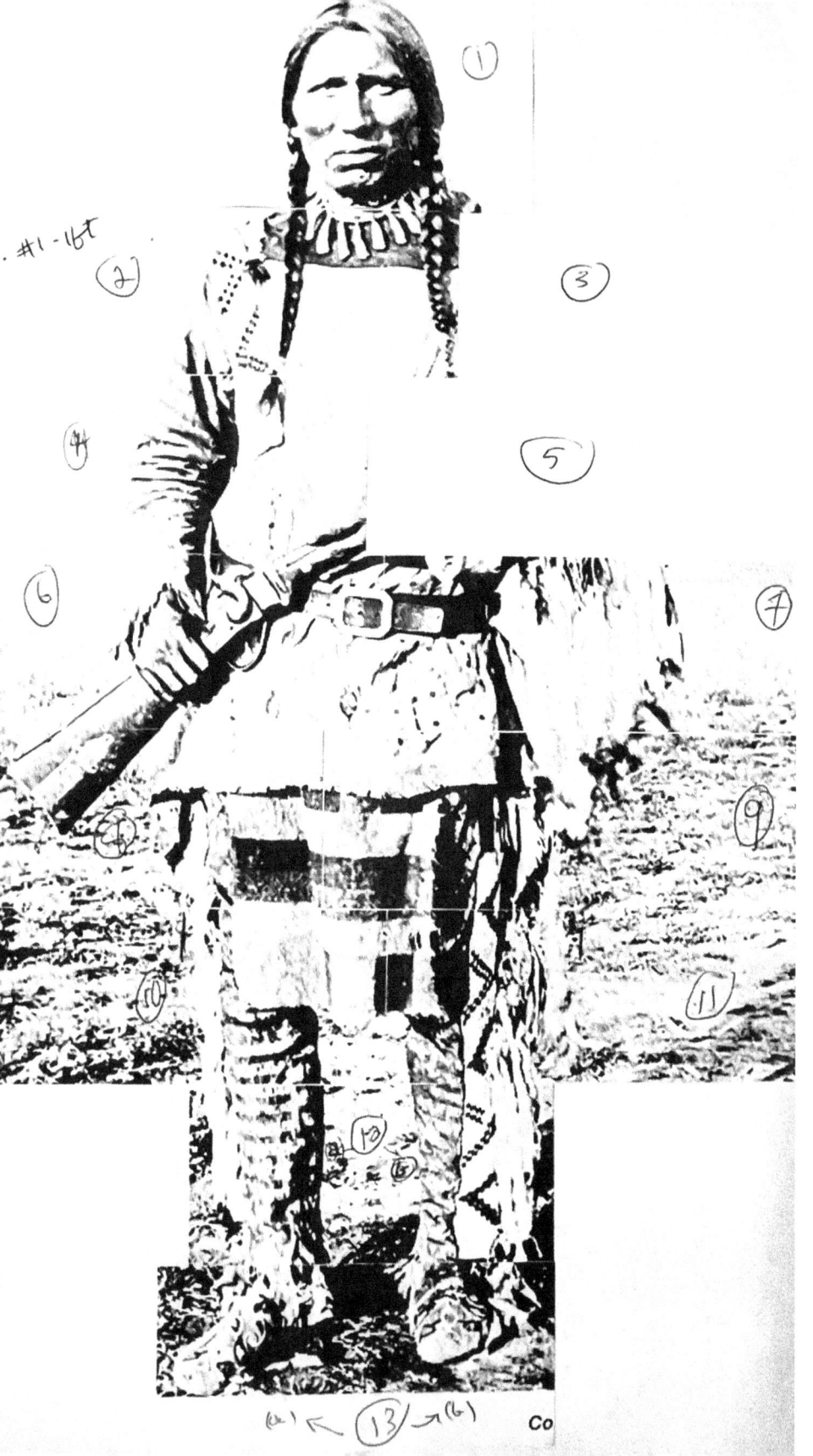

# Winter Morning at Mistik Ridge

Coyote in the grass
with diamonds
Phoebe in a tree
with dawn songs
and Dale in the hot tub
with wraiths of steam
dancing wantonly
in frost shine.

A luxuriously accoutred
fox was sniffing at the sparkling
plexigrass coyote.

Imagine the offspring!

# 79th Winter, Mistic Ridge

Backlit hoarfrost on firs
Diamonds on poplar boughs and fallen snow
Sandra in the hot tub with a book

If the Presbyterians are right
I'll soon be paying for this

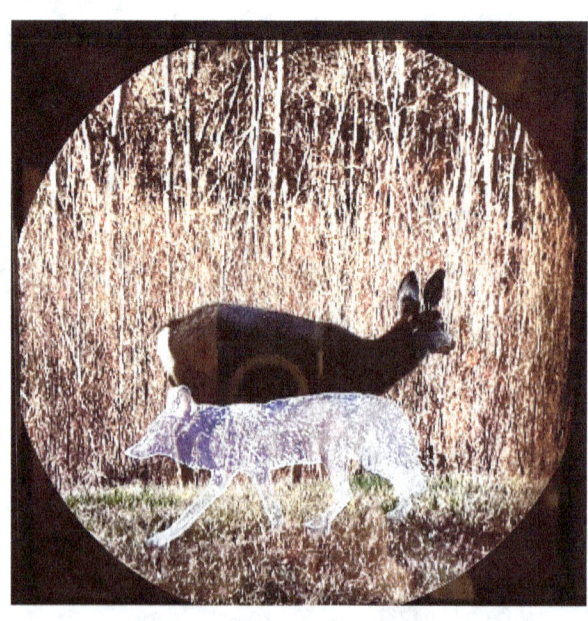

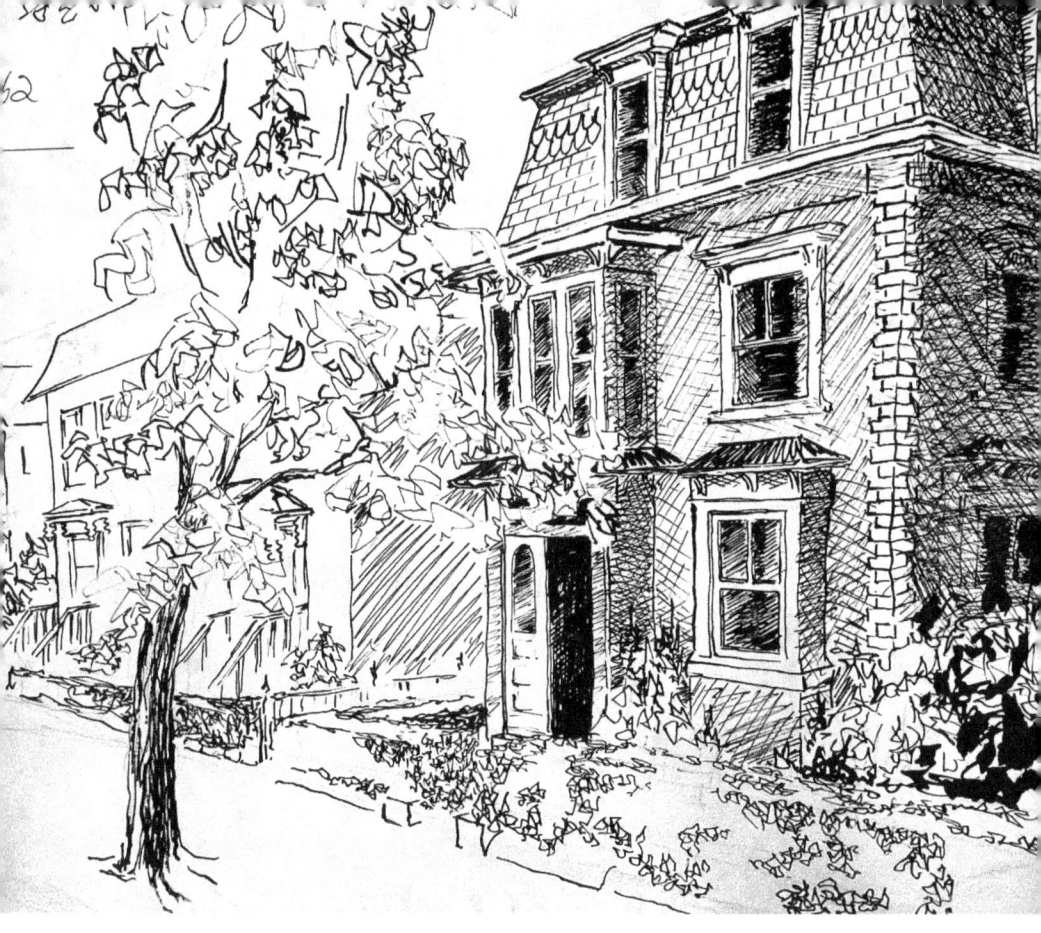

# At the Butterfly House

A waft of trembling symmetry,
music, inaudible, visible,
lights upon a flower
fleetingly,
indispensably.

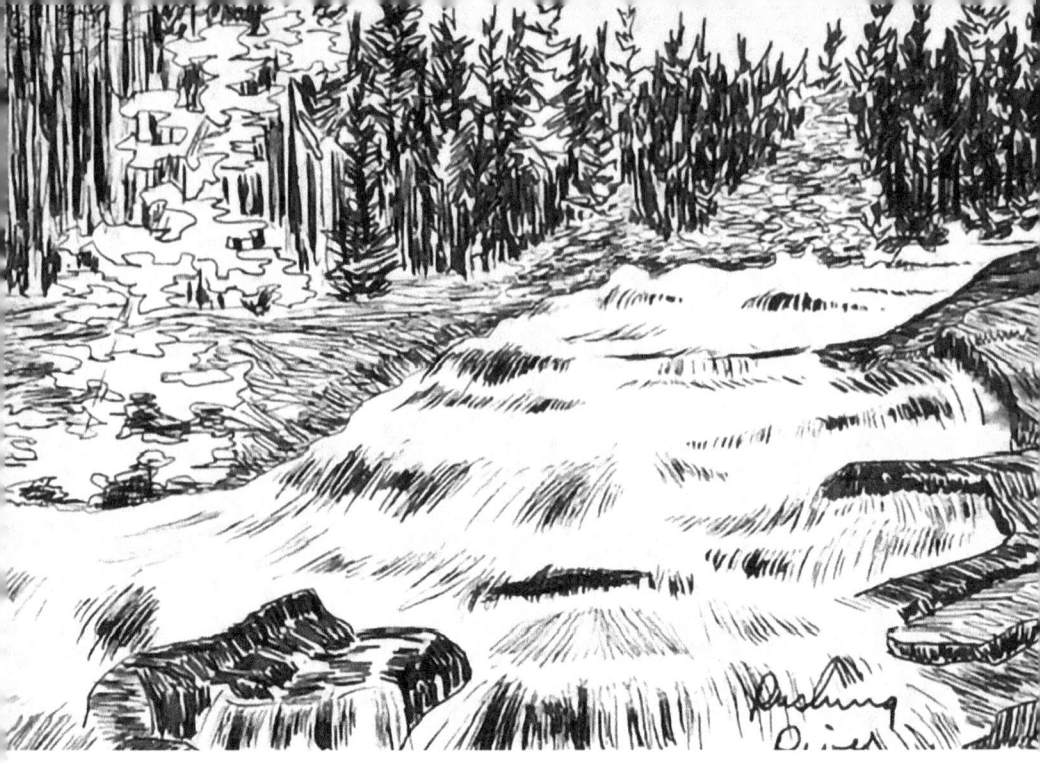

# Thoughts of Calmness by the Athabasca River

The snow's been softened,
the frozen river lies below,
accepting the warmth
of an unexpected thaw,
retaining its composure
but for an underglow of green
from place to place,
the shade of eyes.

# Other Places – China & Asia

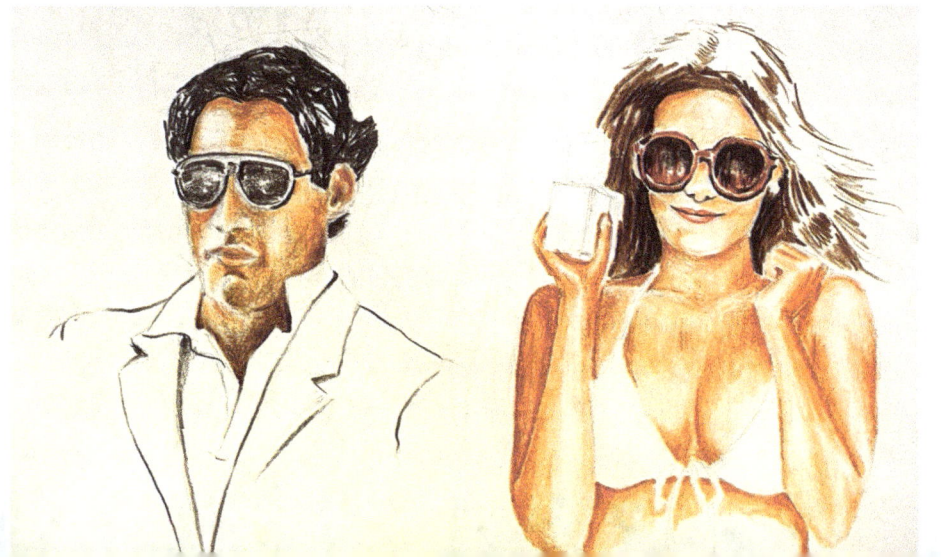

# What Was He Trying to Prove?

I just can't accept that Emperor Qin
that supremely practical man
who so brilliantly
unified

a gigantic polyglot wartorn Asian expanse
in a blink of history's eye

and
produced the world's largest physical structure to boot

was stupid enough to think
that even eternity
could animate sculpture
that had never felt the original shudder of life

But why else
would he lavish so much of his wealth
on this massive baked-clay brigade?

Maybe he thought that lesser minds
would believe in life after clay

or perhaps
like John Paul Getty et al
he simply enjoyed collecting fine art.

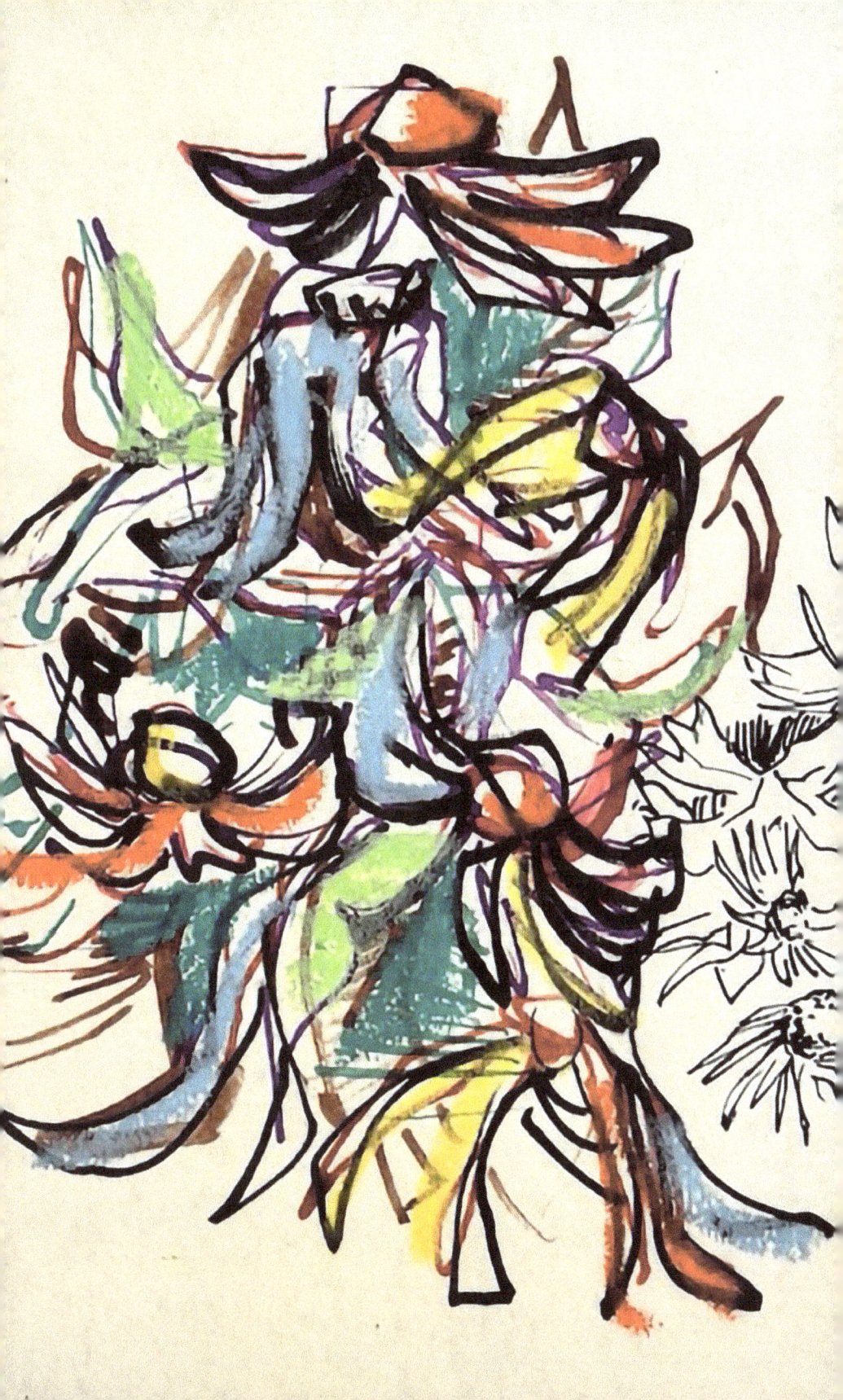

# The Wall

Alluring
droves of the strangers
it was built to repel

the imperial reptile
- masonry Celestial Dragon -
stretches across, slithers along
Emperor Qin's
mountains and vales

visible
to travellers in space
when pollution levels permit

\* \* \*

What cannot ever be seen
are the bones
under the stones

and
under the Appian Way
and
Westminster Abbey
and
Canada's first
(Chinese constructed)
national railway

And what I can't decide is
whether the bones
make structures like those
more or less
worthy of praise?

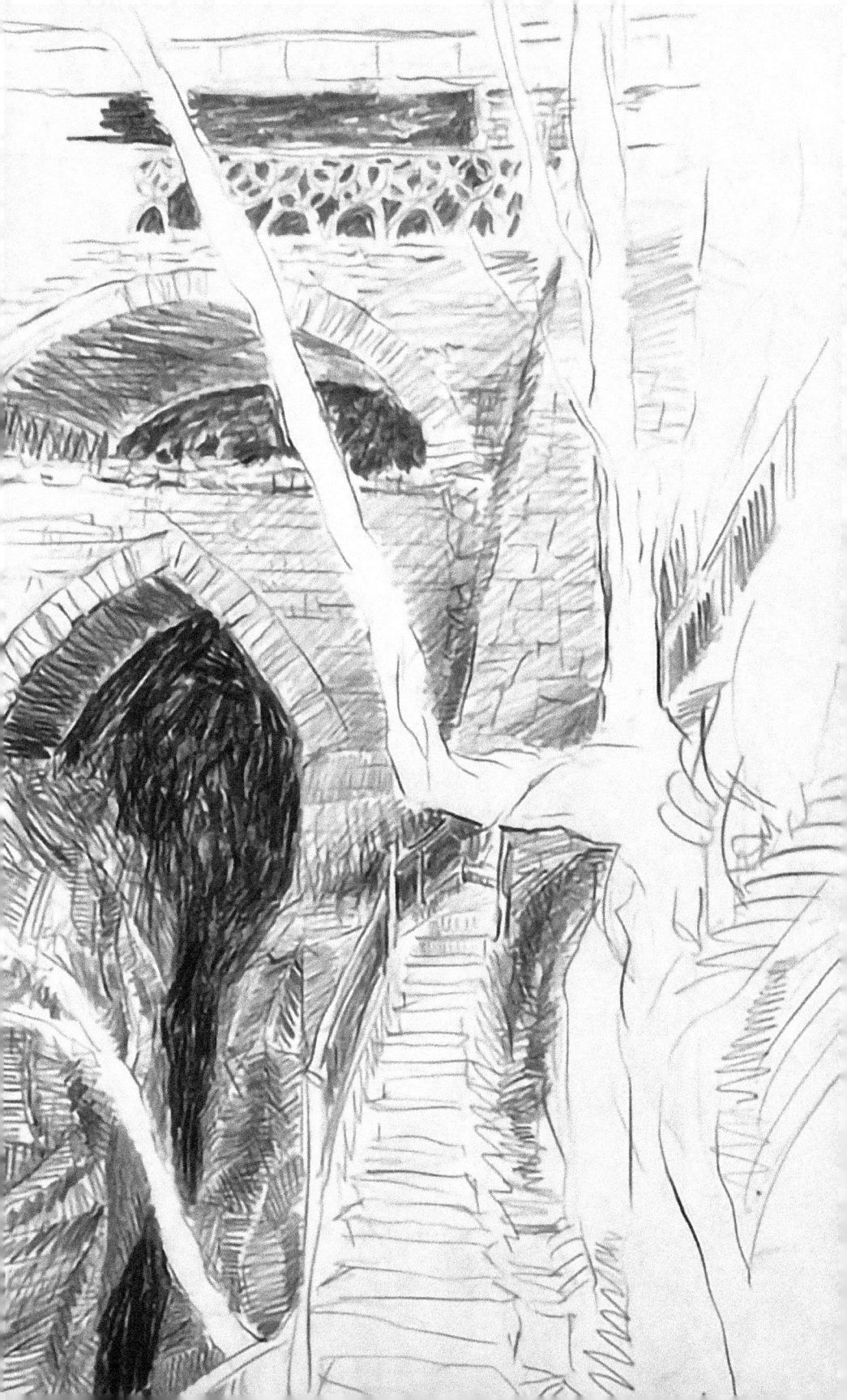

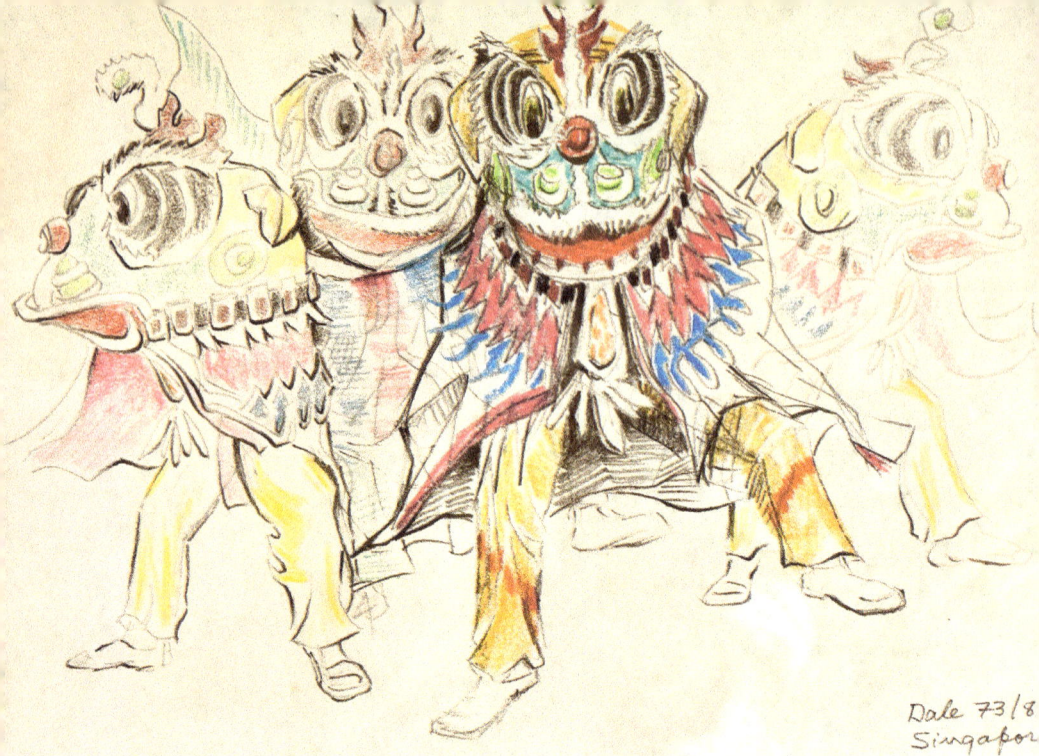

# Singapore Street

Wrinkled woman
walking slowly
home from shopping

straw hat shielding
face from sun

brushing pantaloons unheard
in street cacophony

pauses
at a rubbish bin

inspects

continues
on her
graceful way.

# Other Places – Europe

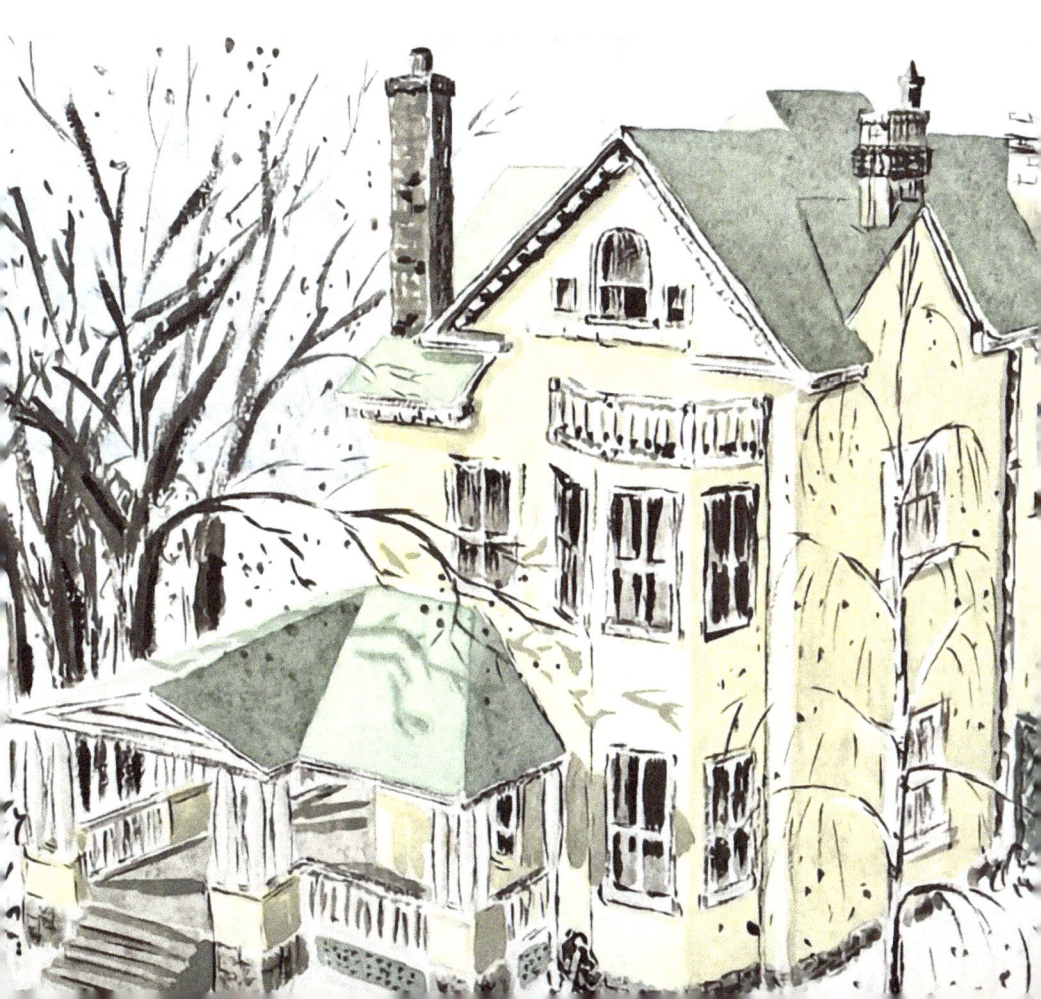

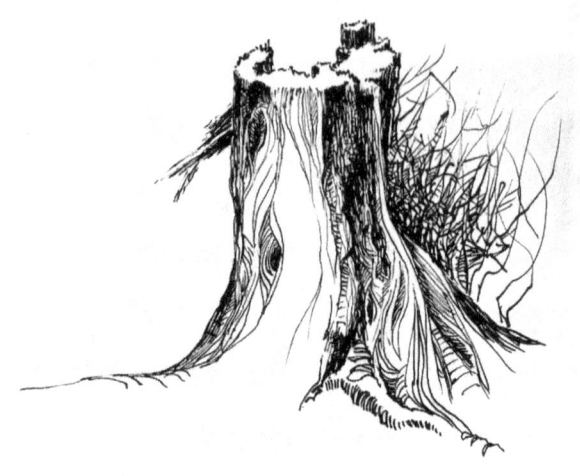

# Metamorphoses

Kafka awoke
to a
Prague transformed.

The sculptured Jew
on the tower clock
had had a
cosmetic nose job.

The Jews
now in the streets
wore jogging shoes
and carried maps.

Synagogues
were now
museums.

# Grafenegg

Many birds are singing
in the ancient trees,
many kinds of birds
though all I recognize
are mourning doves.

Before me
is a once-old castle,
twice restored.

One transformation
after Swedish pillage
in the sixteen hundreds.

The second followed
what is happening
around me now:
Sherman tanks
clawing up the lawns,
bombarding the castle
silencing the birds.

I hide behind a tree
because I'm only twelve
because I'm sixty-three
and I cannot understand
that part of me.

# Chartres Blues

In France,
not far from Orléans,
is Chartres
with famous stained glass windows.

Stained?

In what way stained?

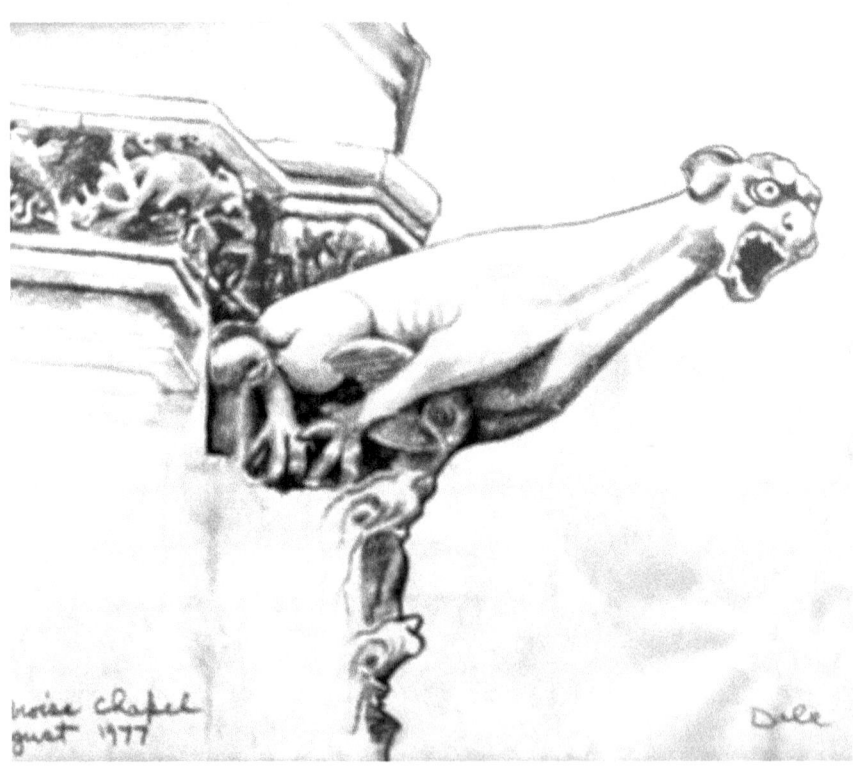

Flashes of ancient light
frozen instants
crimsons, embers, astonishing blues,
pure
as from God's own prism,
arranged
to soften stone
and illumine myth.

Stained?
By what?

By sin.
Bloody crimsons, evil ambers, melancholy blues
extracted
from anonymous penitents,
by priests
swept up from confessional floors by monks,
and put to pious use.

Much later
in New Orleans
shards from other sinners' souls,
picked up in churches brothels and bars
were used to build a different kind of blues.

It's strange
how heavily
art relies on sin.

# A Rose from the Dead – Ronsard's House at Comeau Abbey

Among the monks,
he wrote of love.

Watching
from his study window
wizened brothers
pruning roses
in the monastery garden,
Ronsard fashioned
verbal blossoms
for Cassandra,
urging her to
pluck her pleasures
young.

We, however,
left the perfumed bower
intact,
retreating to our single cells
as celibate as siblings.

In Winnipeg it's winter
when I open Ronsard's poems again,
skeptically,
expecting brown and brittle blooms
to flutter out,

not this overwhelming
waft of summer roses.

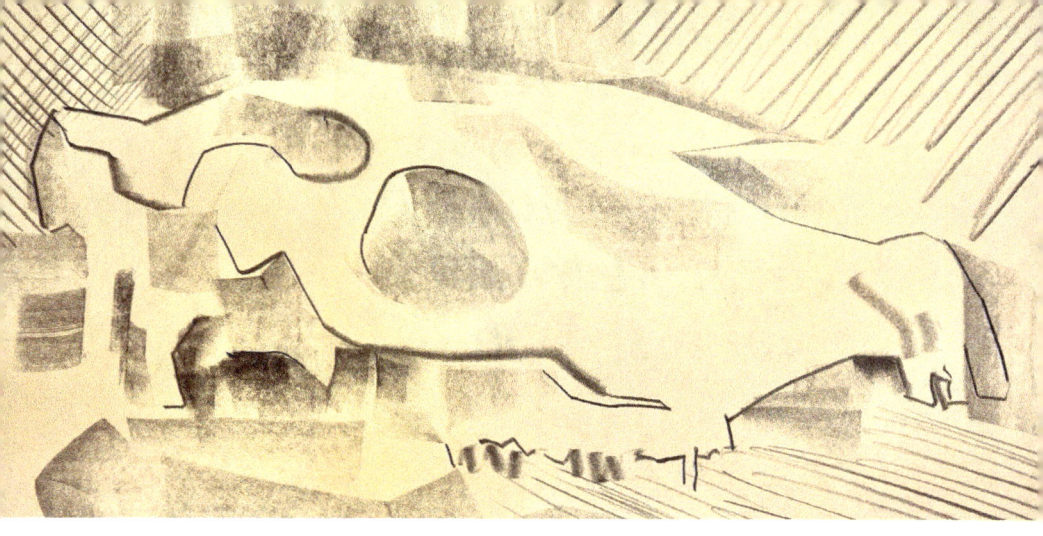

# Stonehenge

Smaller
at first
than imagined

they might
from a distance
be teeth
of some burrowed creature
snapping at low-hanging clouds

from closer they're legs
severed from torsos of gods
and still dancing slowly
to ritual rhythms

but when
I lift up my child
to the altar
I know
the dimensions
are human.

# Abandoned Village Near Aberfan August 1966

The Welsh hills sprawled
like giants in uneasy sleep

Among the tangled limbs
lay mining hills
like this once was
this roofless ruin
forgotten
in a fold of landscape
staring at its slag

Behind a crumbled cottage
sprang a crystal stream
unsummoned
from the hillside

I thought its murmurs
were apologies

but now I know
it warned
the giants
soon would
wake.

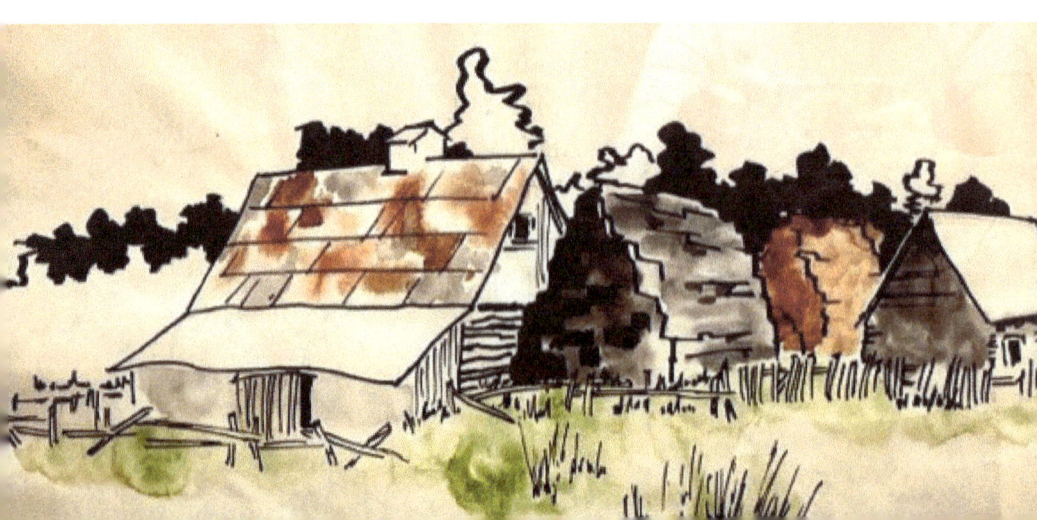

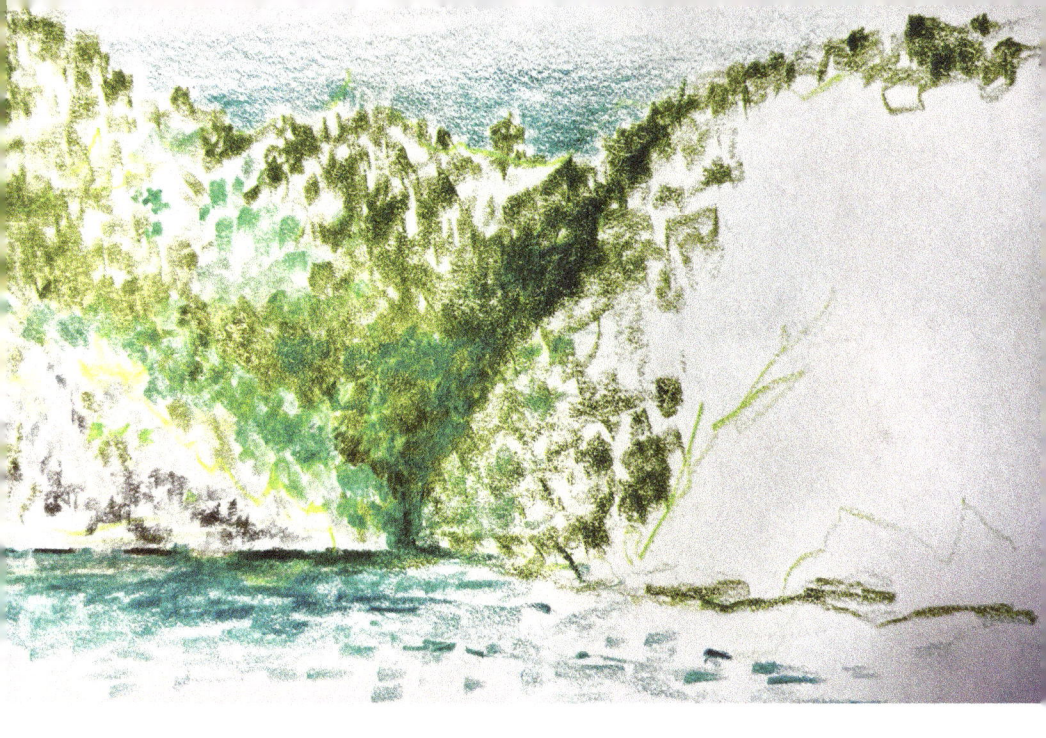

# Other Places – Ireland

# North of Balleyvaughen

The sea
is on our left

and on our right
a limestone tidal wave
crests

about to engulf
in time

whatever's in the path
of its returning to
the sea.

The burren is solid limestone
of course

except in the cracks
where life occurs

and miniature orchids
eight or ten to a stem

applaud and mock
the burren's debates
with the rain and the wind.

except
underneath,
where cave water
patiently dissolves
its innards
and will
eventually
return it
to the sea.

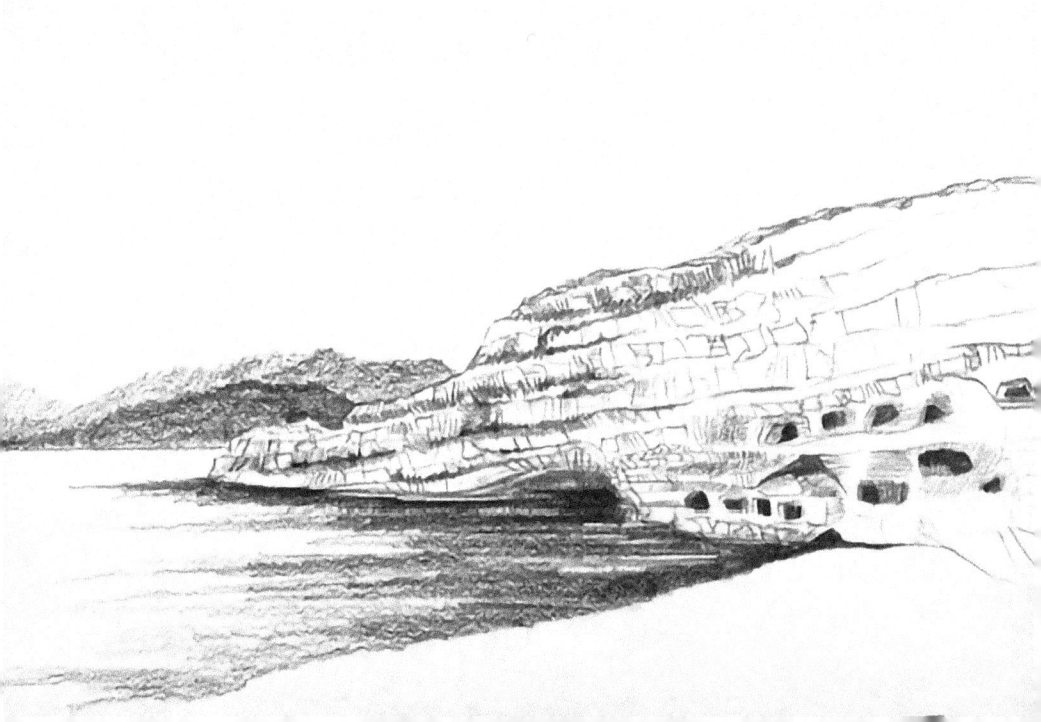

# Irish Stones: Altar Rock

Green mist is mocking my umbrella and
rubbing against me like an unseen crowd.

It saturates everything
except the stone slabs
of this ancient tomb
beside the pulsing surf

erected
several thousand years ago
by forgotten people
at the urging of unknown beliefs

adopted
by the Druids, so we're told,
for rituals now remembered
only in imagination

and
resorted to again, not so long ago
as "altar rock"
for celebrations of forbidden faith

All of which helps me understand, and fear,
Belief.

In the car again
umbrella folded,
heater on,
I shiver still.

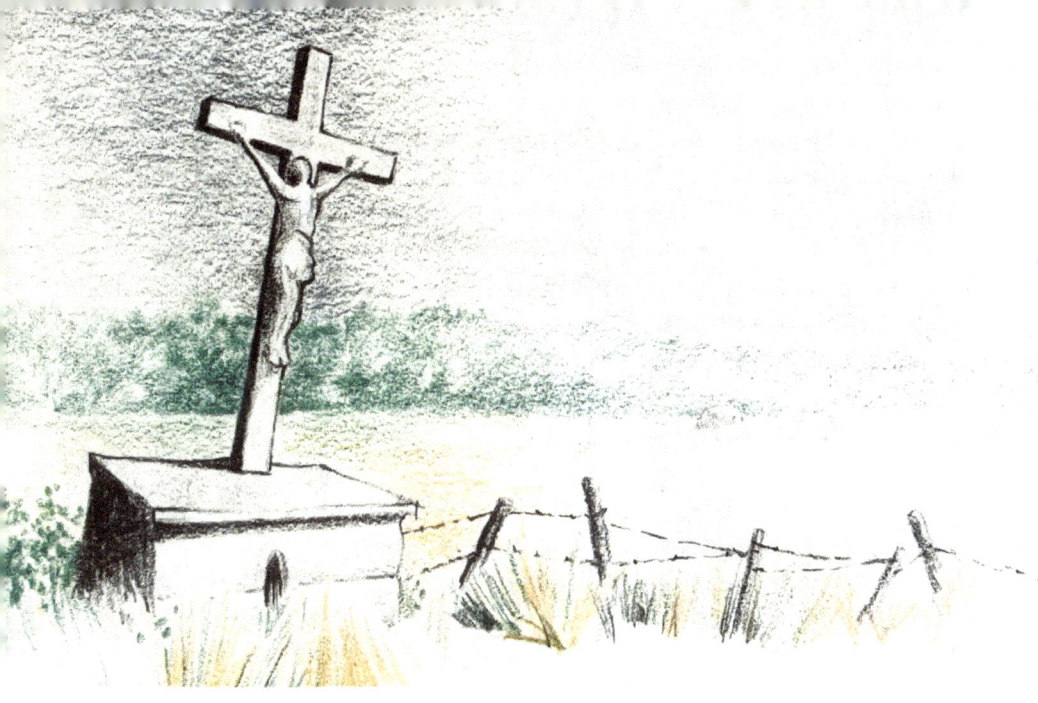

# Irish Stones: Famine Cemetery

There are no stones
for them

only this uneven field,

these slight depressions
shallow as apologies

in the ground
that failed them.

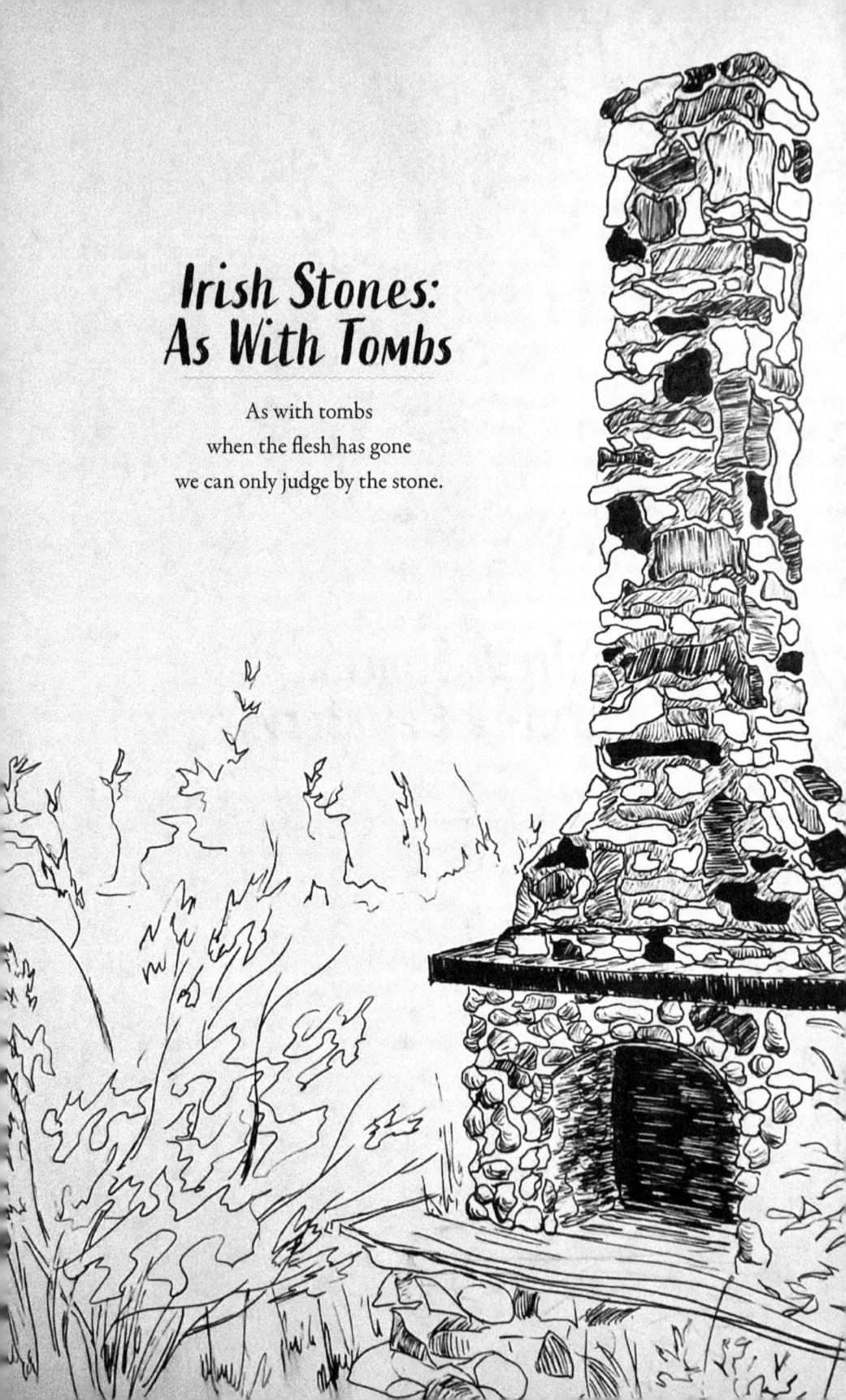

# Irish Stones: As With Tombs

As with tombs
when the flesh has gone
we can only judge by the stone.

# Irish Stones: Yeats

No stones in Yeats
except his soul
upon which
ogham-like
literature was born.

Yeats's tower:
like an empty shell,
chambered nautilus,
pulp removed,
elegant but empty,
gave shape to
the pulp.

His poetry,
After all, was ephemeral stuff,
Awfully soft-edged fluff.

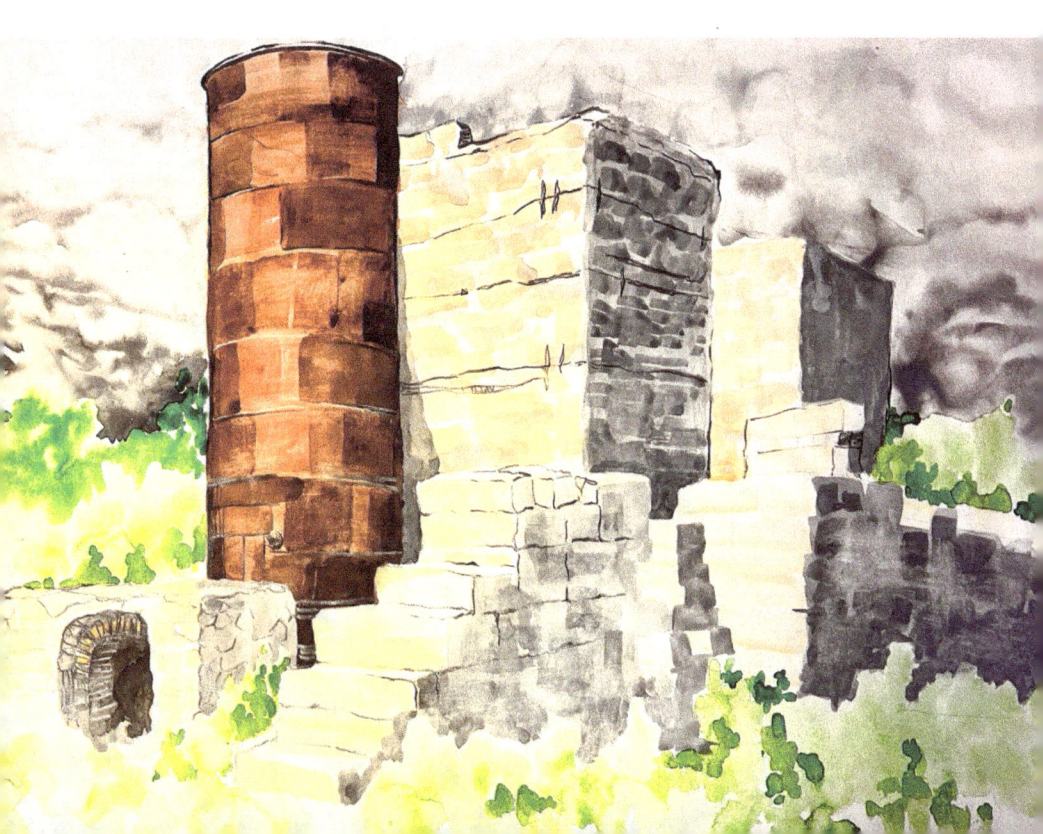

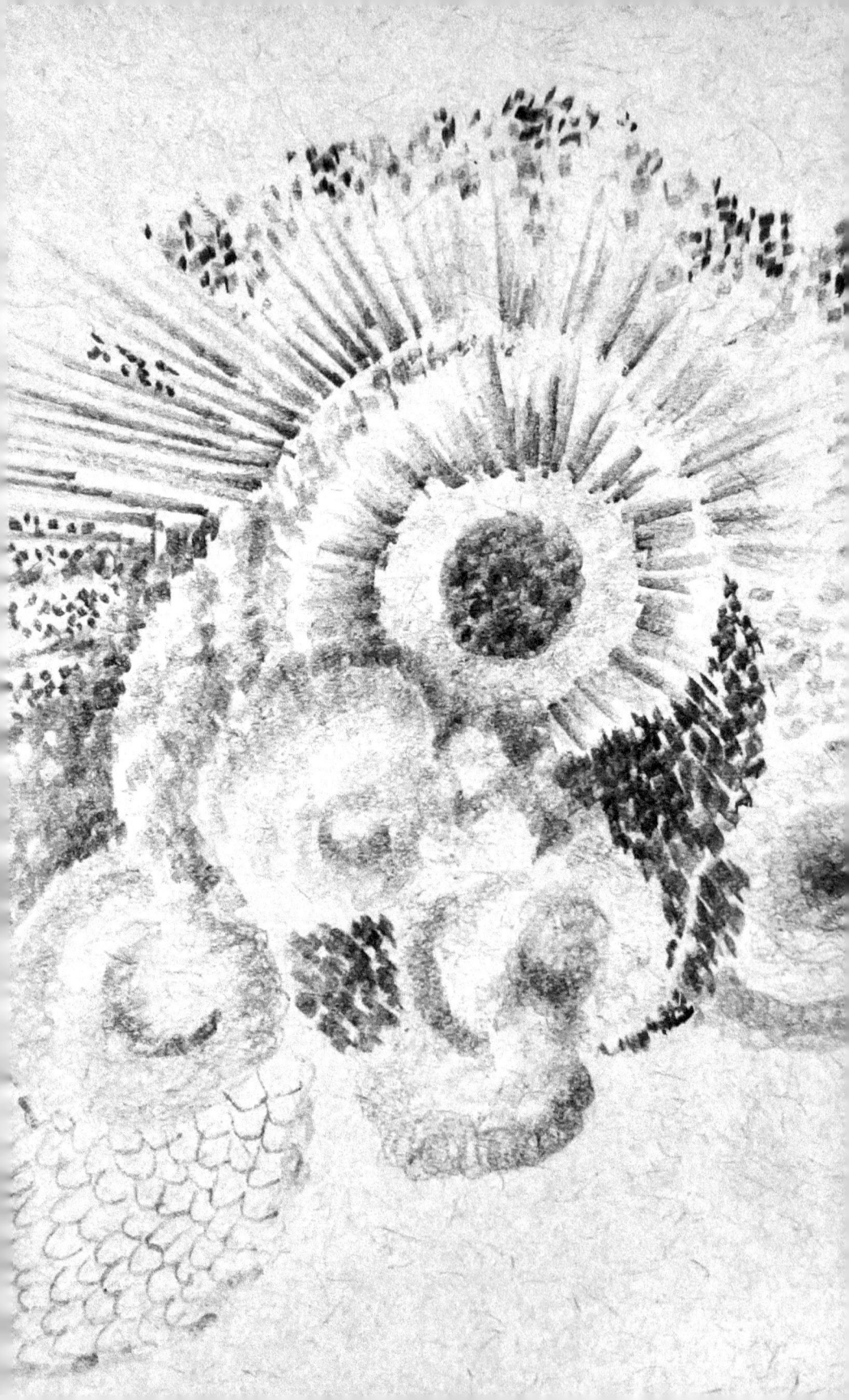

# Other Places – United States

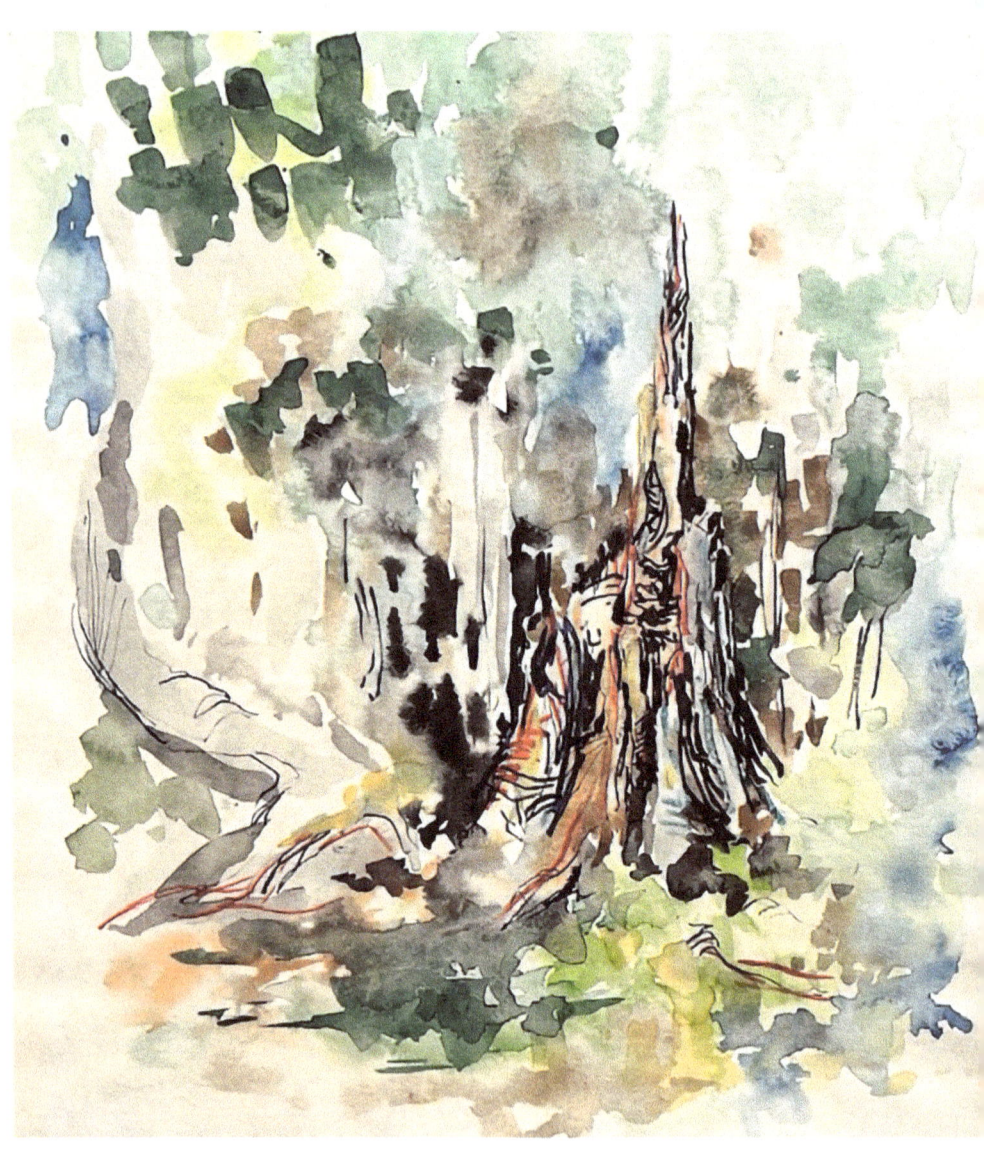

# Fairhaven Beach State Park

The sun performs
its daily
pastel plunge
into Lake Ontario
and
all that's left
to kindle dawn
are sparks:

Venus
and
her
followers
are
first
and
then
the
flirting

fireflies
impersonating
stars
among
the
trees.

"I know the fireflies flash like that
because they want to mate
but how, I wonder,
do they find each other
in between the twinkles?"

"Let me show you,"
says my tentmate in the dark,
her fingertips
a flight of fireflies.

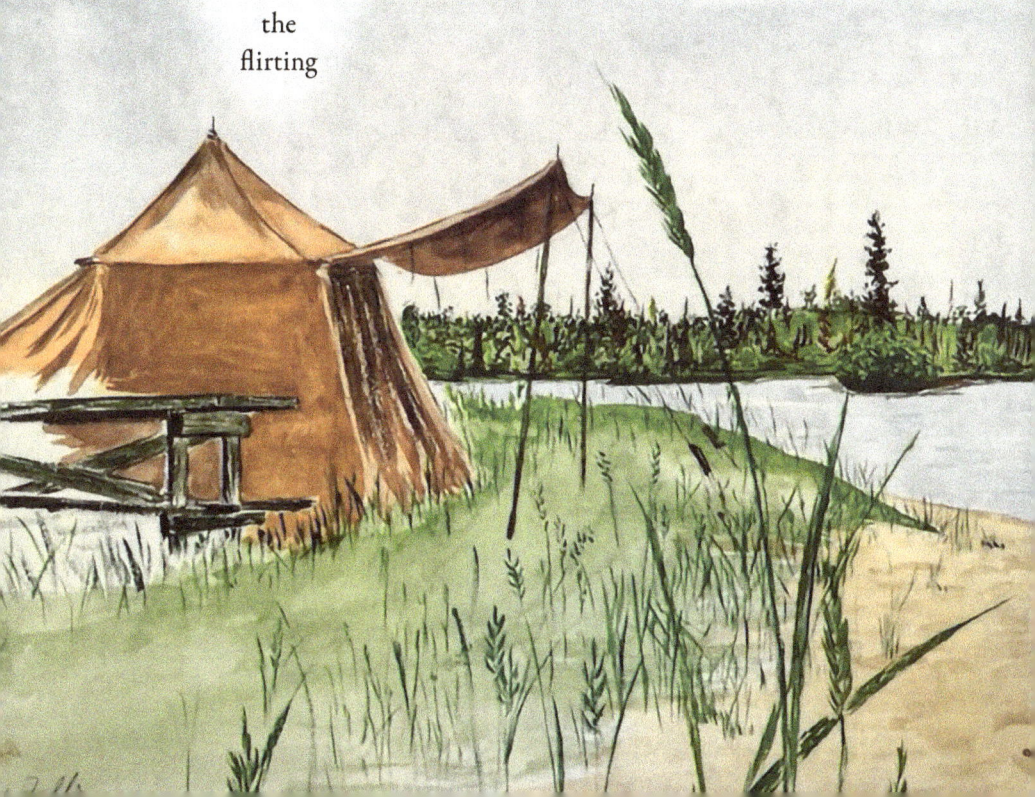

# Pueblo Ladders

the door was a
hole in the roof

the ladder was
entrance and exit

raising the ladder
kept out intruders

the Spanish entered
by tearing doors in the walls

the clergy converted
the ladders to crosses

symbols that Georgia
O'Keefe placed in the sky

between our lives
and the moon

ladders to nowhere
or ladders of hope

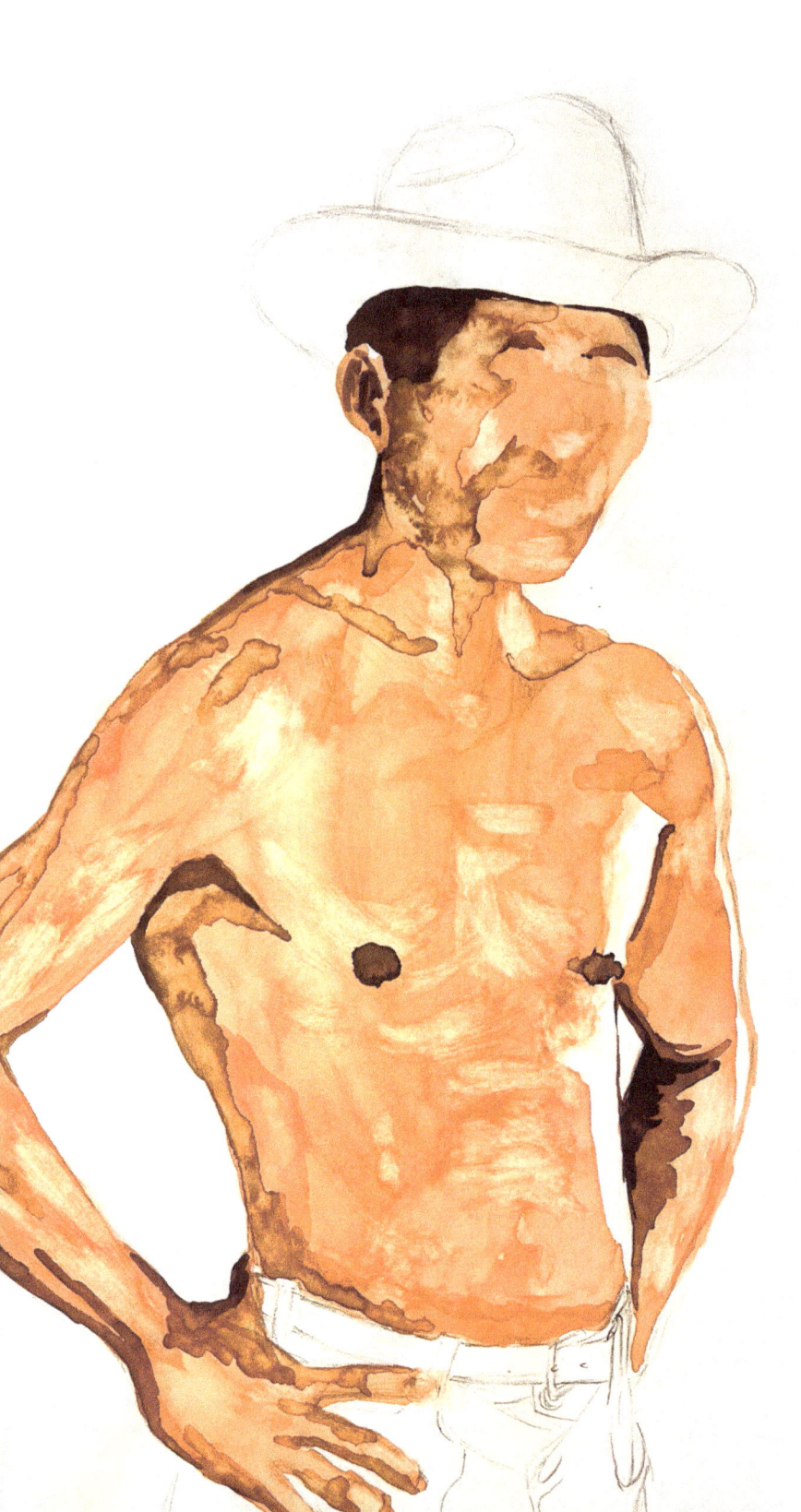

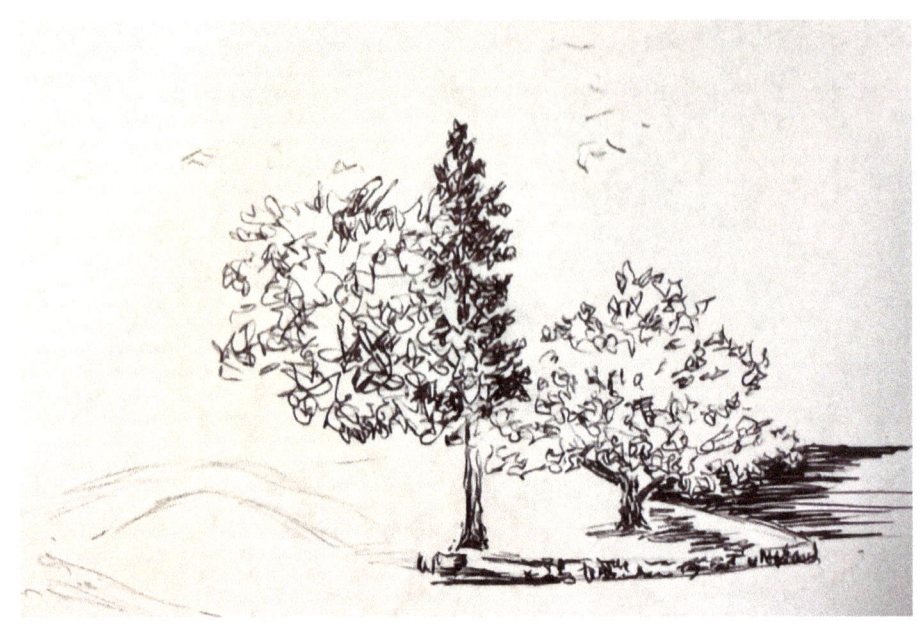

# Washington, D.C., April 7, 1991: I. Cherry Blossoms

Cherry petals
fall
like snow

and
I
wonder
if
the snow
can still be
made to seem
like
cherry petals.

## II. Jefferson Memorial

The cherry trees
are tossing
morning sunbeams
back and forth
like frisbees
bouncing
them off marble walls,

whiter than the blossoms
that incarcerate
in eternal shadow
Tom the redhead

shackled to his fame,
denuded of invention
stripped of mischief
cleansed of personality

imprisoned
in his
retroactive
respectability.

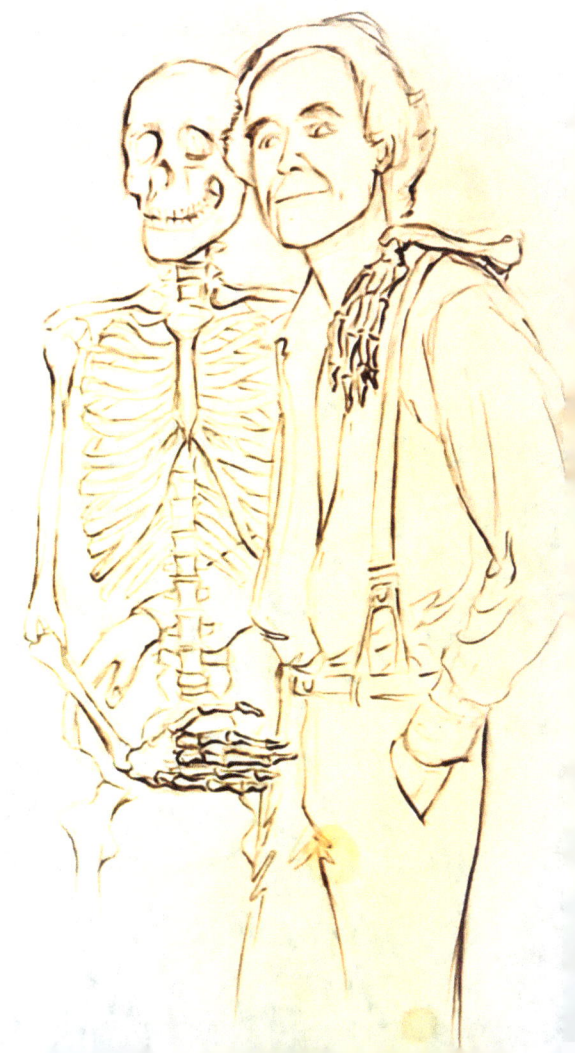

# Viet Nam Memorial

The
symbolism
of the wedge is
slowly driven further in,
as every step we take sinks deeper
into evil, and the victims follow one
another inexorably in geometric multiples

until a hopeless equilibrium is passed, and the

slope inclines a little, lists begin to shrink,
light seems somehow brighter, and
a consciousness returns of grass
of trees of panhandlers
of birds and other
forms of
life.

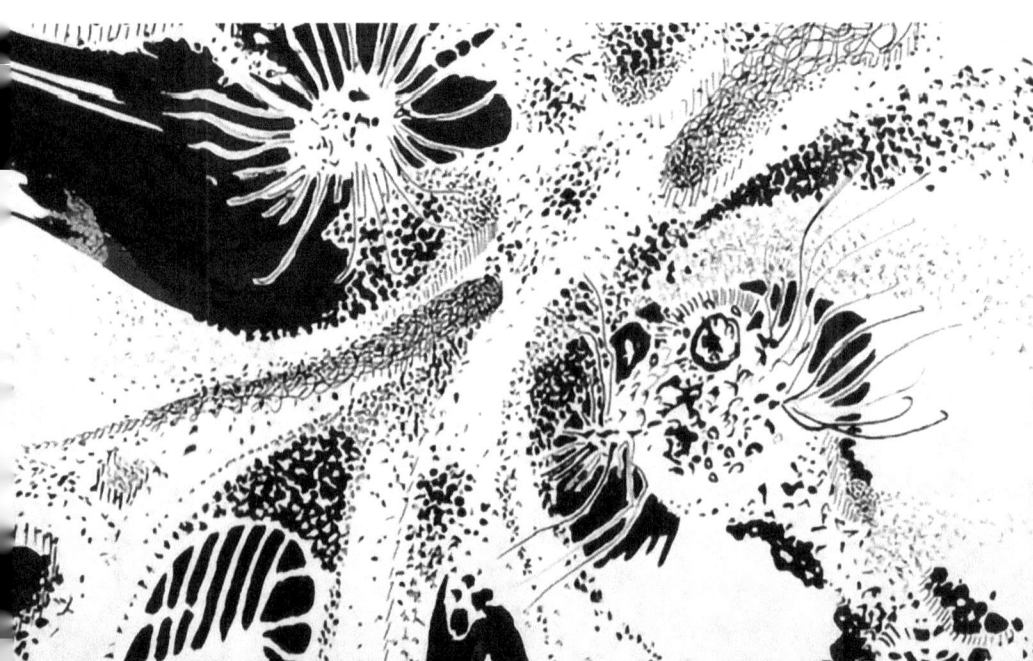

# Glacier Park by Helicopter

Suspended
out-of-body emanation
over
my former self

Between my feet
a lake
a waterfall
a continental divide
stegosaur-sharp

where if we crash
our blood will flow
to the Pacific
or to the Gulf of Mexico
depending on
how the pilot's hand
twitches

Another line
thirty clear-cut feet in width
marches neatly
from vanishing-point to vanishing-point
along the 49th parallel
violating geography, re-arranging reality
making history
as long-dead politicians chose

and present politicians
suspended
with twitching hands
between past and future
now propose
to over-fly

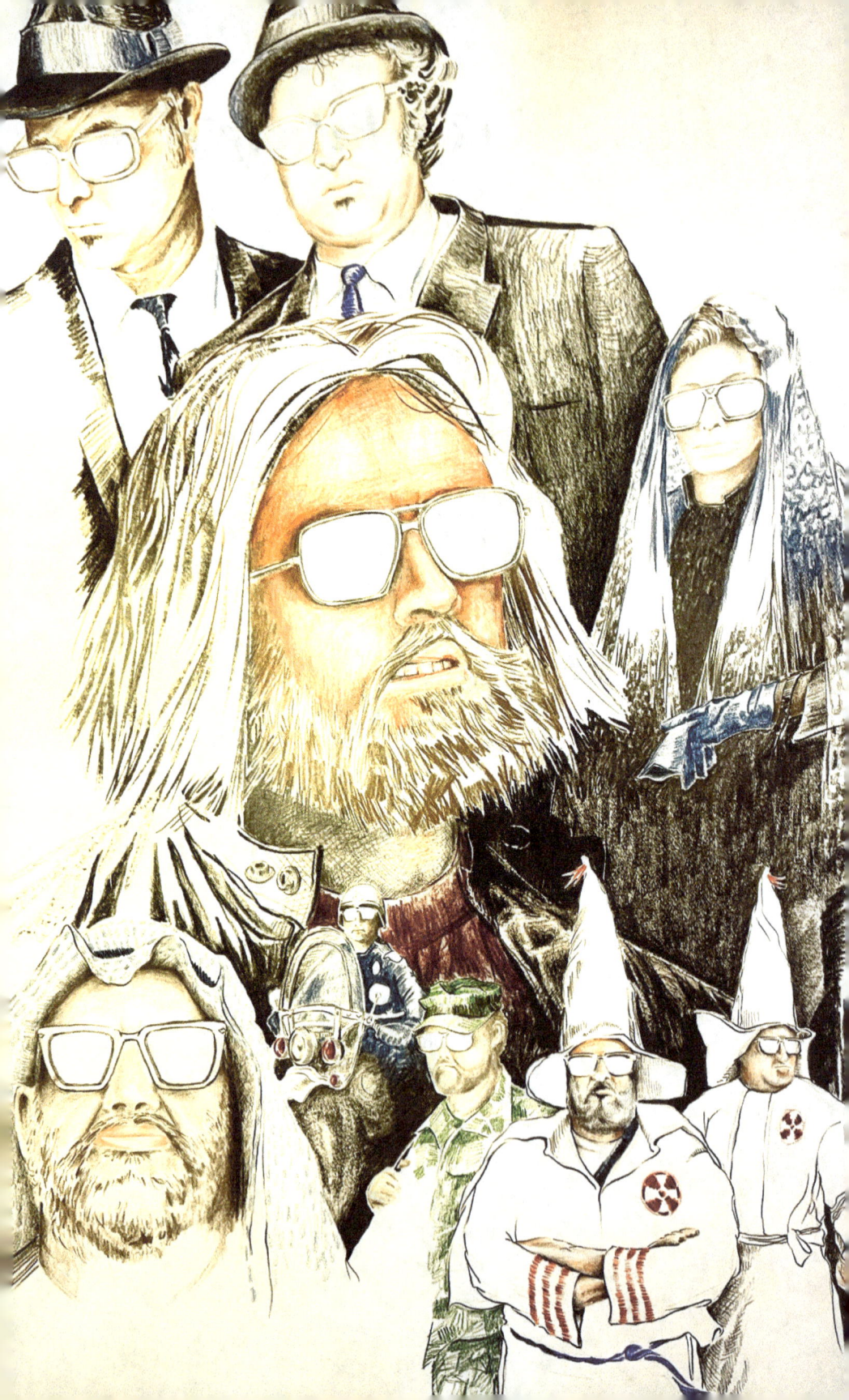

# Ford's Theatre, Washington

Make-believe was murdered
here.

The guilty premises condemned
to masquerade
as warehouse
for a hundred years,
now serves its time
in nineteenth century costume
re-enacting
its true identity.

But something unstaged
lingers
in the empty
presidential box
as the lights
are going out:

awareness
that the audience
is white,
the streets are black.

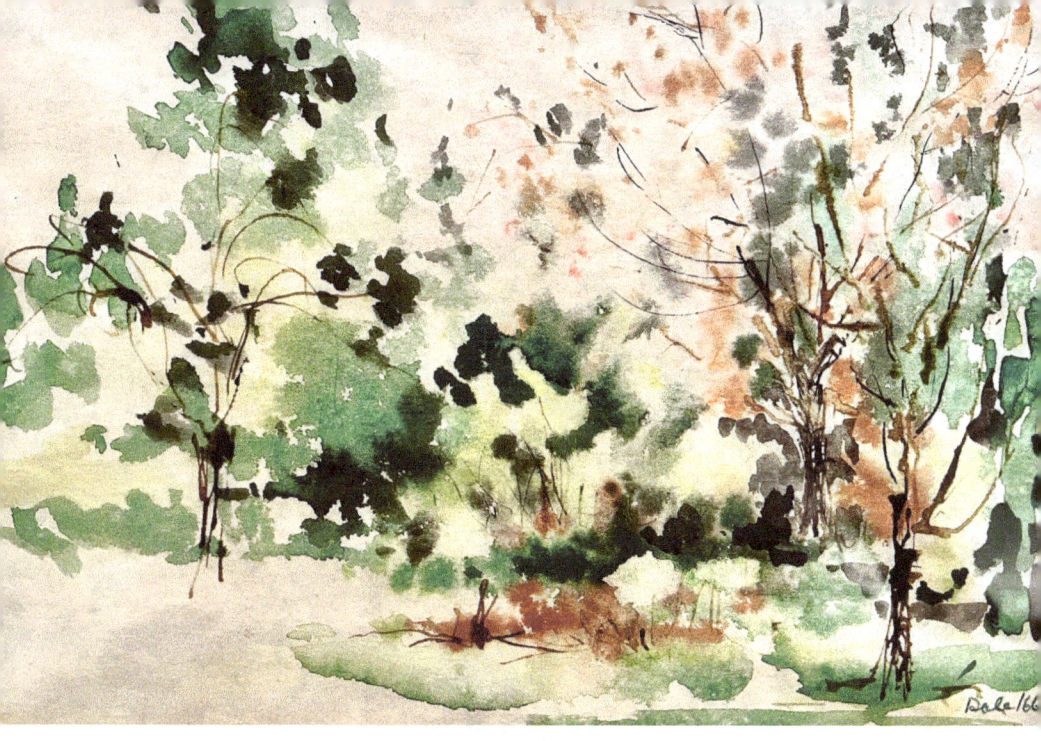

# Nature, General

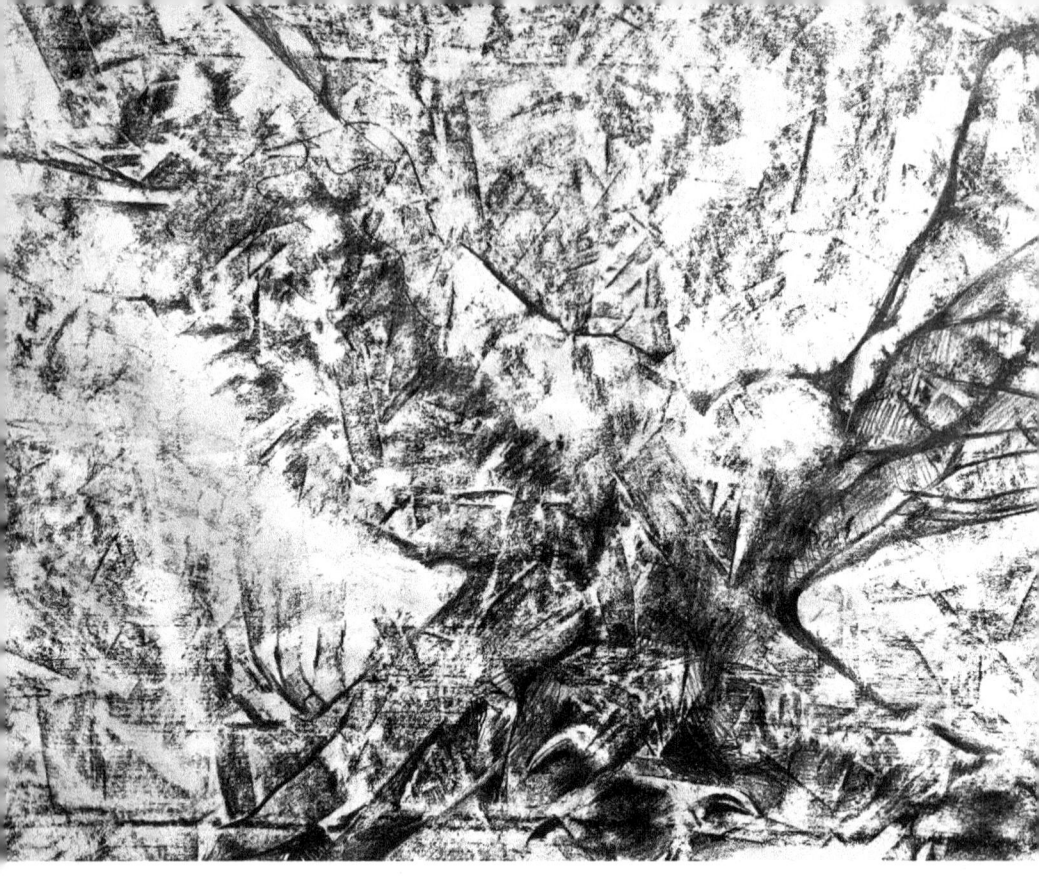

# if You Walk Fast

If you walk fast
through the woods
mosquitoes
won't find you

and you
won't discover
the woods.

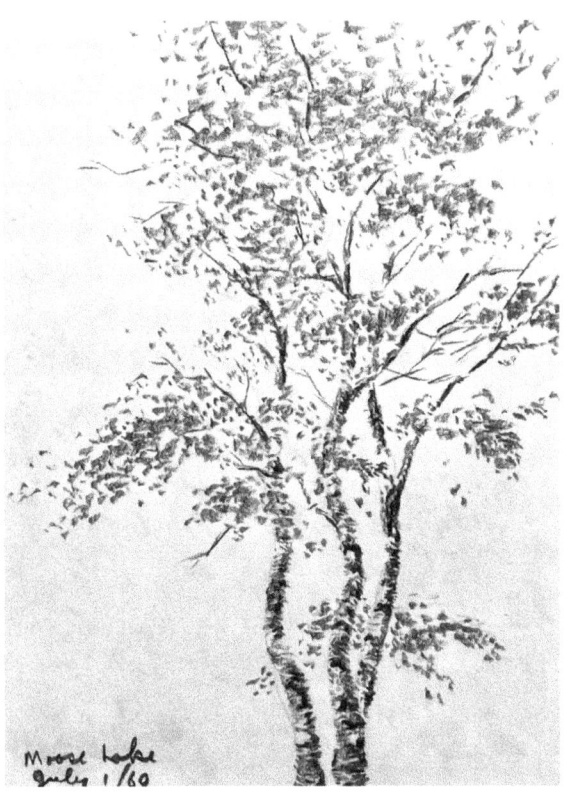

# Swimming in Rain

I'm
now or then
drifting

between here and there
the lake's in the sky
and I'm everywhere

# Spring Vine

Precocious
fence
vine
climbs
its
parents'
corpse.

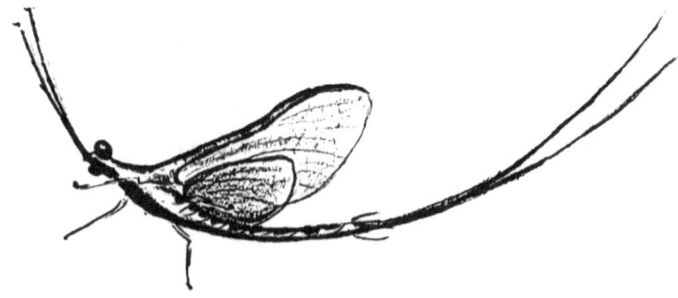

# Walking on Water/ Water Walkers

Trembling shadows,
groups of five, no six,
nervous blotches
spot the sunny bottom
of the pond,
as if from overhanging
clumps of tiny leaves
and yet
there are no leaves.

Then one set
of shadows moves
more quickly than the others,
scurries past them,
and yet
there is no breeze.

Water walkers!
See-through, spider-legged
messiahs of the insect world.

The light
that passes through and past
their bodies
is refracted where
their feet have bent
the water's skin.

# Total Eclipse

Sneaking moon
attempts to steal
the beauty of the sun
but fails.

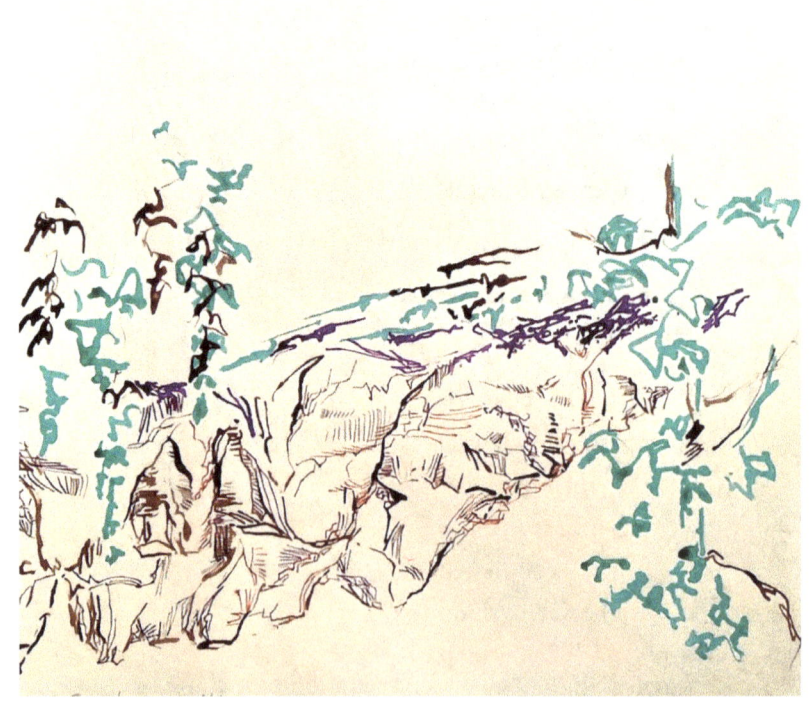

## Rocky Mountains

Some god
trod here
upon a time,
upending
mountains

to
commemorate
a valley orchid

crushed
this morning
by a tourist's
foot.

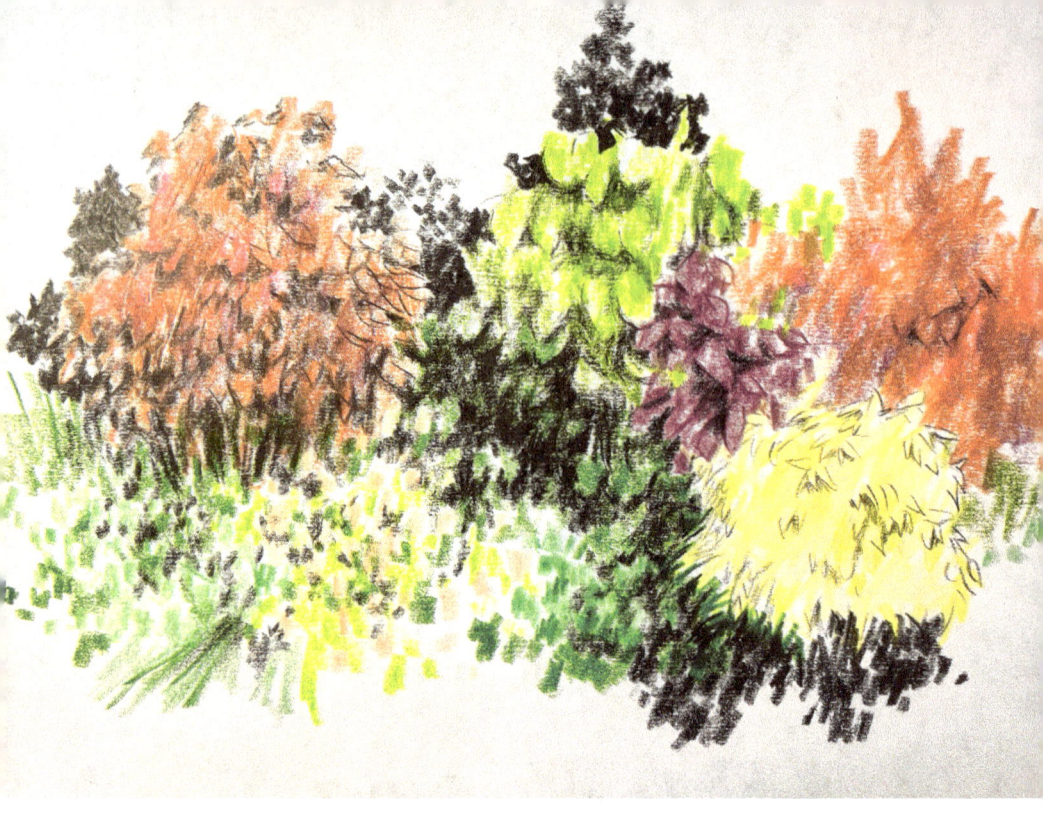

# Lake Shore – Early Evening

Fleeting silhouettes
against the rising moon, bats
like ugly
tantalizing secrets
cruise the whispering shore.

# Epilogue

Years later
I went there once more
with you in my mind
and (forgive me, but poems must be honest)
every plant was you.

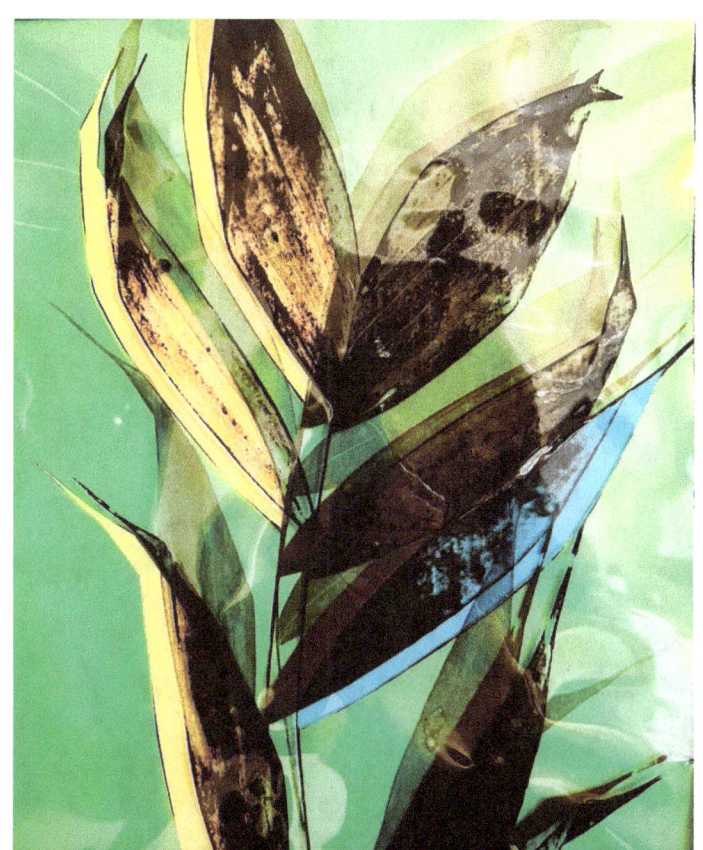

# Winter Magpies

I steal from magpies
what they'll never know
I've stolen: images of
iridescent blacks
on nervous whites.

Eating lunch in my car
on a winter road near Kenora,

I shut the motor off
and sink into
the silent shocking white.

The hills around are
furred with evergreens and
etched with nervous birch.

A sea of snow floods a nearby road-side graveyard,
causing photo-frozen surf
to rear along the roadside.

A crow crosses noisily, carrion in mouth,
leaves it stiller and whiter than before.

A freight train slows,
pulls through the rock cut,
leaving it easier to breathe.

# Adventures in Quetico

Trying to patch
a holed candle
before a looming storm
alone
in Questico

I watch
through parted clouds
a tiny
U.S. bomber
tow its feather
past a thunderhead

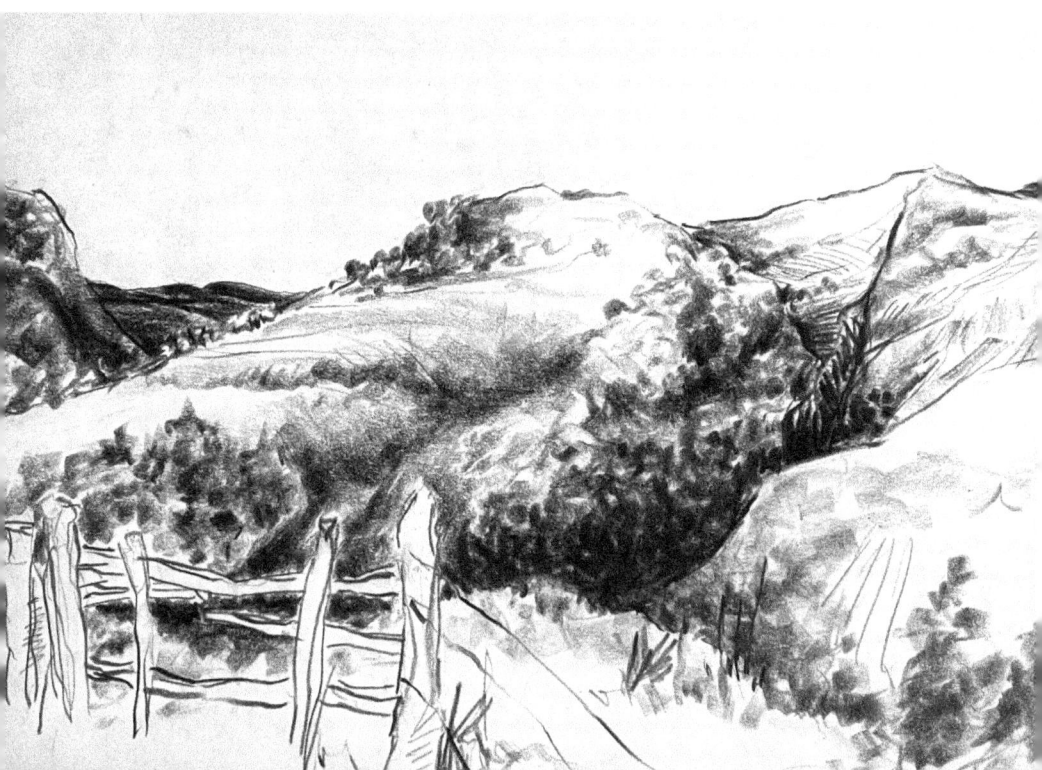

# Winter Night

If you breathe
unduly deep
you'll inhale
a star.

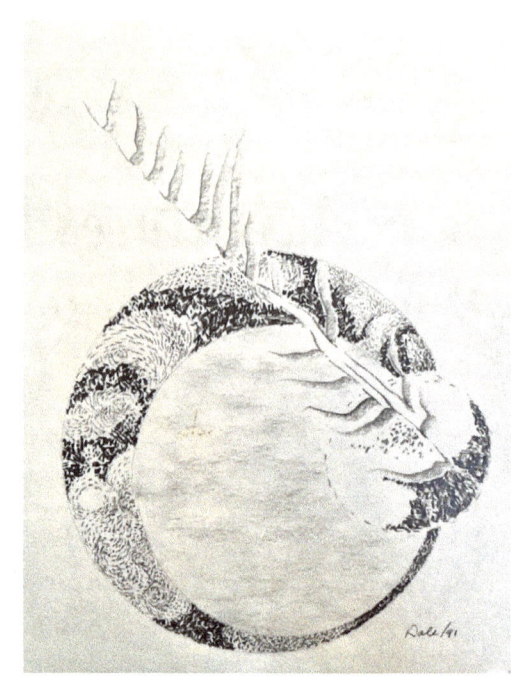

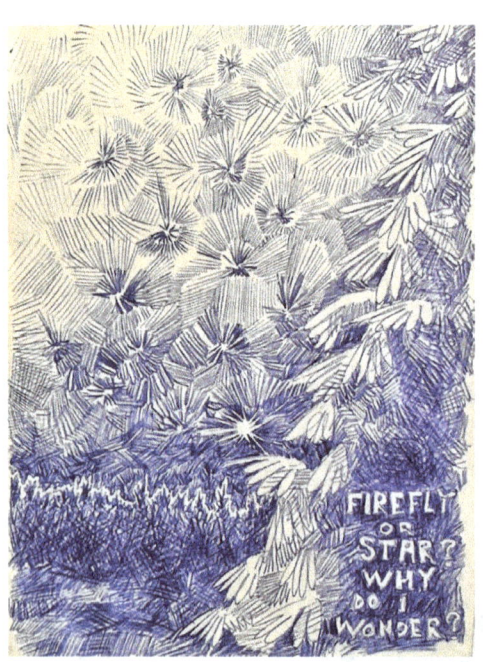

# Firefly or Star

The flicker
in the midnight woods
might have been
a firefly
or a star

Why wonder which?

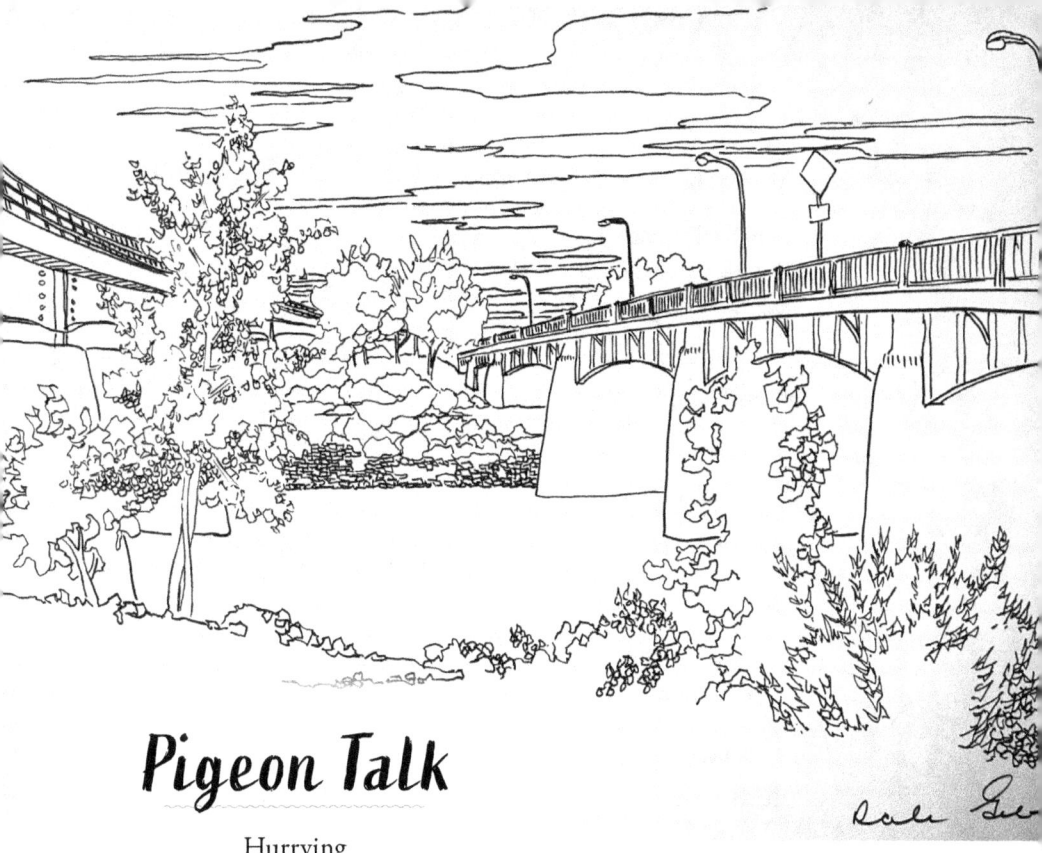

# Pigeon Talk

Hurrying
over the High Level Bridge,
I saw this pigeon
– the usual blue-grey type –
flying past
with a straw
in its beak.

I don't customarily
speak to pigeons
but something
caused me to greet her
(him? Who knows?)
and ask
what's so great
about flying.

"It lets you build nests
out of the reach
of tomcats and dogs
and such-like marauders,"
he/she explained,
words slurred just a bit
by the straw.

"Well, all right,"
I said,
"but what's the point
of the nest?
Do you need it
for rest?"

"My goodness, no!"
said the bird.
"We pigeons can sleep
wherever we perch.
Don't you know that?
Oh poop! Double poop!!"

The straw had slipped
from its beak and fell
to the river below.

"Now
see what your questions
have done!"

I told the
disconsolate bird
that I'd shred up
a memo from my briefcase
as substitute
straw for its nest,
provided, of course, that
my question was answered.

"The nest's for the eggs,
of course!" the pigeon replied.
"And the eggs?
Why lay the eggs?"
I persisted.

"One question's
all that you get
for one sheet of
paper,"
my wily feathered acquaintance
responded.

I offered him (or her)
more paper, but
paper no longer
sufficed.
The pigeon wanted
– and got –
my necktie
(an old one, it's true)
and the conversation
went on.

"Pigeons lay eggs,"
said my friend
with elaborate patience,
"to guarantee
there will always
be pigeons...."

"to fly, and build nests
and lay eggs."

I concluded,
"I guess that
takes us full cycle.
Thanks for the chat."

"Hey, wait!"
said the bird.
"We aren't finished yet.
It's your turn to answer
some questions."

"Like what?"
I rejoined.
"Like what's so great
about hurrying
over the High Level Bridge?"

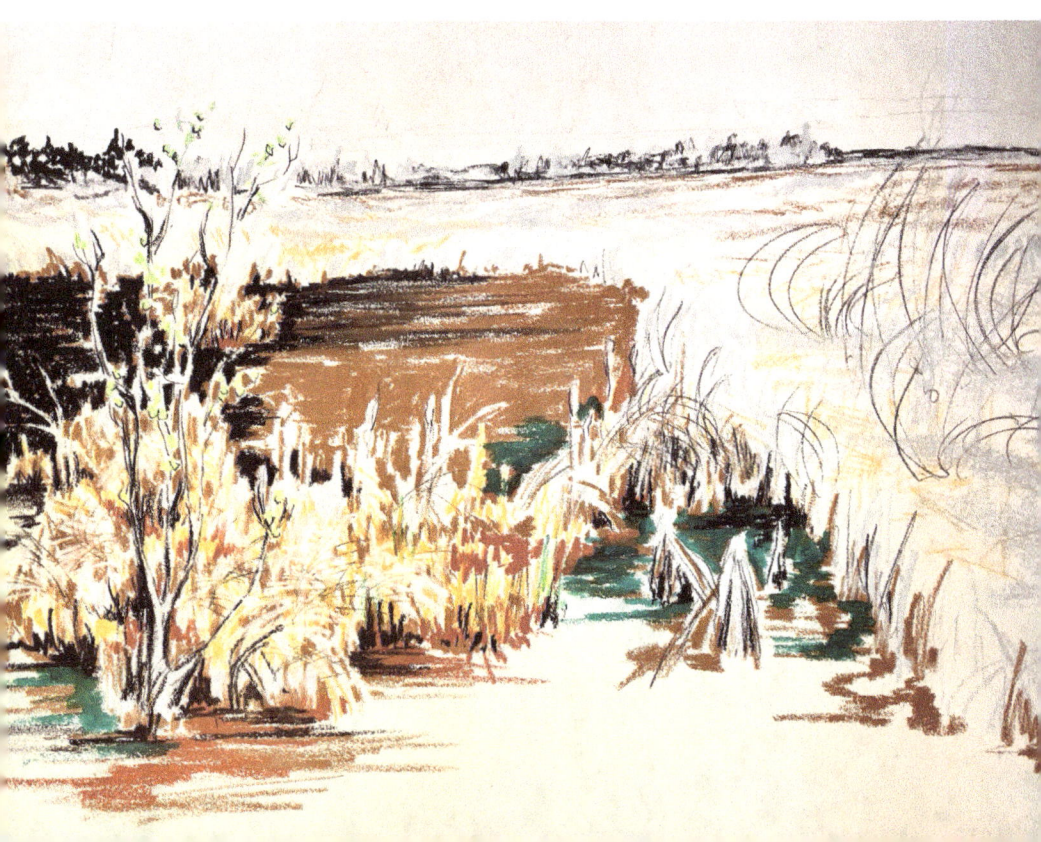

# Wild Violets

Only
in the alien eyes of the tall
do
violets cower.

In their own domain
close to the ground

where congealed snow
lurks in the shade
and
the frost still sears
incautious shoots

violets are regal.

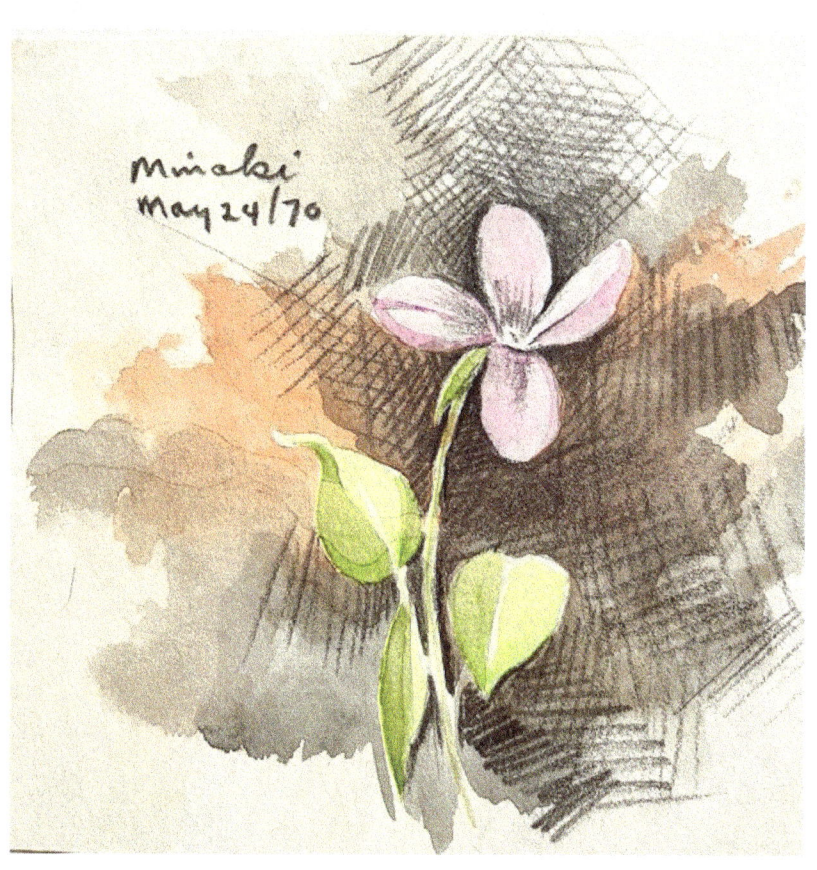

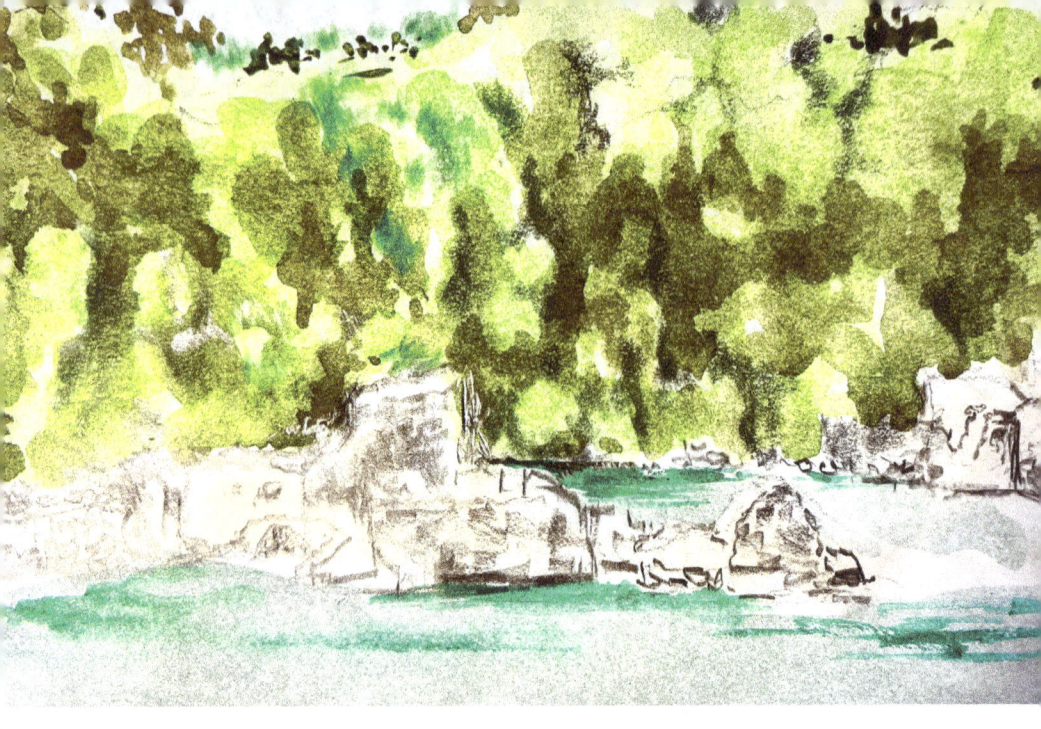

# October Sunrise

Lolling in the arms
of her spent lunar lover,
Venus

stays awake long enough
to observe the voluptuous dawn
and applaud

the still-dancing aspens
scan-lit
in flimsy and tattered
gowns of gold.

# It was a Turbulent Night

It was a turbulent night
where the lightening remained
beyond the horizon

After a tumultuous night,
half of the moon
hurries away
from the
victorious sun
and its brilliantly
uniformed clouds
in search of its
vanquished half-brother.

There were serious casualties
even here
the recently risen sun
reveals shattered clouds
limping eastward toward it

while half of the moon
hurries wanly above them
in search of its dark brother.

# If you walk on Bloor Street

If you walk on Bloor Street
early in the morning
before the swarms become too numerous,
you may see
along the cracks between the paving blocks
a lot of ant hills.

I came upon about a dozen ant hills:

Now, they were relatively small,
as ant hills go,
but even so
there must have been a thousand
grains of sand or more in each,
every one of which
would be a massive boulder
to an ant.

I wonder how the ants react
on learning every morning that
the first few scuffling humans of the day
have unknowingly obliterated
all the hills once more,
like yesterday, and always,
and every other day,
on Bloor Street?

Does the vanguard ant
of each succeeding evening shift
report:
"Our monument has been destroyed again,
so we must begin once more."

Until,
one by one,
his fellow ants
refuse to struggle with their boulders any longer
and huddle in their trembling chambers
two feet under Bloor Street,
waiting for the end?

Or does he shout:
"Rejoice, my friends!
Our prayers have once again been heard.
Last night's diggings
have been cleared away.
You know, it really
is surprising how
efficiently the humans
take away our refuse."

# Manitoba Magpies

There was a time
when magpies were plenteous
in Manitoba,
but something lured them west
a lot of years ago.

Perhaps it was the oil wells
(that may be how
they got their iridescence).

Anyway, I first noticed them
in numbers
when I lived in Edmonton:
overdressed, strutting over lawns proprietorially
like Brian Mulroneys
of the feathered realm
stealing from the nests
of weaker birds.

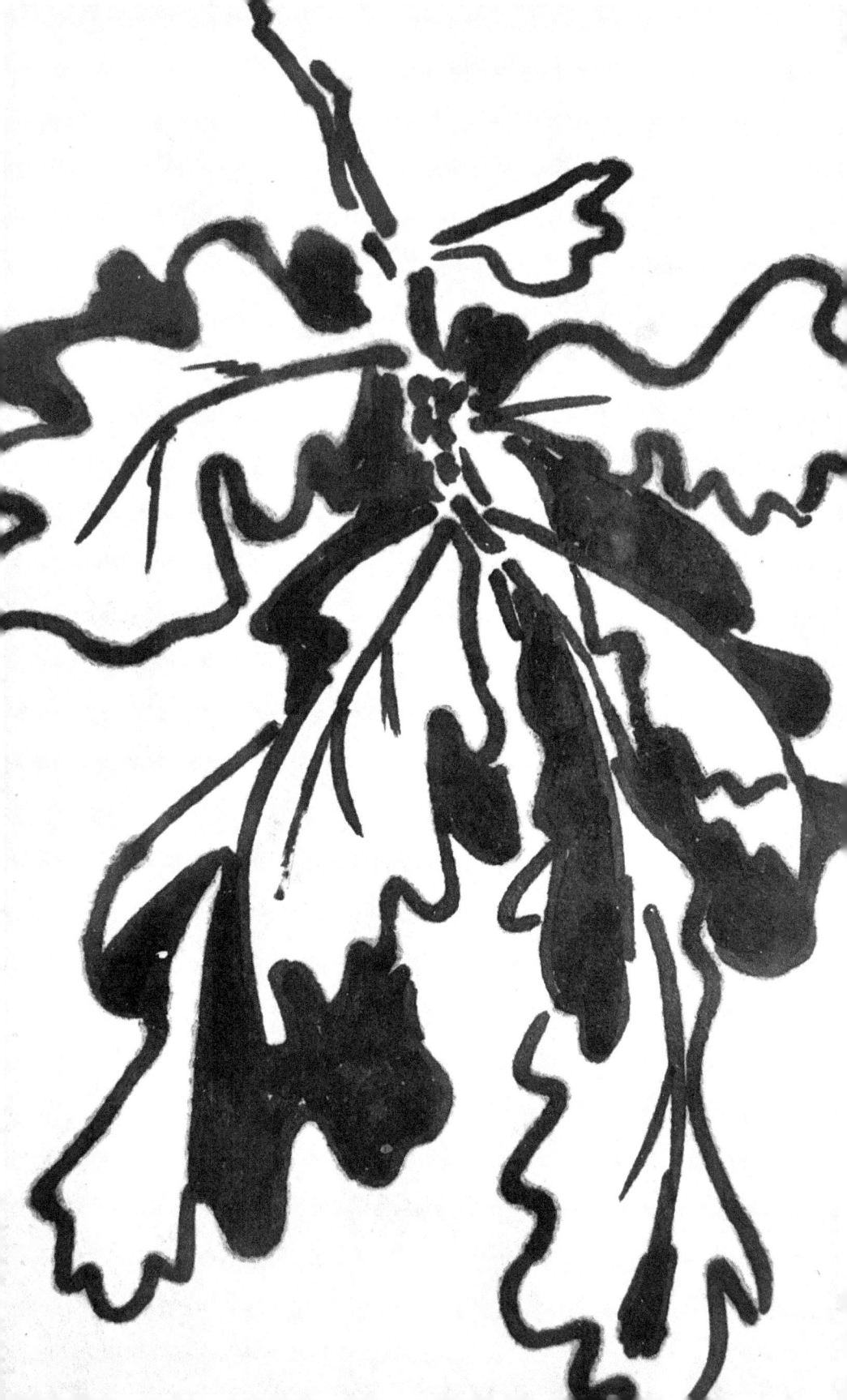

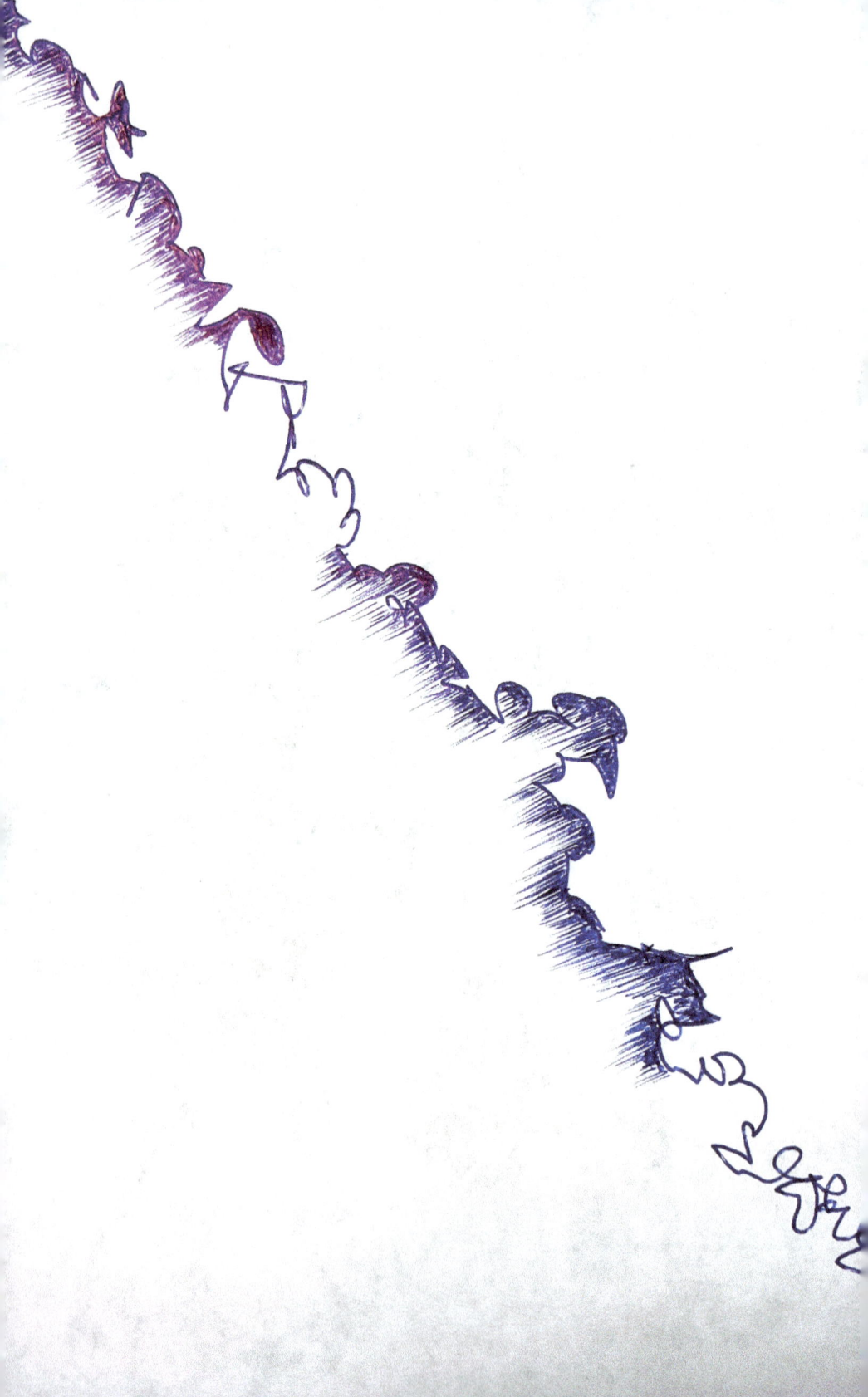

*Art*

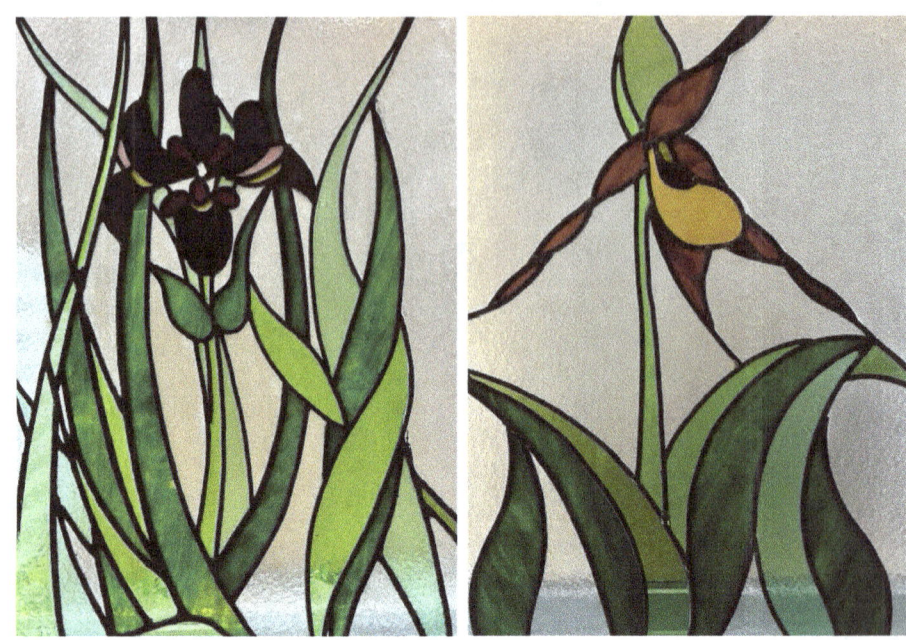

# Beyond

Beyond,
over the valley
gulls glide
on thermals
spiralling higher

as Gould
soars on a fugue
out of sight
out of sound
beyond Bach.

# Archeologists, Historians & Old Farts Rule

It's much harder to write upon stone
than parchment
and on parchment than paper
while paper requires more effort than
cyberspace

On the other hand
cyberspace destructs more easily than paper
paper than parchment
parchment than stone

And so, in the long run, perhaps
cyber jabber
the reputed death of the book
and the current starvation of
historical arts and sciences
really don't matter.

# Julian Barnes Isn't a Writer

Yesterday I finished reading Julian Barnes" short story collection "The Lemon Table". He's a magical writer. There stories are all about aging and the elderly, and they are, apart from being immensely varied in style and setting, eerily accurate in characterisation. How can a middle-aged, worldly, heterosexual, English male become a cranky eightyish woman in a nursing home; Sibelius in his dotage; an elderly henpecked husband, his shrewish wife, and the aging woman he left for her for; a disillusioned gay music lover in a limp relationship; Turgenev in his sixties in platonic love with a young actress; an eight-year-old boy on his first solo trip to a barber shop?

> Julian Barnes isn't a writer
> isn't a man
> isn't a woman, for that matter
> he or she's a
> supernatural
> international, multicultural
> all-generational, cross-gender
> pirate of souls

**Journal, May 9, 2005**

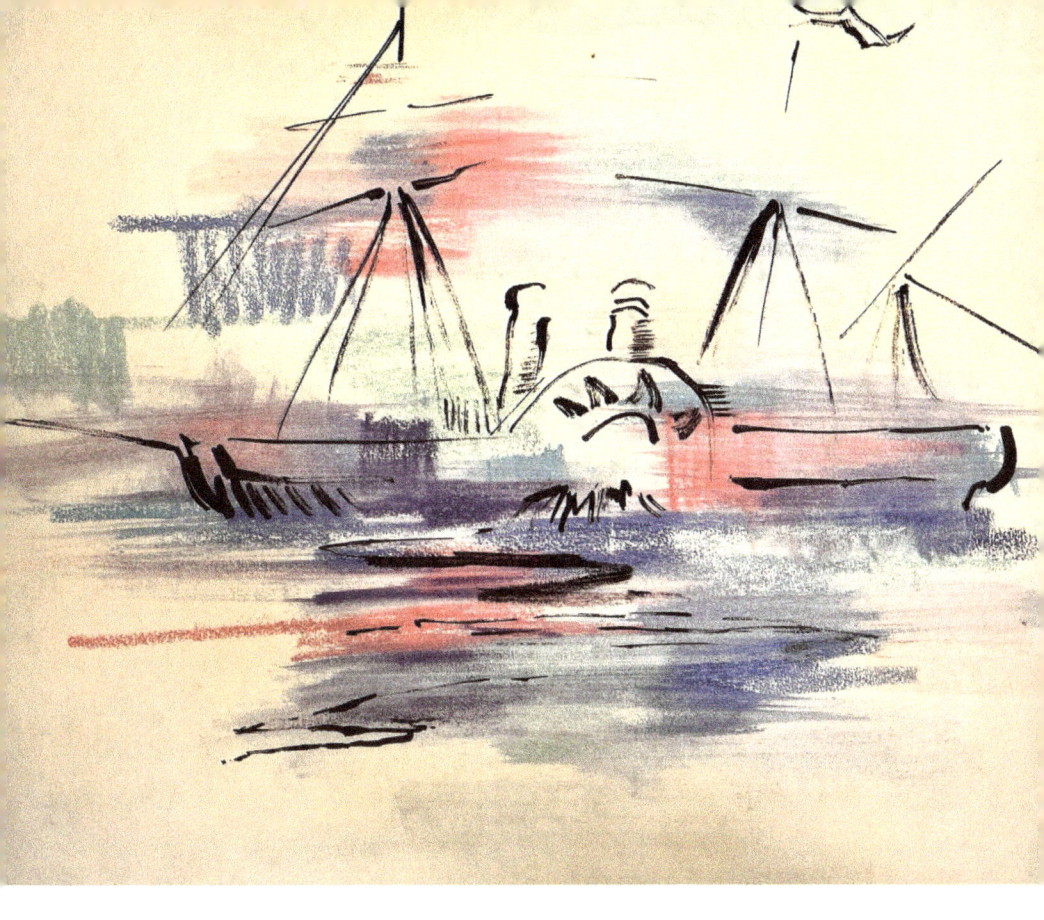

# Frank Scott

Frank Scott
loped through crowds,
seeing everything
at once.

# Three for Frank
thinking about lawyer-poet
F.R. Scott 1899-1985

## I: Past Perfect

It may be true
as Frank Scott said
that Was
is an Is that died

but
Is
is growing older
by the day
while

Was
remains forever young

and almost as perfect as
Will Be
or
Might Have Been

\* \* \*

When
Frank became a Was
the tenses blurred.

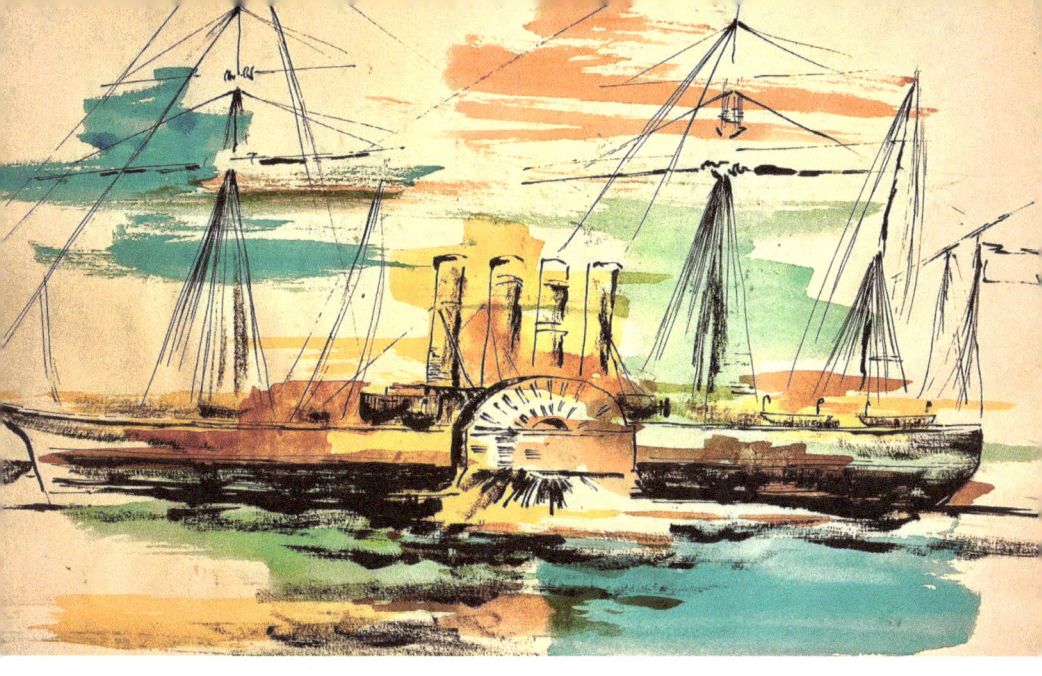

# II: Either/Or

Either and Or
rule by exclusion.

Their realms have
barbed-wire boundaries.

Nothing is shared between them.

Neither
Either nor Or
leaves any doubt.

The pleasures they seek
and treasures they take
are
certain, finite
and incomplete.

# III: And

And
is acquisitive.

And
throws nothing away.

And
is
affirmative
companiable
polygamous

and

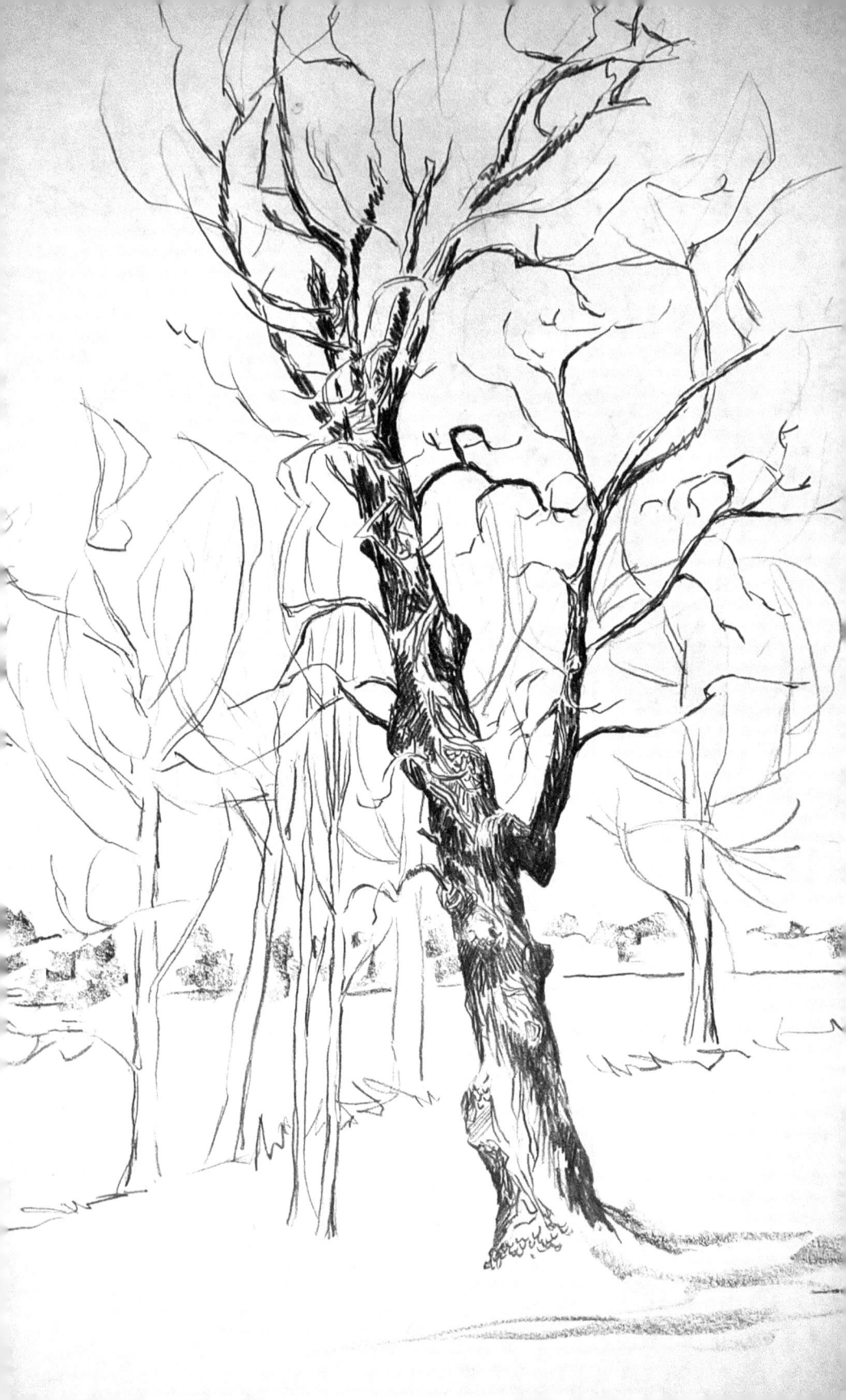

# Repast

The future
feeds the present
while the past,
too much present,
eats the future.

\*\*\*

The past,
too present,
devours the future.

WITH THESE POEMS, DALE KEPT A COPY OF SCOTT'S POEM, "WAS IS AN IS THAT DIED" FROM F.R. SCOTT, SELECTED POEMS (1966), P. 163:

# Frank Scott, Moving, and Things

When Frank Scott was moved
from his university office
he wrote of the anguish of
seeing strangers commit

"murder in my cathedral"

watching them
violate his space, pack his files
take his pictures off the walls
sunder
the juxtapositions of
his things and his thoughts.

"These are all cells to my brain, a part of my total,"
he protested.

But he resiled at the end of the poem
apologizing for
"a moment of weakness"
and claiming the move would be beneficial:
would strip off impediments
to meeting the challenges yet to come.

That was bravado.
I'm sure he was right in the first place.

There was more than divestment
there must also have been severe amputation.
Why else devote nine-tenths of the poem
to his pain?

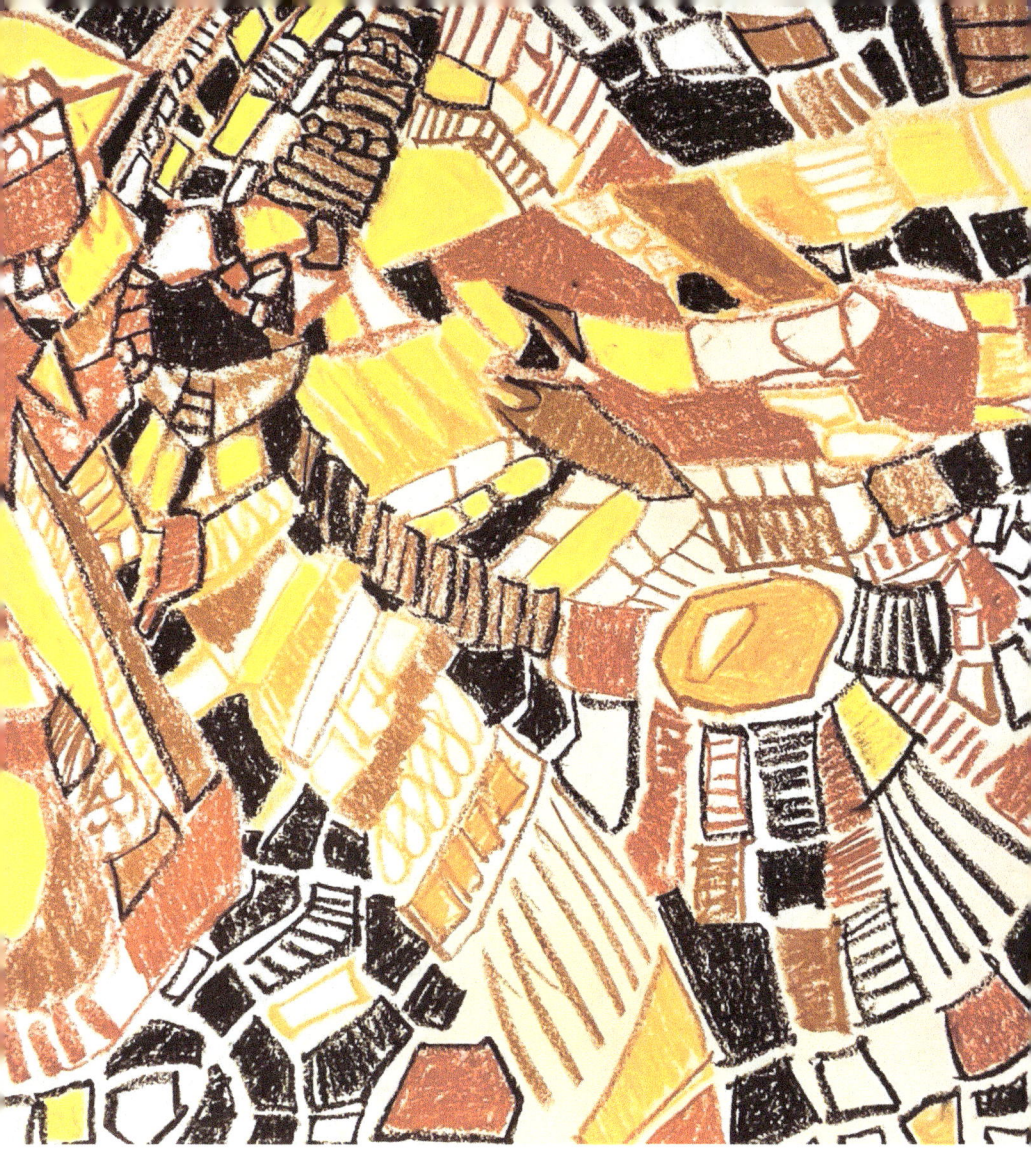

These thoughts kept nagging
like flies
while I was moving my things
from a university office to a more
and more cluttered study at home.

But why should they have?
I was just merging cathedrals.

# Death of an Artist

(On reading Leonard Cohen's "Death of A Lady's Man")

Returning from exile
again,
he carries a box:

a small golden box
encrusted with delicate
ornamentations.

a former container of spices
now filled,
so he tells us,
with gems:

burnished epitomes
essences of art
and experience,
exquisite distillations
of beautiful losses,
fashioned from
unspeakable sorrow
and fired in the
Mediterranean sun.

When revealed,
they turn out to be
bunions
and fingernail clippings.

But O
what a beautiful box!

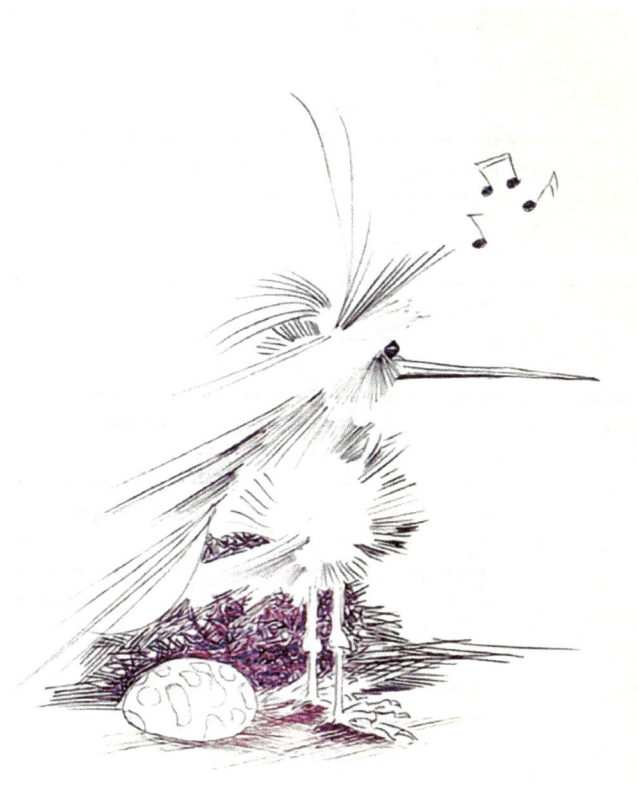

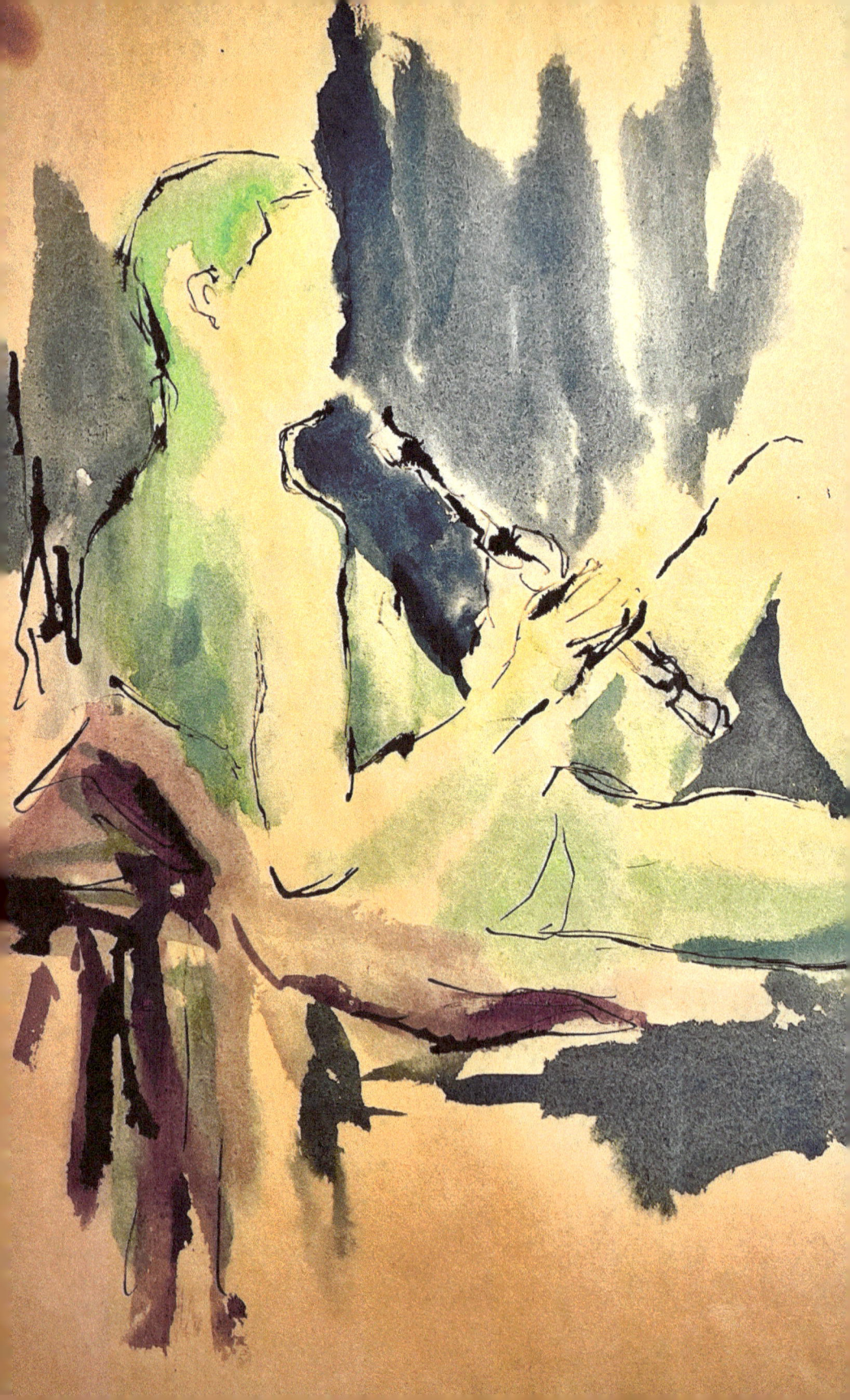

# In Music

In music
there aren't any
really pure notes.

If there were,
you couldn't distinguish
a flute from a fiddle.

Every sound
an instrument makes
is a choir

and the character
comes from the voices
you're not quite certain
you heard.

"There!"
said my cousin
who tunes pianos.
"Hear the harmonics?
Just as the main note decays?"

I couldn't.

But I can tell
a flute from a cello
and I don't doubt his word.

And then we got talking religion.
We usually do;
he's a born-again something.

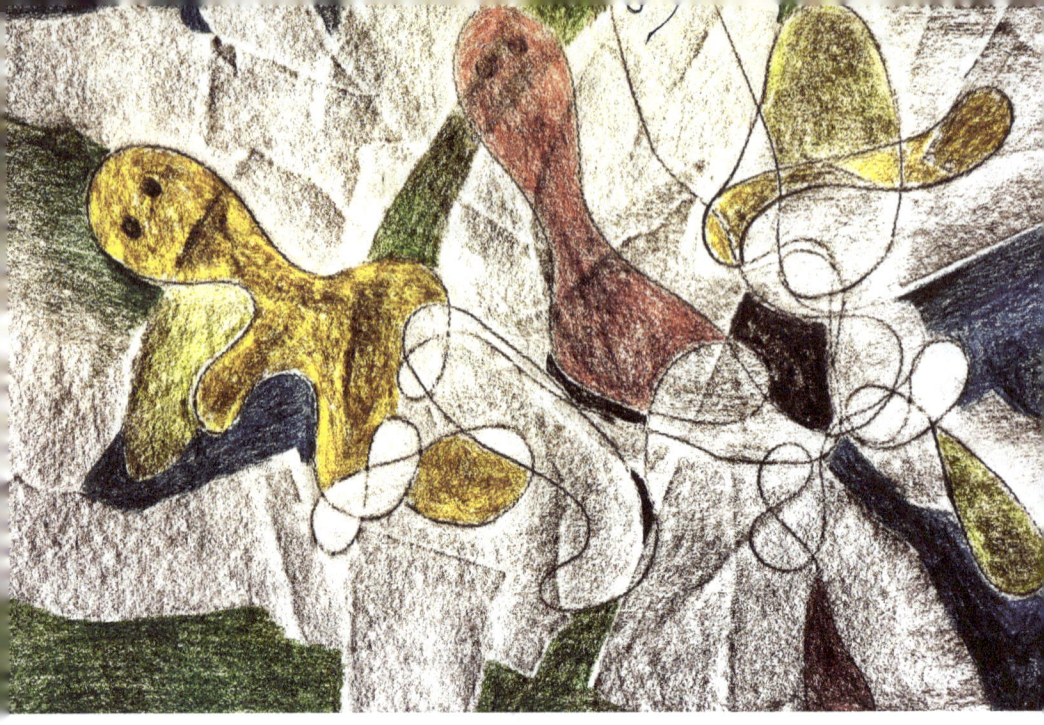

# Can You Hear?

Distortion
gives each instrument
its character

subtle
overtones and undertones
you're not quite sure
you heard.

# Hey Leonard

I loved you, Leonard
Well, at least I loved
the image you projected.

Anyway,
I followed you
from time to time
until the end,

enjoyed some of your writing,
some of your songs
and the one concert I took in.

At the end I decided
your talents were modest,
but your merchandising
was
magnificent.

Bon voyage – if any.

# The Lawyer and the Poet

Offstride and grinning
in the lawyer's doorway
like a Smokey Stover portrait
climbing from its frame,
Purdy
thrust a book of poems
as a calling card.

*\*\*\**

Drunk and surly
on the lawyer's doorstep,
Purdy
brought another book
to dinner,
but refused to read.

*\*\*\**

They planned to lunch
before the poet

left the city,
but they never did.

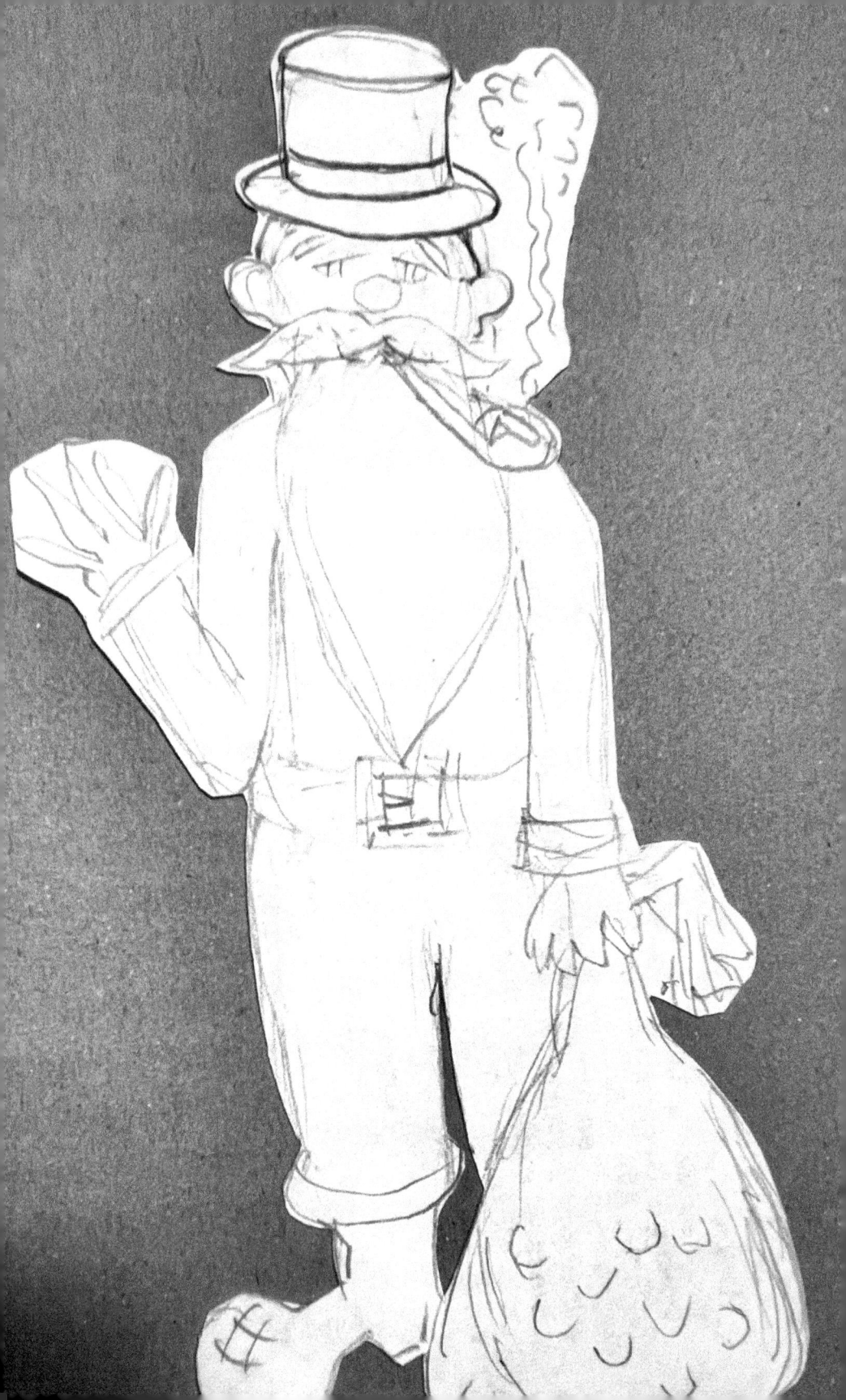

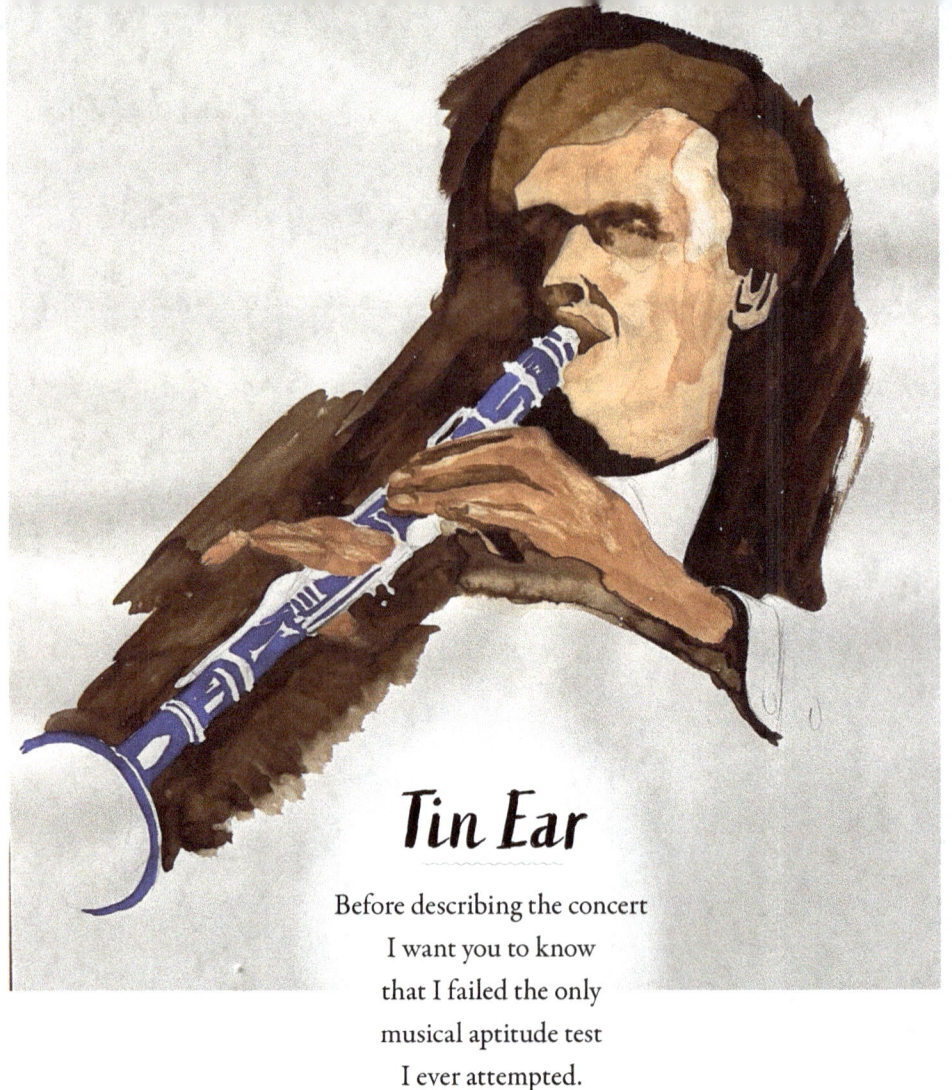

# Tin Ear

Before describing the concert
I want you to know
that I failed the only
musical aptitude test
I ever attempted.

The featured event
was a new piano concerto
composed by a young
Canadian-Vietnamese,
who explained that her aim
was to marry eastern and western
musical styles.

I thought she did.

Gongs and glissandos cavorted,
polyglot rhythms consorted.
The Roar of the Lion
caroused with the strings,
typani and tablas disported.

Melodies
slipped through the clatter
like Humphrey Bogart pursuing his prey
through the streets of Shanghei.

I sat transfixed and vibrating,
expecting us all to
shatter like goblets at
some emphatic crescendo.

But only a few were a-quiver.

The applause
was barely polite,
and when it was over
my friend in the orchestra
told me the music was trash.

Young Albert
kept failing mathematics exams
'til mathematics finally
failed his.

The man who discovered ancient Troy
didn't know it was only a myth.
And Ludwig, of course,
heard a lot of his music
when deaf.

Perhaps it takes a tin ear
to hear the future approaching.

# King's College Choir Boys

Spring lambs in top hats
are herded through traffic
into a musical abattoir.

King's College Chapel
soars fit for Henry
and God,
but the walls
and arteried ceilings
are pallid as flesh.

An organ erupts,
and the slaughter begins.

Lambs squeal deliciously
each time the murderous
baton descends.
Aisles run with blood:
cutlets are stacked
on the alter
for sale.

"What nonsense!"
someone protests.
"This isn't murder,
it's training,
the best that there is.
These are the Bachs
of the future."

But Bachs
don't travel in flocks.

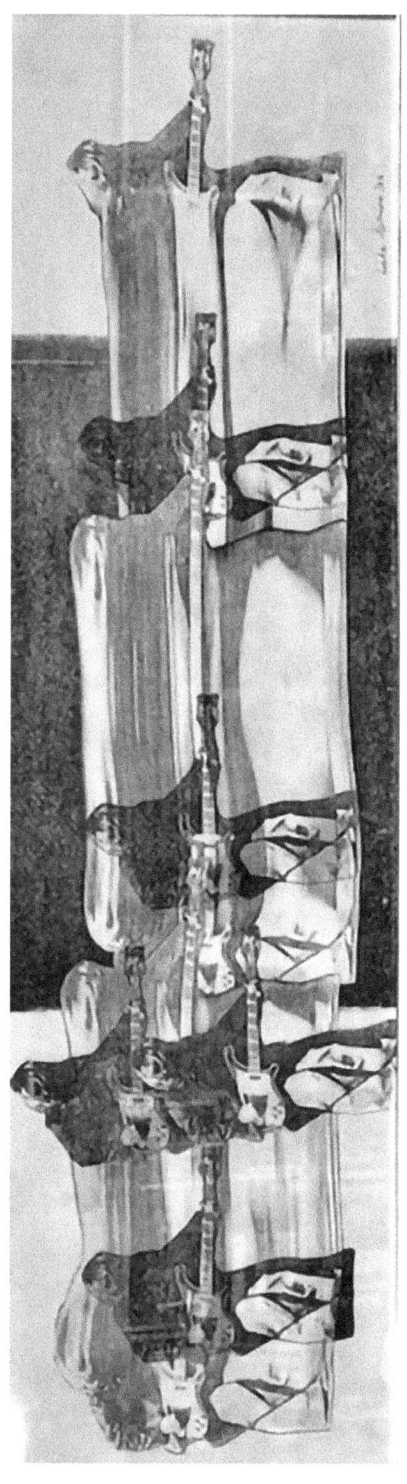

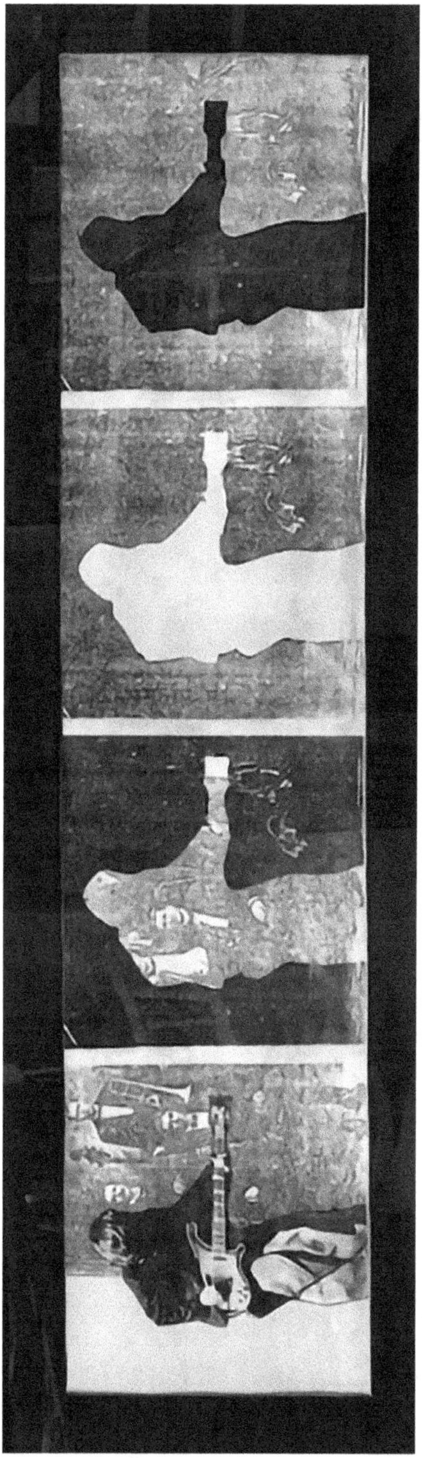

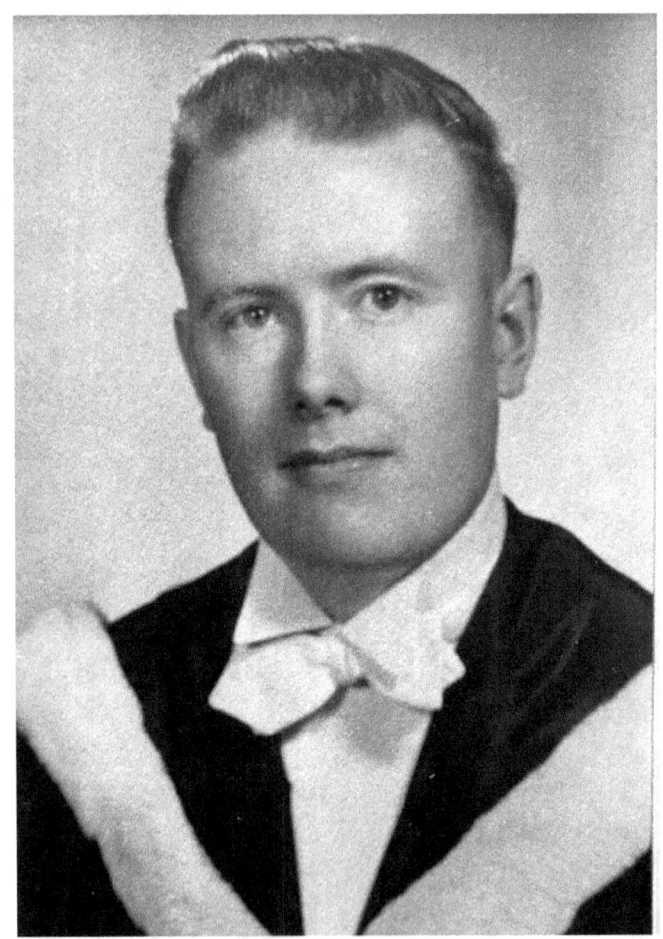
Dale Gibson, age 25, 1958

# Dale's First Court Case

## (May 1, 1962, Dressler v. Tallman)

I consider my articling experience to have been satisfactory for the most part. My year with Robertson and Long left me quite well trained in two major areas of solicitor skills: real estate transactions and administration of estates. And the three years I was with the Canadian Pacific Railway Law Department offered, in addition to ongoing, semi-clandestine, real estate experience, constant opportunities to research interesting legal problems of wide-ranging types, and to draft contracts of many sorts.

Sadly, however, apart from a one-day opportunity to observe a trial in the Manitoba Court of Queen's Bench, one solo assignment conducting what I recall as a small arbitration in Thunder Bay, and one County Court case involving a minor collision between a CPR truck and someone's car which my principal Herb Pickard and the opposing lawyer agreed to let their respective students handle (a case so minor that the judge held the trial in his office, which suited me well, since my opponent – classmate Arnold Sigesmund – won), I received very little litigation training.

After returning to Winnipeg from Cambridge and being called to the bar, I ached for some courtroom experience. But the only type I could find was – at a time before formal legal aid existed in Manitoba – volunteering for about a year to "speak to sentence" free of charge in Magistrates' Court on behalf of persons who had pleaded guilty to minor offences. Speaking to sentence involved attempting to persuade the presiding magistrate to impose a light sentence on the ground that the convict in question was a really sweet person who had uncharacteristically strayed from his or her normally law-abiding ways and was now bitterly repentant and determined to walk the straight and narrow thereafter.

Aside from those very minor experiences, my first significant courtroom appearance was in the Supreme Court of Canada! This was in the early 1960s, and my circumstances were very much like those often faced by the renowned, if fictitious, English barrister Horace Rumpole: "alone and without a leader." I was 27 years old but looked about 17.

How in earth did I manage to get a Supreme Court gig with absolutely no relevant experience? I was a last-minute replacement for a much more seasoned Manitoba lawyer I knew who had been told by the Supreme Court, a few days before the case in question was due to be heard in Ottawa, that he would not be allowed to appear on behalf of his client because the Court file disclosed that he, rather than a process-server, had sworn an affidavit relating to the service of some legal document on someone involved in his case. While it was a very minor, not to say picayune, slip on the lawyer's part, it had the effect of making him a witness in the case, which therefore disqualified him from also acting as an advocate therein!

For understandable reasons, the disqualified lawyer did not come immediately to me when searching for a replacement lawyer to represent his client. He had approached several veteran litigators, all of whom turned him down, before he came desperately upon me at the bottom of the advocates' barrel.

An even more understandable reason that the others had all refused the assignment was that there was no fee involved. The client, for whom the lawyer in question did considerable other legal work, was a small and not very well-to-do trade union that had already spent a lot of money litigating an important issue unsuccessfully at two lower court levels and was not confident that success at the Supreme Court level was likely.

The lawyer, on the other hand, knew that the issue involved was very important to all Manitoba workers, and believed that it was a winnable case. He had therefore volunteered to present the Supreme Court appeal *pro bono*: for no payment other than expenses. No wonder he had difficulty finding a replacement. For me, however, fees were not a significant matter; I was a reasonably well-paid junior law professor lusting for courtroom exposure, and I leaped at the opportunity being offered to me. I never knew whether the client was even made aware how totally inexperienced I was.

Having agreed to take the case, I studied the file in the very few days I had to do so before leaving for Ottawa, rearranged the factum (written argument) the first lawyer had prepared into a sequence I preferred, borrowed a court gown from my friend and law partner Al Mackling, and boarded the only flight I could get to Ottawa – an overnight "milk run" with a couple of stops *en route*. I got no sleep to speak of.

But I had a big day ahead of me, and, arriving at Ottawa's Château Laurier hotel around lunch-time – about an hour before I was due in court – I was eager to get on with it. I grabbed Al's court gown from my suitcase, which I left with the desk clerk, asked him to point me in the direction of the Supreme Court of Canada, and ran full tilt, gown flapping in my afterbreeze, the several blocks separating the two buildings, happily recognizing the Supreme Court building when it hove into view from photographs I had seen.

After checking in with a very anxious-looking court clerk, and racing to the court library to acquire a number of books I thought I might need to refer to in argument, I was starting to wheel my book-filled cart toward the courtroom when I suddenly remembered a vital question I had intended, but had forgotten, to ask Al. "Well," I thought, "a librarian should know." So I sidled up to the first librarian I saw and whispered: "I'm on for the appellant. Which side of the courtroom should I sit on?"

Trying hard to suppress his astonishment that a barrister entrusted to argue a case in the highest court in the land should be so ignorant of court procedure, the librarian replied: "The right side." Whew! And so, confidence renewed, I wheeled the cart to the courtroom, entered, turned right, and arranged my books and other paraphernalia on the table I found there, finishing about five minutes before the members of the court were due to enter.

My pounding heart was just beginning to settle down when my opponent entered, looked at me in puzzlement, and said: "Mr. Gibson, you're on the wrong side of the courtroom!" The librarian's directions had been from the judges' perspective! So I scrambled to shift everything across the aisle, any confidence I might previously have felt in complete tatters, and slumped breathless into my chair just moments before the clerk summoned us all to rise for the entry of the nine awesomely-attired members of Canada's highest court.

In those rather less regimented days, not many Canadian courts imposed time limits on hearings. This included the Supreme Court of Canada, and I had been informed by the Court Clerk's office that the case ahead of us was still in progress. "Thank God!" I thought, "I can at least catch my breath." But the barristers contending ahead of us – both aging QCs – provided me with much more than breathing space. They were terrible! They droned and stuttered and stumbled, while the judges yawned but appeared nevertheless to be listening; and I began to realize that I could not possibly be as bad as they were.

About mid-afternoon, the Chief Justice interrupted the proceedings and said something like "Since it seems likely that this case will occupy most of the afternoon, counsel waiting for the next case to be heard might as well go home and come back tomorrow morning."

Wow! I returned to the hotel, had an early – though sumptuous and wine-filled – dinner (after all, I'd had no lunch), and went straight to bed thereafter. The next morning, after arising early to review my argument and breakfasting well, I strolled back to the Court, donned my borrowed gown, and took my (correct) place at counsel table, considerably less nervous than on the previous day.

I opened my argument in the same way the factum prepared by the lawyer I was replacing had – with a summary of the legislation applicable to the situation – and was almost immediately met with a question from the bench. Halfway through my response to that question, another judge fired another question at me, my answer to which was interrupted by a third query from yet another member of the court about something else. It was obvious that the judges were restless about something. And all three questions seemed to be less about legislative detail than about my client's basic complaint.

Now, it is a fundamental rule of litigation ethics that lawyers are forbidden to refer in court to facts that are not either disclosed in the trial court testimony or are commonly known by all humankind. And I had not had time, given my teaching responsibilities, to read the transcripts of the trial evidence before flying to Ottawa; so I did not know what was, and what was not, contained therein.

I did know, however, what the lawyer in whose place I was appearing had told me as to why his client was suing the employer; and I decided that, at the risk of possibly getting myself into deep trouble with the Court and my Law Society, I needed to explain the basic importance of both my client's basic complaint as I understood it (hoping against hope that what I said could be found in the recorded evidence) and the rather dry procedural grounds upon which its claim had been rejected.

So I stepped back from the podium and said something like: "Perhaps it would assist the Court if I explain why my client brought this matter to the courts. The chief legal issue involved is a very important one concerning overtime wage laws in Manitoba. My client sued this employer because the employer has been getting around the law requiring time-and-a-half wages for overtime work by means of a compensation scheme – my client calls it a scam – that pays $X per hour "wages" for <u>regular</u> work hours, <u>plus</u> an alleged "bonus" of $Y per hour. In the case of overtime work, however, although a time-and-a- half "wage" is indeed paid as required by law, <u>there is no "bonus."</u> In the result, my client and his fellow employees receive precisely the same amount of money for overtime work as for regular work!

"But when my client attempted to have the legality of this evasive scheme determined by the Manitoba Court of Appeal, they were prevented from doing so by the Court's application of several procedural rules that I hope to persuade your Lordships were not properly applicable to the situation."

To my intense relief, my opponent did not attempt to refute or object to what I had said, and the judges seemed to relax thereafter, settling back in their chairs, and listening to my presentation concerning the procedural grounds on which my client lost in the Court of Appeal with few further interruptions. Although I had no idea whether I was persuading them, either during my main presentation or by my rebuttal of my opponent's very competent presentation for the respondent, I felt that my contentions were understood and considered relevant by all members of the bench.

Then when, after the session was over, the judges had retired, and my opponent and I were re-packing our briefcases in the otherwise empty courtroom, a clerk came down the aisle and handed me a slip of paper. It was a form used by the judges to request books from the library, and read as follows:

**BOOKS REQUIRED FROM SUPREME COURT LIBRARY**
BY MR. JUSTICE MARTLAND
I CONGRATULATE YOU ON A CLEAR ARGUMENT WELL PRESENTED.
K. M.

The unbolded text was handwritten in pencil. Justice Martland was widely considered to be the strongest member of the Court at the time, and I was totally gob-smacked that he had taken the trouble to congratulate me on my first significant venture in advocacy. Was it because he'd never before been addressed in court by an apparent 17-year-old? As I later told the lawyer who had taken the risk on me, I almost felt as though I could fly home without the aid of an airplane. I framed the note, and it has been on my office or study wall ever since.

More good news followed in due course. The Supreme Court ruled completely in our favour and awarded our client substantial court costs! Then, after consulting the client, my instructing lawyer informed me that the award of court costs – a much larger sum than I had expected to be awarded – would be paid entirely to me for my services! How could a lawyer's first court case possibly have gone better?

# Index of Poems

| | |
|---|---|
| 249 Ottawa Ave. | Feb/91 |
| A Conceptual Bestiary | *circa* 2017 |
| A Rose from the Dead – Ronsard's HouseAt Comeau Abbey | Nov/77, Jan/78, Sep/79 |
| A Winter Morning at Mistik Ridge | After 1998; Dale had created a coyote from etched plexiglass which attracted living animals, here, a deer; see photo. |
| Abandoned Village Near Aberfan August 1966 | Feb/68, Jan/77, Jul/83 |
| Accommodating the French | Nov/68, Jan/77 |
| After the Play (Niagara-on-the-Lake) | Jul/01 |
| Alone | Sep/87 |
| Ann's Funeral | Mar/16 |
| April 14, 1991-April 14, 2001 | May 26/01 |
| April in Ottawa | 2002 |
| Archeologists, Historians & Old Farts Rule | Oct/14 |
| A Rose from the Dead – Ronsard's House at Comeau Abbey | Nov/77, Jan/78, Sep/79 |
| At the Butterfly House | Oct 13/96 (at the Devonian Gardens) |
| Atoms [or: Decision] | Jan/91 (in Winnipeg), Apr/98 |
| August | Aug/85 (at Minaki) |
| Autokleptia | Dec/11 |
| Baskets | *circa* 1982 ("Gene Blues") |
| Bayeux Tapestry | Aug/77, Jan/78, Nov/78, Mar/79, Jul/83 |
| Beasts of Academe | Mar/06 |
| Before the Flowers | Apr/94 |
| Beyond | May/89, Sep/89, Jan/90 (Edmonton) |
| Can You Hear? | Undated |
| Can't Be Sure (For Mo) | Jun 28/03 |
| Chartres Blues | Dec/79, Jan/80, Feb/80, May/80 |
| Collision Course | Mar/91 (Winnipeg), Apr/98 |
| Crossroads | Undated |

| | |
|---|---|
| Death of an Artist (On reading LeonardCohen's "Death of A Lady's Man") | Dec/78, Mar/79, Apr/79, Sep/79 |
| Devon Dawn I | Dec 6/98 |
| Devon II | Feb 21/99, Jul 17/99 |
| Devon Dawn III (Howl(s)) | Mar 21/99, 7:00 a.m., Jul 18/99 |
| Dilemma | Dec/11 |
| Don Quixote's Mid-Life Crisis | Oct/12, Nov/12 |
| Eating lunch in my car | Undated |
| Ecocracy [August Styles] | Aug/86 (Minaki) |
| Eiffel Tower | Nov/97 |
| End Game | *circa* May/96 |
| Endgame | May 10/02 |
| Epilogue | Jul/84 |
| Fairhaven Beach State Park | Aug/97 |
| Farewell to Former Friends | Oct 8/17 |
| Firefly or Star? | Aug 72, Dec 82 |
| Fe(de)ral Bureaucrat | Oct/94 |
| Fires of Iceland | *circa* 2018 |
| Flowers became beads | Apr 10/01 |
| Ford's Theatre, Washington | Apr/80, Aug/80, Jan/81, Dec/82, Feb/90 |
| Frank Scott | Feb/68, Jan/77, Oct/79, Jun/83, Apr/98 |
| Frank Scott, Moving, And Things | *Journal*, Aug/01 |
| Future Imperfect | Sep/Nov/85 |
| Generational | Jan/08 |
| Genuine Pariahs | *Journal*, Jul 5/94 |
| Glacier Park by Helicopter | Aug/95 |
| Going to the Cottage to Get Some Work Done | May 7/70 |
| Good Friday | Apr 21/00 |
| Grafenegg | May/96 (Northern Austria) |
| He was only 16 | Undated |
| Hey Leonard | After 2017 |
| High Art | Jan/74, Aug/74, Mar/78 |

| | |
|---|---|
| Homecoming Away From Home | *Journal*, May 22/16 (during a Winnipeg trip) |
| I've got the flu | Undated |
| If You Walk Fast | Aug/89 (at Minaki) |
| If You walk on Bloor Street | Undated |
| In Music | Undated |
| Irish Stones: Altar Rock | *Journal*, Jun 11/00 |
| Irish Stones: As With Tombs | 2001 |
| Irish Stones: Famine Cemetery | *Journal*, June 14/00 (near Newcastle West, Ireland) |
| Irish Stones: Yeats | *circa* 2001 |
| It was a turbulent night | Undated |
| It's in Me | Sep/06 |
| Julian Barnes Isn't a Writer | Journal, May 9/05 |
| King's College Choir Boys | Aug/89, Dec/89 |
| Lake Agnes | Aug/90, May/98 |
| Lake S hore – Early Evening [3] | Aug/80, Jan/81, Jun/82, Jul/83, Jan/90 |
| Late Afternoon, Edmonton | May/90 [imprinted on the drawing] |
| Loons are Laughing | Jul/81, Dec/82, Jan/90 |
| Lower Bankhead | *circa* 2018 |
| Manitoba Magpies | *circa* late 1980s |
| March Butterfly | Apr/72, Jan/77, Oct/78, Jan/81, Dec/82[imprinted on the drawing] |
| Metamorphoses | May/96 (Prague) |
| Microcosmos | Feb, Mar/97 |
| Mobius | Jan, Jun/83 |
| Mrs. C's Ashes | Aug/86 |
| My dear Lady Swan | *circa* 1990 |
| Near where | Undated |
| North of Balleyvaughen | Jun/00 |
| October Sunrise | Oct/07 |
| Omelettes | Jan/97 |
| One Prairie Province Conference | Aug/70, Aug/74, Jan /77 |
| Paleo – Love | Aug/90 |
| Past Perfect...Either /Or...And | Jul/83 |

| | |
|---|---|
| Peace River Road | *Journal*, Feb 11-17/91, Apr/98 |
| Pigeon Talk | Jun/92 |
| Pisew Falls in Winter | Jan/83, Jun/83, Jun/87 |
| Poems are the least of things | Undated |
| Policy Evaluation Seminar [1] | Nov/68, Aug/74, Jul/83 |
| Policy Evaluation Seminar [2] | Nov/68, Aug/74, Jul/83, Feb/90 |
| Prairie Dragon | Feb/79, Oct/79, Aug/83 |
| Pueblo Ladders | *Journal*, Dec 31/97 (in Santa Fé) |
| Red River Saga | *circa* 2017 |
| Repast | Undated |
| Richard the Turd | Feb/95 |
| Rocky Mountains | Jun/75, Jan/78 |
| Running | Jul/83 |
| Sandra by Moonlight | Sep/95 |
| Sandra, my Love | Feb/97 |
| Schizography | Dec/83, Jul/85, Dec/85, Aug/86, Sep/86 |
| Seeming to Return/ Mirages | Jul/95, Jan/96 |
| Senior Partner | Jun/94 |
| September/Walking to the Class | Undated |
| Seven Dales | Jan/12 |
| Shards | Mar/97 |
| Shazam! | early 1960's, revised Aug/74 |
| Singapore Street | May/73, Jul/83 |
| So long as the rivers flow | Undated |
| Some Say Law | Sep/77 |
| Something beside me | *Journal,* Jun 5-12/90 |
| Somewhere Between | Jul/84, Aug/86 |
| Sorting Myself Out | Undated |
| Spirit Sands: Spruce Woods Provincial Park | Aug/97 |
| Spring in the Vineyard | Apr 30/99 (Niagara-on-the-Lake) |
| Spring Vine | Jan/72 |
| Squaring the Great Circle | *Journal,* Jun 25/15 (flying to Geneva on KLM) |

| | |
|---|---|
| Stone and Feathers | *circa* 2017 ("see my drawing in Sandra's and my dining room") |
| Stonehenge | Oct/83, Dec/83, Jun/84, Feb/85, Aug/85, Nov/85, Aug/86 |
| Swimming in Rain | Jul/82, Jun/83 |
| Swimming Stones: Quadra Island | Oct/79, Mar/80, May/80, Dec/82 |
| Symbol Searching for a Poet | Aug/17/93 |
| Taras Shevchenko sits | *circa* 2018 |
| The Birds | Mar/92 |
| The Canadian Charter of Rights and Freedoms | Undated |
| The Clerics Explain Cycle | Undated |
| The Client | Feb/24, Jul 18/99 |
| The Day I Became an Atheist | Undated |
| The Dual Aspect Tango: Part I: Ultra Vires | Jan/81 (by Dale Gibson) |
| The Dual Aspect Tango: Part II: An Aroused Response | Jan/81 (by Class 2B) |
| The Foreigner | 91/92 |
| The Free Enterprise Pussy-Willow | Feb, Apr/77 |
| The Game | Undated |
| The Lawyer and the Poet | May/76, Jul/83 |
| The library | Undated |
| The Magic Hat | Jan/71 |
| The Magnets | Aug/90 |
| The Night My Mother Didn't Die | Feb 1/87 (in Auckland) |
| The Rising Sun [or: Decision] | Apr 13/91 (in Winnipeg) |
| The stone, you see, wasn't thrown | Undated; referring to an incident circa 1939; described in an essay, "The Beach" |
| The symbolism | Apr/81, Dec/82 |
| The Wall | *Journal*, Apr 19/13 (on seeing the Great Wall of China) |
| Thoughts of Calmness by the Athabasca River | Undated |
| Three for Frank – I Past Perfect | Jul/83, Sep/09, Oct/12 |
| Three for Frank – II Either/Or | Jul/83, Sep/09, Oct/12 |
| Three for Frank – III And | Jul/83, Sep/09, Oct/12 |

| | |
|---|---|
| Tin Ear | Mar/85, May/85, Aug/86 |
| To Dale, with Profoundest Love | Feb/95 [by Sandra] |
| Total Eclipse | Undated |
| Unsure Weather | *Journal*, Apr 11/15 |
| Upon a Hill (1) | May/95 |
| Upon a Hill (2) | May, Jun/95 |
| Viet Nam Memorial | Apr/91, Sep/14 (Washington, D.C.) |
| Walking in Brilliance | Feb/85, May/85, Jun/85, Sep/86 |
| Walking into a Glass Door | *Journal*, Feb 21 - Mar 3/91 |
| Walking on Water/ Water Walkers | Undated |
| Washington, D. C., I. Cherry Blossoms | Apr 7/91 |
| Washington, D. C., II. Jefferson Memorial | Apr/91 |
| West of Saskatoon | Aug 13/88 |
| What Have I Learned? | *circa* 2008 |
| What Was He Trying To Prove? | *Journal*, Apr 17/13 (on seeing China's Terra Cotta Warriors) |
| What's Left | Undated |
| Why Dress? | Aug/90 |
| Wild Violets | Spring/99 (at Mistik Ridge) |
| Winnipeg Blizzard | Jan, Feb/75 |
| Winnipeg International Airport | Feb 15/68 |
| Winnipegers are Masochists | Undated |
| Winter is Finished | Apr/98 |
| Winter Magpies | Dec/95 |
| Winter Night | Oct/68 |
| World without End | Mar/75 |
| Yesterday I killed a bird, | Undated [circa mid-1970s; Dale was traumatized when he shot the bird and vowed never to hunt again] |
| You sang for me | *circa* 1991 |
| Your present is | dated "1991/2" by Dale [by Sandra] |

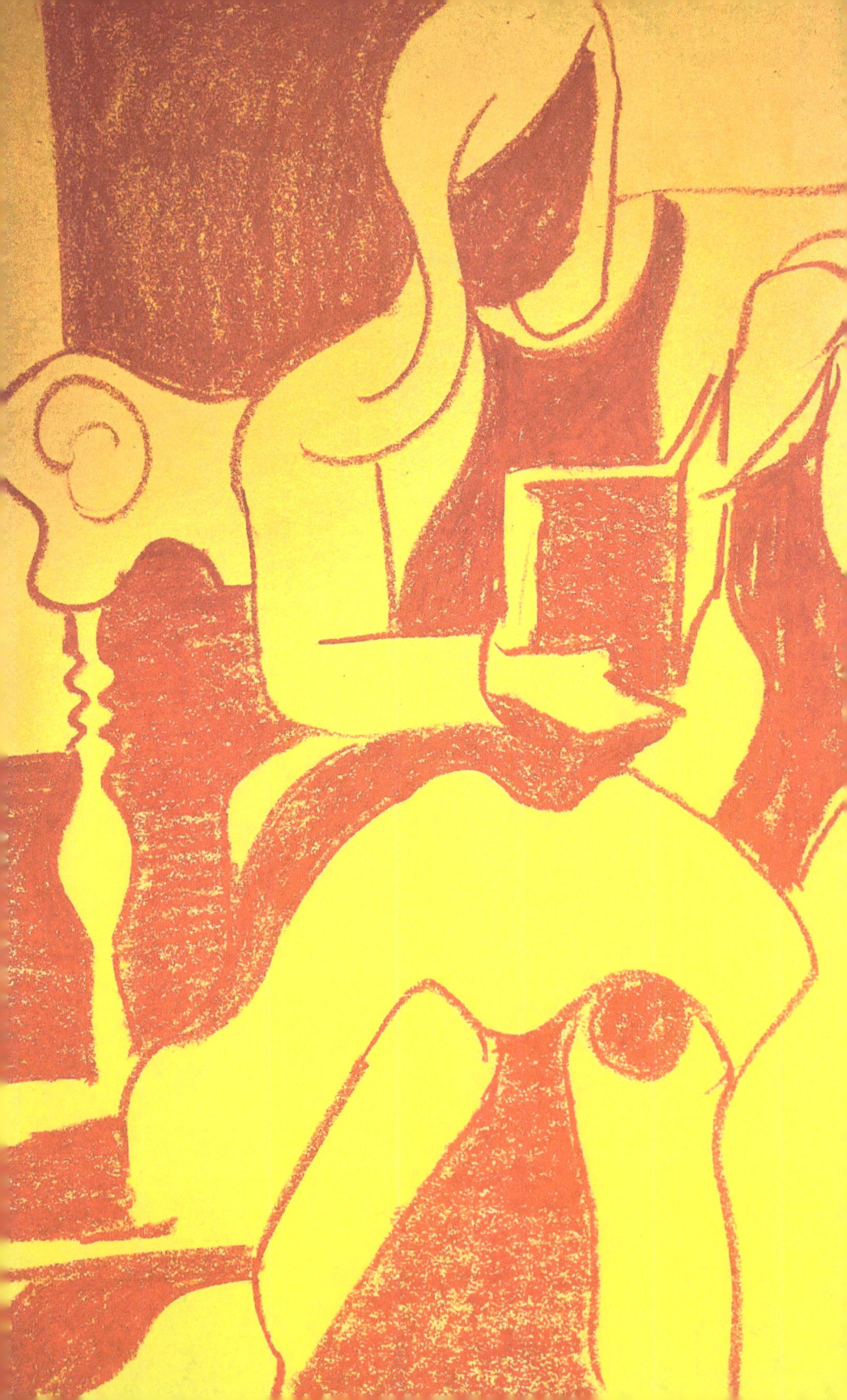

# Curriculum Vitae
## Ronald Dale Gibson

### EDUCATION

| | | | |
|---|---|---|---|
| B.A. | - | 1954 | - United College, University of Manitoba |
| LL.B. | - | 1958 | - Manitoba Law School, University of Manitoba |
| LL.M. | - | 1959 | - Harvard Law School |

### CALL TO THE BAR:

Manitoba  -  1959

Alberta -  1991

### ACADEMIC APPOINTMENTS:

| | |
|---|---|
| Assistant Professor, Manitoba Law School (U. of M.) | 1959-1964 |
| Associate Professor, Manitoba Law School (U. of M.) | 1964-1968 |
| Professor, Faculty of Law, University of Manitoba | 1968-1991 |
| Belzberg Professor of Constitutional Studies, University of Alberta | 1988-1991 |
| Bowker Professor of Law, University of Alberta | 1991-1993 |
| Belzberg Fellow of Constitutional Studies, Faculty of Law, University of Alberta | 1993-2001 |

### PRACTICE OF LAW:

| | |
|---|---|
| Canadian Pacific Railway Law Department | 1958 |
| Mackling and Gibson, Winnipeg | 1959-1966 |
| Consulting practice, Winnipeg | 1966-1991 |
| Milner Fenerty, Edmonton | 1991-1994 |
| Sole practice, Edmonton | 1994-1995 |
| Dale Gibson Associates, Edmonton | 1995-2000 |
| Dale Gibson, Consulting Barrister, Edmonton | 2000-2007 |

## OTHER APPOINTMENTS:

| | |
|---|---|
| Founding Editor, Manitoba Law Journal | 1963-1966 |
| Constitutional Consultant, Government of Canada | 1969-1970, 1980-1981 |
| Constitutional Consultant, Government of Manitoba | 1970-1977, 1982-1987 |
| Constitutional Consultant, Yukon Government | 1988-1989, 1995-1996 |
| Chairman, Study Group on the Canadian Constitution | 1970-1975 |
| Chairman, Legal Research Institute, University of Manitoba | 1968-1982 |
| Director, Archives of Manitoba Legal History | 1970-1980 |
| Member, Manitoba Law Reform Commission | 1971-1979 |
| Chairperson, Manitoba Human Rights Commission | 1982-1984 |
| Chair, Canadian Association of Statutory Human Rights Agencies | 1983-1984 |
| Manitoba Official Representative, Federal-Provincial Continuing Committee of Human Rights Officials | 1982-1984 |
| Director, Legal History Project, University of Manitoba | 1990-1991 |
| Consultant and Writer, Royal Commission on Aboriginal People | 1994-1995 |

## AWARDS

| | |
|---|---|
| University of Manitoba and Law Society of Manitoba Gold Medals in Law | 1958 |
| University of Manitoba Rh Institute Grant for Outstanding Contributions to Scholarship & Research in the Social Sciences | 1975 |
| Designated "Distinguished Professor" University of Manitoba | 1984 |
| Elected Fellow of the Royal Society of Canada | 1985 |
| Law Reform Commission of Canada/Canadian Association of Law Teachers Award for Contributions to Legal Research and Reform | 1986 |
| Manitoba Association for Rights and Liberties Volunteer Medal | 1988 |
| Appointed Belzberg Professor of Constitutional Law, University of Alberta | 1988 |
| Appointed "Distinguished Professor of Law Emeritus" University of Manitoba | 2005 |
| Edmonton Bar Association Distinguished Service Award | 2006 |

# BOOKS:

*Substantial Justice - Law & Lawyers in Manitoba 1670 – 1970*, with Lee Gibson
    Winnipeg, Peguis Press (1972)

Aspects of Privacy Law: Essays in Honour of John M. Sharp, Editor and
    Contributor
    Toronto, Butterworths, 1980

The Role of the United Kingdom in the Amendment of the Canadian
    Constitution
        background monograph (unattributed) prepared for Jean Crétien,
        Minister of Justice for Canada
        Ottawa, [Government] Publications Canada, March, 1981, and
        News Release, Minister of Justice and Attorney General of Canada,
        March 24, 19[81, on which Dale wrote: "Blurb for the pamphlet ["The
        Role of the United Kingdom," etc.] I wrote for Chrétien's signature.
        DG"

Attorney for the Frontier: Enos Stutsman, with Lee Gibson and Cameron
    Harvey
    Winnipeg, University of Manitoba Press, 1983

Law In a Cynical Society: Opinion and Law in the 1980's, Editor and
    Contributor, with Janet Baldwin
    Calgary, Carswell, 1985

The Law of the Charter: General Principles
    Calgary, Carswell, 1986

The Law of the Charter, Equality Rights
    Agincourt, Ontario, Carswell, 1990

Glimpses of Canadian Legal History, Editor, with Wesley Pue
    Winnipeg, Legal Research Institute, University of Manitoba, 1991

The Bear That Wouldn't Dance: Failed Attempts to Reform the Constitution
    of the Former Soviet Union, Editor and Collaborator with Alexander
    Yakovlev
    Winnipeg, Legal Research Institute, University of Manitoba, 1992

Law, Life & Government at Red River, Vol. 1: Settlement and Governance,
    1812-1872
    Montreal & Kingston, McGill Queens University Press, 2015.

Law, Life & Government at Red River: 1844-1872, Vol. 2: Annotated Records
    of the General Quarterly Court of Assiniboia
    Montreal & Kingston, McGill Queens University Press, 2015.

Peter of the Prairies: the 19th Century Red River Diaries of Peter Garrioch,
    Fur Trader, Teacher, Contrarian, Smuggler, Trail-Blazer, editor and
    annotator, completed by Sandra M. Anderson
    Edmonton, PageMaster Publishing, 2025.

# PUBLICATIONS:

(excluding newspaper articles, broadcast scripts, and some unpublished conference presentations)

- "Remoteness of Damage in Tort"
  (1962) 34, 2 Manitoba Bar News 33

- "The Wagon Mound in Canadian Courts"
  (1963) 2 Osgoode Hall L. J. 416

- "The Status of Certified Cheques - A Choice of Analogies"
  (1964) 35(1) Manitoba Bar News 1

- "The B.C. Power Case: New Restrictions in Provincial Control over Federal Companies"
  (1963) 2 Manitoba L. J. 155

- "Liability for Damage Caused by Dogs"
  (1964) 42 Canadian Bar Review 143

- "Province of Ontario Report of the Joint Committee on Legal Aid"
  (1964-65) Manitoba L. J. 306

- "Let's Abolish Guest Passinger Legislation"
  (1965) Manitoba Bar News 274

- "An Ombudsman for Manitoba"
  (1966) 2(1) Manitoba L. J. 61

- "An Ombudsman for Manitoba" + "Appendices"
  (1966) 35 (15) Manitoba Bar News 467;
  (1966) 36(1) Manitoba Bar News 1

- "Torts"
  (1966) 2(1) Manitoba L. J. 130

- "Constitutional Law – Federalizing the Judiciary"
  (1966) 44 Canadian Bar Review 674

- "Civil Disobedience and the Legal Profession"
  (1966) 31 Saskatchewan Bar Review 211

- "The Fulton-Favreau Formula in Manitoba"
  (1966-67) 12(4) McGill L. J. 485

- "Constitutional Amendment and the Implied Bill of Rights"
  (1966-67) 12(4) McGill L. J. 497

- "Torts"
  (1967) 2(2) Manitoba L. J. 277

- "Constitutional Law"
  (1967) 2(2) Manitoba L. J. 283

- "Non-Fault Automobile Insurance"
  (1968) Canadian Bar Journal 172

- "Guest Passenger Discrimination"
  (1968) 6(2) Alberta Law Review 211

- "A New Alphabet of Negligence"
  in: A.M. Linden (ed.) Studies in Canadian Tort Law, Toronto, Butterworths, 1968, 189

- "Privacy & Commercial Reporting Agencies"
  Pamphlet with John M. Sharp (1968)

- "The Forensic Lottery: A Critique on Tort Liability as a System of Personal Injury Compensation, by Terence G. Ison"
  (1968) 46 Canadian Bar Review 321

- "The Judicial Committee and the British North America Act – An Analysis of the Interpretative Scheme for the Distribution of Legislative Powers, by G. P. Browne."
  (1968) 46 Canadian Bar Review 153

- "Constitutional Aspects of Water Management," 2 vols., Editor of essays
  (1969) Agassiz Centre for Water Studies, University of Manitoba, Vol. II.

- "The Constitutional Context of Canadian Water Planning"
  (1969) 7(1) Alberta Law Review 71

- "Interjurisdictional Immunity in Canadian Federalism"
  (1969) 47 Canadian Bar Review 40

- "Torts – Illegality of Plaintiff's Conduct as a Defence"
  (1969) 47 Canadian Bar Review 89

- "Legal Education in Manitoba"
  (1969) Pamphlet

- "Robson Hall – Faculty of Law, University of Manitoba"
  (1969) Pamphlet

- "Techniques of Law Reform," with C. Sharp
  (1969) Pamphlet, Legal Research Institute, University of Manitoba

- "Constitutional Jurisdiction over Environmental Management in Canada"
  (1973) 23 U. Toronto L. J. 53 (reprinted in revised form in: O.P.

Dwivedi (ed.) Protecting the Environment, Toronto, Copp Clark, 1974 page #

- "Canadian Negligence Law, by Allen M. Linden"
  (1973) 23 University of Toronto L. J. 373

- "Unobtrusive Justice - Mr. Justice R.G.B. Dickson"
  (1974) 12(2) Osgoode Hall L. J. 339

- "Legal Education - Past and Future"
  (1974) 6(1) Manitoba L. J. 21

- "And One Step Backward - The Supreme Court and Constitutional Law in the Sixties"
  (1975) 53 Canadian Bar Review 621

- "The Trial of Guillaume Sayer" - script for an audio-visual presentation - University of Manitoba, 1975

- "The 'Federal Enclave' Fallacy in Canadian Constitutional Law"
  (1976) 14 Alberta Law Review 167

- "Measuring 'National Dimensions' - The Federal Peace, Order and Good Government Power"
  (1976) 7(2) Manitoba L. J. 15

- "Power of Provincial Courts to Determine Constitutionality of Federal Legislation"
  (1976) 54 Canadian Bar Review 372

- "A Good Case for Raising [Constitutional] Ceilings"
  (1977) 1(2) Canadian Lawyer 14

- "Common Law Protection of Privacy: What to Do Until the Legislators Arrive,"
  in: Lewis Klar (ed.), Studies in Canadian Tort Law, (Butterworths), 1977, Chapter 12, 343

- "An Anecdotal Sampler,"
  in: C. Harvey (ed.), The Law Society of Manitoba: 1877-1977 (1977), Chapter 9, 191

- "A Comment on Athans v. Canadian Adventure Camps - Appropriation of Personal Attributes"
  (1978) 4 Canadian Cases on the Law of Torts 37

- "The High Court Leans to the Right – Again"
  (1978) 2(4) Canadian Lawyer 16

- "Repairing the Law of Damages"
  (1978) 8(4) Manitoba L. J. 637

- "Torts - Negligence and Occupiers Liability - Role of Jury - Confusing Words from the Oracle"
  (1978) 56 Canadian Bar Review 693

- "Charter or Chimera - A Comment on the Proposed Canadian Charter of Rights and Freedoms"
  (1979) 9(4) Manitoba L. J. 363

- "The Right to be Left Alone: Legal Protections of Privacy in Canada"
  in: R. St. J. Macdonald and J.P. Humphrey (eds.) The Practice of Freedom,
  (1979), 179

- "Report of the Citizens' Task Force on the Manitoba Human Rights Act"
  Chairperson and Author (1979) A Report Prepared for the Manitoba Association of Rights
  and Liberties

- "The New Tort of Discrimination: A Blessed Event for the Great-Grandmother of Torts"
  (1980) 11 Canadian Cases on the Law of Torts 141

- "Regulating the Personal Reporting Industry," Chapter 5
  in: Dale Gibson (ed.), Aspects of Privacy Law: Essays in Honour of John M. Sharp, Toronto, Butterworths, 1980, 111

- "Stare Decisis and The Action Per Quod Servitium Amisit - Refusing to Follow the Leader: R. v. Buchinsky"
  (1980) 13 Canadian Cases on the Law of Torts 309

- "The Constitutional Position of Local Government in Canada"
  (1980) 11 Manitoba L. J. 1

- "Comments on Submissions to Kershaw Committee [Foreign Affairs Committee of the British House of Commons]," submitted to R. Tassé, Deputy Attorney-General from Dale Gibson, March 17, 1981 (unpublished)

- "Interpretation of the Canadian Charter of Rights and Freedoms: Some General Considerations, Chapter 2
  in: Walter S. Tarnopolsky and Gérald-A. Beaudoin (eds.), The Canadian Charter of Rights and Freedoms: Commentary, Toronto, Carswell, 1982, 25

- "Enforcement of the Canadian Charter of Rights and Freedoms," 2nd version, with Scott Gibson, Chapter 16 in: Walter S. Tarnopolsky and Gérald-A. Beaudoin (eds.), The Canadian Charter of Rights and Freedoms: Commentary, Toronto, Carswell, 1982, 489, and in: Gérald-A. Beaudoin and Ed Ratushny (eds.), The Canadian Charter of Rights and Freedoms, Second Edition, Toronto, Carswell, 1989, 781

- "The Charter of Rights and the Private Sector"
  (1982) 12(1) Manitoba L. J. 213

- Discrimination and Unfair Hiring Practices in Making University Appointments, chairperson & principal author
 (1982) A Report prepared for Canadian Association of University Teachers

- Impact of Canadian Charter of Rights and Freedoms on Manitoba Statutes, supervisor & author
 (1982) A Report prepared for the Legal Research Institute, University of Manitoba, and Attorney-General of Manitoba

- "Dale Gibson – You helped make it happen. Barry S." Note inscribed on: "The Patriation and Legitimacy of the Canadian Constitution" by B. L Strayer, Assistant Deputy Minister (Public Law), Department of Justice
 (1982) Dean Emeritus F. C. Cronkite, Q. C. Memorial Lectures, College of Law, University of Saskatchewan, 3rd series,

- "Constitutional Arrangements for Environmental Protection and Enhancement Under a New Canadian Constitution"
 in: Stanley M. Beck and Ivan Bernier (eds.) Canada and the New Constitution: the Unfinished Agenda, Institute for Research on Public Policy, 1983, Vol. 2, 113

- "Determining Disrepute: Opinion Polls and the Canadian Charter of Rights and Freedoms," with Kristin Lercher & Steven Vincent
 (1983) 61 Canadian Bar Review 377

- "Shocking the Public: Early Indications of the Meaning of 'Disrepute' in Section 24(2) of the Canadian Charter of Rights and Freedoms"
 (1983) 13(4) Manitoba L. J. 495

- Distinguishing the Governors from the Governed: The Meaning of 'Government' Under Section 32(1) of the Canadian Charter of Rights and Freedoms"
 (1983) 13(4) Manitoba L. J. 505

- "Developments in Tort Law: The 1983-84 Term"
 (1985) 7 Supreme Court Law Review 387

- "Public Opinion and Law: Dicey to Today"
 in: Dale Gibson and Janet Baldwin (eds.), Law in a Cynical Society: Opinion and Law in the 1980's, with Janet Baldwin, Calgary, Carswell, 1985, 1

- "Teaching Human Rights in Canada, chairperson and principal author
 (1985) A Report Prepared for the Continuing Federal/ Provincial/ Territorial Committee of Officials Responsible for Human Rights in Canada

- "Protection of Minority Rights Under Canadian Charter of Rights and Freedoms: Can Politicians and Judges Sing Harmony?"
 in: Neil Nevitte and Allan Kornberg (eds.) Minorities and the Canadian State, Oakville, Mosaic, 1985, 31

- "Protection of Minority Rights Under Canadian Charter of Rights and Freedoms: Can Politicians and Judges Sing Harmony?" (revised) (1985) 8(2) Hamline Law Review 343 [St. Paul, MN]

- "Stereotypes, Statistics and Slippery Slopes: A Reply to Professors Flanagan & Knopff and Other Critics of Human Rights Legislation" in: Neil Nevitte and Allan Kornberg (eds.) Minorities and the Canadian State, Oakville, Mosaic, 1985, 125

- "Reasonable Limits Under the Canadian Charter of Rights and Freedoms" (1985) 15(1) Manitoba L. J. 27

- "The 'Special Nature' of Human Rights Legislation: Re Winnipeg School Division and Craton" (1985-86) 50(1) Saskatchewan Law Review 175

- "Accentuating the Positive and Eliminating the Negative: Remedies for Inequality under the Canadian Charter" in: Lynn Smith et al. (eds.), Righting the Balance: Canada' s New Equality Rights, Selection of papers originally presented at the National Symposium on Equality Rights in January 1985 in Toronto, Saskatoon, Canadian Human Rights Reporter, 1986, 311

- "Developments in Tort Law: The 1984-85 Term" (1986) 8 Supreme Court Law Review 357

- "Reliance on Unconstitutional Laws: The Saving Doctrines and Other Protections" (with Kristin Lercher) (1986) 15 Manitoba L. J. 305

- "Developments in Tort Law: The 1985-86 Term" (1987) 9 Supreme Court Law Review 455

- "The Rule of Non-Law: Implications of the Manitoba Language Reference" Transactions, Royal Society of Canada, 1986

- "The Rule of Non-Law: Some Implications of the Manitoba Language Reference" (1986) V, 1 Transactions of the Royal Society of Canada 31

- "Canadian Equality Jurisprudence: Year One" in: Sheilah L. Martin and Kathleen E. Mahoney, eds., Equality and Judicial Neutrality, Toronto, Carswell, 1987, 128

- "Blind Justice and Other Legal Myths: The Lies That Law Lives By" (1987) Dalhousie Review 432

- "Tort Law and the Charter of Rights" (1987) 16(1) Manitoba L. J. 1

- "Judges as Legislators: Not Whether but How" (1987) 25(2) Alberta Law Review 249

- "So What Can Be Done About It? An Overview of Charter Remedies," Chapter 9
  in: Gérald-A. Beaudoin, ed., Charter Cases: 1986-7, Proceedings of the October, 1986, Colloquium of the Canadian Bar Association in Montreal, Cowansville, Québec, Éditions Yvon Blais, 1987, 225

- "Constitutional Entrenchment of Environmental Rights,"
  in Nicole Duplé, ed., Le Droit à la Qualité de l'Environnement: Un Droit en Devenir, un Droit à Définir, Fifth International Conference on Constitutional Law,
  Montreal, Éditions Québec/Amérique, 1988, 273

- "Constitutional Law - Public Funding for Denominational Secondary Schools - Are Some Supreme Laws More Supreme Than Others?"
  (1988) 67 Canadian Bar Review 142

- "What Did Dolphin Deliver?"
  in: Gérald-A. Beaudoin, ed., Your Clients and the Charter (1988), 57

- "The Free Trade Agreement and the Provinces: A Counter For the Sale of Constitutional Wares" in: M. Gold and D. Leyton-Bown, eds., Trade-Off on Free Trade (1988), 117

- "Can Lame Ducks Lay Golden Eggs? The Power of Defeated Governments to Make Binding Agreements"
  (1988) 17 Manitoba L. J. 324

- "Developments in Tort Law - The 1986-7 Term"
  (1988) 10 Supreme Court Law Review, 345

- "Domestic Models of Reform"
  In: The Canadian Senate: What is to be Done?, Proceedings of the National Conference on Senate Reform, May 5-6, 1988
  (1988) Centre for Constitutional Studies, University of Alberta, 95

- Not-So-White, The Ten Dwarfs, and The Nine Wise Ones:
  A Constitutional Fairy-Tale"
  (1989) 18 Manitoba L. J. 1

- "Senate Reform - The Case for Abolition," in The Canadian Senate (Proceedings of Alberta Centre for Constitutional Studies Conference on Senate Reform),
  (1989), 9

- "The Crumbling Pyramid: Constitutional Appeal Rights in Canada"
  (1989) 38 University of New Brunswick L. J. 1

- "Non-Destructive Charter Responses to Legislative Inequalities"
  (1989) 27 Alberta Law Review 181

- "The Clapman Omnibus Meets the Trudeau Express: Tort Implications of the Canadian Charter of Rights and Freedoms"
  (1989) Pitblado Lectures, Law Society of Manitoba

- "Equality Rights Under the Charter"
  (1989) Cambridge Lectures: Canadian Institute for Advanced Legal Studies)

- "The Nature of Equality: Apples and Oranges / Chests and Breasts"
  (1989) 1(1) Constitutional Forum 3

- "Starr Trek: The Unfinished Mission"
  (1990) 1(3) Constitutional Forum, 1

- The Real Laws of the Constitution"
  (1990) 28(2) Alberta Law Review 358

- "Section 27 of the Charter: More Than A 'Rhetorical Flourish'"
  (1990) 28(3) Alberta Law Review 589

- "Freedom of Commercial Expression Under the Charter: A.-G. Quebec v. Irwin Toy Ltd."
  (1990) 69 Canadian Bar Review 339

- "Scandal at Red River: The Case of the Judge and the Serving Girl"
  (Oct./ Nov. 1990) 70(5) The Beaver 30

- "Heritage Languages and the Constitution"
  in: D. Schneiderman (ed.) Language and the State: The Law and Politics of Identity, Cowansville, Québec, Éditions Yvon Blais, 1991, 313

- "Railroading the Train Robbers: Extradition in the Shadow of Annexation," with Lee & Scott Gibson
  in: Gibson and Pue (eds.) Glimpses of Canadian Legal History, Legal Research Institute, University of Manitoba, 1991, 71

- "Equality for Some"
  (1991) 40 University of New Brunswick L. J. 2

- "What Constitutes an Analogous Ground?"
  in: Third Annual Conference on Human Rights and the Charter, Department of Justice, June 21, 1991, Proceedings.

- "Analogous Grounds of Discrimination Under the Canadian Charter: Too Much Ado About Next to Nothing"
  (1991), 29(4) Alberta Law Review 772

- "Manifest Justice: A Biographical Sketch of Chief Justice Brian Dickson"
  in: Roland Penner (ed.) The Dickson Legacy, Winnipeg, Legal Research Institute, University of Manitoba, 1992, and (1991) 20(2) Manitoba L. J. 268

- "Now What?" Comment in Report, After Allaire and Bélanger-Compeau Symposium
  (1991) 3(1) Constitutional Forum 10

- "'As I see it, René...' said Sir John"
    (1991) 3(1) Constitutional Forum 18

- "Sir James Aikins' Seamless Web: Finding Fortune and Fame as a Lawyer in the Adolescent Canadian West," with Lee Gibson
    (1992) 21(2) Manitoba L. J. 161

- "Founding Fathers-in-Law: Judicial Amendment of the Canadian Constiution"
    (1992) 55 Law and Contemporary Problems, 261

- "Coping with Quasi-ness: Ombudsmen and Quasi-Judicial Tribunals"
    (1992) 10 Ombudsman Journal, 17; Re-printed in Linda C. Reif (ed.), The International Ombudsman Anthology, The Hague, Kluwer Law, 1999, 479

- "Breu Sinopsi de La Constitucid Del Canada,"
    in: Generalitat de Catalunya, Institut d'Estudis Autonòmics: Seminari Sobre "El Federalisme Canadenc," Barcelona, 1992

- "Constitutional Law ... Prostitution, Pimps, Presumptions and Preposterous Laws"
    (1992) 71 Canadian Bar Review 727

- "Fearful Symmetry: Constitutional Uniformity and the Federal Amendment Proposals"
    (1992) 3(3) Constitutional Forum 54

- "The Development of Federal Legal Institutions," Working Paper 92-17
    in: University of Manitoba Canadian Legal History Project (unpublished)

- "The Constitutionality of Christmas"
    (1992) Milner Fenerty Newsletter

- "Free Trade in Criminals: Canadian-American Extradition Before 1890,"
    in: W. Kaplan and D. McRae, Law, Policy, and International Justice: Essays in Honour of Maxwell Cohen, Montreal & Kingston, McGill Queens University Press, 1993, 144

- "The Deferential Trojan Horse: A Decade of Charter Decisions"
    (1993) 72(4) Canadian Bar Review 417

- "Endangered Species and the Parliament of Canada"
    Study for Sierra Legal Defence Fund, 1994, unpublished

- "The Canada Health Act and the Constitution"
    (1996) 4 Health Law Journal [Health Law Institute, University of Alberta], 1

- "Company Justice: Origins of Legal Institutions in Pre-Confederation Manitoba"
    (1996) 23(3) Manitoba L. J. 247; reprinted in D.J. Guth and W.W.

Pue (eds.): Canada's Legal Inheritances, Faculty of Law, University of Manitoba, 2001

- "Development of Federal Legal and Judicial Institutions in Canada" (1996) 23(3) Manitoba L. J. 450; reprinted in D.J. Guth and W.W. Pue (eds.): Canada's Legal Inheritances, Faculty of Law, University of Manitoba, 2001

- "Métis Rights and the Royal Commission on Aboriginal Peoples" (1996) Presentation to C.B.A. Constitutional and Aboriginal Law Subsections. (unpublished)

- "Notwithstanding Notwithstanding: How to Side-Step a Charter Opt-Out" (June 19, 1998) Lawyers Weekly

- "Monitoring Arbitrary Government Authority: Charter Scrutiny of Legislative, Executive and Judicial Privilege" (1998) 61(2) Saskatchewan. Law Review 297

- "Dickson and the Environment" in: DeLloyd J. Guth (ed.), Brian Dickson at the Supreme Court of Canada, Winnipeg, Supreme Court of Canada Historical Society, 1998, 175

- "Will the Supreme Court of Canada Restore Effective School Board Governance in Alberta?" in: W.F. Foster and W.J. Smith (eds.), Reaching for Reasonableness: The Educator as Lawful Decision-Maker, Montreal, Lisbro, 1999, 1

- "Constitutional Aspects of Canadian Administrative Law," with Ritu Khullar in: D.P. Jones and A.S. de Villars, Principles of Administrative Law (3d ed), Toronto, Carswell, 1999, 21

- "The Firearms Reference in the Alberta Court of Appeal" (1999) 37(4) Alberta Law Review 1071

- "Who may Drink from the Holy Grail? Charter Remedies by Administrative Tribunals" (November, 1999) Dale Gibson Associates (unpublished)

- "Constitutional Vibes: Reflections on the Secession Reference and the Unwritten Constitution" (1999) 11 National Journal of Constitutional Law 49

- "Paying the Piper without Calling the Tune: Legal and Policy Implications of Provincial Certification of Local Education Property Taxes" (1999) Presentation to Canadian Association for the Practical Study of Law and Education (CAPSLE) (unpublished)

- "Local Property Taxation, Equity, and Educational Excellence: A Position Paper Developed for Calgary Board of Education" (April, 1999) (unpublished)

- "Collective Labour Law in Canada, 1812-1982: The Branch Plant Has a Few Ideas of Its Own"
  in: Marcel Van der Linden and Richard Price (eds.), The Rise and Development of Collective Labour Law, Bern et al, Peter Lang, 2000, 97

- "Some Implications of Delgamuukw"
  (May 17, 2000) Presentation to Legal Education Society of Alberta (unpublished)

- "William Lightening v. Muskwachees Fire & Ambulance Authority Ltd.,"
  (March 1, 2001) Adjudication of Complaint of Unjust Dismissal under Canada Labour Code, Part III, Division XIV (unpublished)

- "Fulfilling the Promise of Bill C-31: Strategies for General Challenges. Case Development Report for Court Challenges Program of Canada," National Round Table – Bill C-31 Court Challenge, December 7-9, 2001 (May, 2001) (unpublished)

- "When is a Métis an Indian? Some Consequences of Federal Constitutional Jurisdiction over Métis," Chapter 7
  in: Paul L. A. H. Chartrand (ed.), Who are Canada's Aboriginal Peoples? Saskatoon, Purich Publishing (2002), 258

- "Teachers and their Families as School Trustees: Legislative Limits and Constitutional Rights"
  in: Law in Education: Help or Hindrance?, ed. Roderick Flynn, Proceedings of the Fourteenth Annual Conference of the Canadian Association for the Practical Study of Law and Education, held in Jasper, Alberta, April 27-30, 2003, Toronto, CAPSLE, 2004, 431

- "The Rights Balance in Public Education: Moving Tightropes and Variable Scales"
  (2004) Presentation to B. C. School Trustees Association AGM (unpublished)

- "Constitutional Aspects of Canadian Administrative Law"
  (with K. Hurlburt), (2005) 28S.C.L.R. (2d) 481, and in: D.P. Jones & Anne S. De Villars, Principles of Administrative Law (4th), Scarborough, Thomson/Carswell, 2004

- "Bible Bill and the Press Barons: The Alberta Origins of Canada's Implied Bill of Rights," Chapter 7
  in: Richard Connors & John M. Law (eds.) Forging Alberta's Constitutional Framework, Edmonton, University of Alberta Press, 2005, 191

- "Enforcement of the Canadian Charter of Rights and Freedoms," 3rd version with Scott Gibson, co-author of 2nd & 4th ed., & John Gee, co-author of 3rd ed. (2005) 28(2d) Supreme Court Law Review, 481, and in: Gérald-A. Beaudoin & Errol P. Mendes (eds.), Canadian Charter of Rights and Freedoms (3rd), Montreal, Wilson & Lafleur, 1996, 1085, and in: Gérald-A. Beaudoin & Errol P. Mendes (eds.), Canadian Charter of Rights and Freedoms (4th), Markham, Butterworths, 2005, 1323

- "History in the Courtroom: An Alberta/Saskatchewan Centennial Sampler,"
  paper prepared for Joint Meeting of Her Majesty's Superior Courts for the Provinces of Alberta and Saskatchewan
  (May 30-31, 2005) 66 pages, unpublished

- "The Supreme Court of Alberta Meets the Supreme Law of Canada: Constitutional Law in Alberta,"
  in: J. Swainger (ed.), The Alberta Supreme Court at 100: History and Authority, Edmonton and Toronto, University of Alberta Press and Osgoode Society, 2007, 99

- "Backing Into the Future: Law Practice in 2007"
  in: J. Watson (ed.), Just Works: Lawyers in Alberta, 1907-2007, Toronto, Irwin Law, 2007, 268

- "The People's Charter: Thoughts on the 25th Anniversary of the Canadian Charter of Rights & Freedoms"
  (April 16, 2007) Presentation at Edmonton City Hall (unpublished)

- "The Constitutional Right of Parents to Educate their Children and Alberta Education's Private School Evaluation Model"
  (March, 2008) unpublished

- "Independent Schools and the Law in Alberta: A Legislative and Constitutional Overview"
  (March, 2008) 68 pages, unpublished

- "Towers, Bridges and Basements: The Constitutional and Legal Architecture of Independent Schooling"
  (2010) 19 Education & Law Journal 155

- "Robson Hall, Faculty of Law – 100 Years,"
  Documentary CD, featuring interviews with Dale Gibson inter alia (who describes it in his Journal entry for October 12, 2014)
  (2012-2014) University of Manitoba

- "The First Hanged Was Indian: Capital Punishment in the Quarterly Court of Assiniboia,"
  in: Papers of the Rupert's Land Colloquium, 2008. CD. Winnipeg: Centre for Rupert's Land Studies, University of Winnipeg, May 14-16, 2008

- "Doing Justice in Rupert's Land: 1835-1870,"
  in: Papers of the Rupert's Land Colloquium, 2010. CD. Winnipeg,

- Centre for Rupert's Land Studies, University of Winnipeg, May 19-22, 2010

- "Louis Riel as Governor: 1869-70,"
  in: Selected Papers of the Rupert's Land Colloquium, 2012. CD. Winnipeg, Centre for Rupert's Land Studies, University of Winnipeg, May 16-19, 2012

- Self-help Justice in Rupert's Land"
  in: Selected Papers of the Rupert's Land Colloquium, 2014 Centre for Rupert's Land Studies, University of Winnipeg

## BOOK REVIEWS

- "The Life and Times of Confederation, by P. B. Waite" (1963) 41 Canadian Bar Review 488

- "Civil Liberties and the Constitution, by Paul G. Kauper" (1963) 41 Canadian Bar Review 316

- "The Function of Criminal Law in 1962, by J. D. Morton" (1963) 1(2) Manitoba L. J. 120

- "The Government of Manitoba, by M. S. Donnelly" (1963) 1(2) Manitoba L. J. 209

- "Manual of Motor Vehicle Law, by David B. Horsley" (1963) 1(2) Manitoba L. J. 214

- "Civil Liberties in Canada, by D. A. Schmeiser" (1965) 43 Canadian Bar Review 385

- "Law in Red River – Four Recorders of Rupert's Land, by Roy St. George Stubbs" (1967) 36 Manitoba Bar News 178

- "Pollution, Property and Prices, by J. H. Dales" (1969) 3(2) Manitoba L. J. 101

- "Judicial Review of Legislation in Canada, by B. L. Strayer" (1969) 3(2) Manitoba L. J. 107

- "In the Last Resort: A Critical Study of the Supreme Court of Canada, by Paul Weiler" (1974) 6(1) Manitoba L. J. 215

- "Attitudes Towards Crime and Punishment in Upper Canada, 1830-50, by J. M Beattie; The North-West Mounted Police and Law Enforcement, 1873-1905, by R. C. MacLeod" (1978) 8(3) Manitoba L. J. 611

- "Governmental and Intergovernmental Immunity in Australia and Canada, by Colin H. H. McNairn" (1978) 28 University of Toronto L. J. 445

- "Commentary on the British North America Act," by W. H. McConnell; Constitutional Law of Canada, by Peter W. Hogg" (1978) 56 Canadian Bar Review 533

- "History with Hyperbole without the Law: Administrative Justice and Legal Pluralism in Nineteenth Century England, by H. W. Arthurs" (1985) 15(1) Manitoba L. J. 125

- "Constitutional Biorhythms: Equal Justice under Law: Constitutional Development 1835- 1875, by Harold M Hyman and William M. Wiecek; The U. S. Bill of Rights and the Canadian Charter of Rights and Freedoms, by William R. McKercher, ed.; Towards Increased Judicial Activism: The Political Role of the Supreme Court, by Arthur Selwyn Miller" (1986) 17(3) Canadian Review of American Studies 375

- "Defending Logic from a Bum Rap: Pragmatism and Theory in English Law, by P. S. Atiyah" (1988) 17(2) Manitoba L. J. 227

- "Twain Never Meets at Political Hub; The Unmaking of Canada, by Robert Chodos, Rae Murphy, & Eric Hamovitch; Deconfederation: Canada without Quebec, by David Bercuson & Barry Cooper" (1991) Quill & Quire, 49

- "How Not to Write Constitutional History," Supreme Court of Canada Decision-Making: The Benchmarks of Rand, Kerwin, and Martland, by Randall Balcome, Edward McBride, and Dawn Russell" (1991) 29(2) Alberta Law Review 532

- "New-Age Constitutionalism: A Review of Reasoning with The Charter, by Leon E. Trakman" (1994) 2(1) Review of Constitutional Studies 123

- On Having Cake and Eating It: A Review of Jer emy Webber' s Reimaging Canada" (1995) 41(1) McGill L. J. 311

- "Emerging Justice? Essays on Indigenous Rights in Canada and Australia, by Kent McNeil" (2002) 40(2) Alberta Law Review 523

- "Law and the Modern Mind, by Jerome Frank; Courts on Trial: Myth and Reality in ` American Justice, by Jerome Frank; Casebook for 'The Legal Process', by Henry Hart and Albert Sacks" (Section on "A Book that Shaped your World") (2013) 50(4) Alberta Law Review 916

# UNPUBLISHED PAPERS,

likely to have been written by Dale Gibson for use by Ministers of Manitoba and Canada in the course of discussions concerning the repatriation of the *Canadian Constitution*

"Notes for an Opening Statement at the First Ministers' Conference on the Constitution by Sterling Lyon, Premier of Manitoba"

8 September, 1980 ("Notes only – check against delivery"), Document 800-14-034

"Notes for a Statement on the Entrenchment of a Charter of Rights by Sterling Lyon, Premier of Manitoba," First Ministers' Conference on the Constitution

9 September, 1980 ("Notes only – check against delivery"), Document 800-14-072

"Notes for a Statement on Patriation and an Amending Formula by Sterling Lyon, Premier of Manitoba," First Ministers' Conference on the Constitution

10 September, 1980 ("Notes only – check against delivery")

"Notes for a Closing Statement to the First Ministers' Conference on the Constitution by Sterling Lyon, Premier of Manitoba"

13 September, 1980 ("Notes only – check against delivery"), Ottawa, Ontario

"Notes for a Speech by the Honourable Jean Cretien, P. C., M. P., Minister of Justice and Minister of State for Social Development, to the Canadian Bar Association, Montreal, August 25, 1980"

"Prime Minister's Remarks at Close of Discussion on the Charter of Rights, September 10, 1980," Document: 800-14/078

Thank you for completing this book.

*We would love if you could help by posting a review at your book retailer and on the PageMaster Publishing site. It only takes a minute and it would really help others by giving them an idea of your experience.*

Thanks

PM Store Author's QR Code
https://pagemasterpublishing.ca/by/sandra-anderson/

To order more copies of this book, find books by other Canadian authors, or make inquiries about publishing your own book, contact PageMaster at:

PageMaster Publication Services Inc.
11340-120 Street, Edmonton, AB T5G 0W5
books@pagemaster.ca
**780-425-9303**

catalogue and e-commerce store
**PageMasterPublishing.ca/Shop**

www.ingramcontent.com/pod-product-compliance
Lightning Source LLC
Chambersburg PA
CBHW071624220526
45469CB00002B/469